Perspectives
in
Mental Health
Nursing

Perspectives in Mental Health Nursing

EDITED BY

TOM SANDFORD
BA (Hons), Dip N, RGN, RMN
Adviser in Mental Health, Royal College of Nursing

AND

KEVIN GOURNAY
MPhil, PhD, CPsychol, AFBPsS, RN
Professor of Psychiatric Nursing, Institute of Psychiatry

with 8 contributors

FOREWORD BY

CHRISTINE HANCOCK
General Secretary, Royal College of Nursing

Baillière Tindall
PUBLISHED IN ASSOCIATION WITH THE RCN

London Philadelphia Toronto Sydney Tokyo

Baillière Tindall

24–28 Oval Road
London NW1 7DX

The Curtis Center
Independence Square West
Philadelphia, PA 19106–3399, USA

Harcourt Brace & Company
55 Horner Avenue
Toronto, Ontario, M8Z 4X6, Canada

Harcourt Brace & Company, Australia
30–52 Smidmore Street
Marrickville
NSW 2204, Australia

Harcourt Brace & Company, Japan
Ichibancho Central Building
22–1 Ichibancho
Chiyoda-ku, Tokyo 102, Japan

A catalogue record for this book is available from the British Library

ISBN   1-873853-29-7

Typeset by Words & Graphics Ltd, Anstey, Leicester
Printed and bound in Great Britain by
WBC Book Manufacturers, Mid Glamorgan

For Sam, and Paul and Sylvia Sandford

CONTRIBUTORS

Peter Campbell Mental Health System Survivor, Member of Survivors Speak Out and Survivors' Poetry

Stuart Darby BA(Hons), RGN, RMN, RHV, DPSN
Formerly Head of Community Nursing Development Team
Camden and Islington Community Health Services NHS Trust, London
and Chair of the RCN Membership Group Focus on Older People,
Nursing and Mental Health

Jean Faugier RMN, RCNT, RNT, DANS, DipN, MSc, DipPsych
Regional Director of Nursing, North West Regional Health Authority
NHS Executive, and Honorary Senior Fellow, University of Manchester

Kevin Gournay MPhil, PhD, CPsychol, AFBPsS, RN
Professor of Psychiatric Nursing, Institute of Psychiatry

Sally-Ann Newton BA, RMN, RGN, CertEd(FE), RNT, RCNT
Head of Nursing Services, Northern Ireland Prison Service

David Sallah SEN, RMN, MSc, FETC
Postgraduate Doctoral Research Student, Public Sector Management,
Aston University, Birmingham and Nurse Consultant, Ashworth
Hospital, Liverpool

Tom Sandford BA(Hons), DipN, RGN, RMN
Adviser in Mental Health, Royal College of Nursing, London

Antony Sheehan BEd(Hons), MPhil, RMN, FAETC, HEPS, MHSM
Regional Mental Health Manager, West Midlands Regional Health
Authority

John Tait OBE, RGN, RMN
Deputy Chief Nursing Officer, Department of Health, London

Paul Tarbuck SRN, RMN, DipN, TCert, RNT, DipM, BA
Clinical Manager, Services for Individuals with a Personality Disorder,
Ashworth Hospital, Liverpool

CONTENTS

Foreword

CHRISTINE HANCOCK

We have heard a great deal recently about the challenges confronting mental health services in the rest of this decade. We are becoming more familiar with feedback from users, in terms of programmes and interventions that they have valued and with respect to experiences that they would not wish to see repeated.

In the past year we have heard an enormous amount about the agenda being developed by the Department of Health and by purchasers and GPs and their perspectives on how they will reconcile some of the dilemmas currently being experienced in terms of the type and volume of services being commissioned in the mental health field.

One of the clearest conclusions we have to draw from analysing this material is that if provider organisations are going to be successful in responding to the diverse aspirations and expectations being developed, one of their biggest challenges is going to lie in the area of realising and maximising the contribution of different professionals, individually and collectively, to the UK mental health agenda. Given the extent of their involvement in service provision the contribution of nurses has to be seen as of paramount importance. Contemporary mental health services are littered with evidence of missed opportunities in relation to realisation and maximisation of the nursing contribution to mental health service provision. If I had to identify an example that illustrated the scope of both the problem and of the potential gains to be derived from a clearer strategy for the future, I would use women and their experiences of mental health services as a cameo.

The experience of women within mental health services had become so problematic that MIND recently decided to adopt the issue as their major campaign and policy initiative. Their *Stress on Women* (MIND, 1992) campaign not only raised the profile of the subject very successfully but it also provided helpful and pragmatic material and service solutions which purchasers and providers could use to address the problem locally. The Royal College of Nursing decided to align itself closely to the campaign because we recognised the enormous potential that nurses and nursing have to create a different outcome for women using mental health services at either little or no extra cost to the provider.

As we looked at the prevalence of problems it became clear that nursing strategies had in many areas already prevented or minimised incidence of harassment and abuse of women within inpatient units. Women are still the substantial majority among practitioners and we found that in many places they were already using that position to systematically ensure that women as users had access to women as nurses as an important component of the interventions on offer. Indeed, one could go so far as to say that some of the MIND proposals, such as the user being provided with the choice of gender of key worker, could be operationalised almost single-handedly by nurses.

I would not want this to be seen to be simplifying the problems in relation to either nursing or to the experiences of women in the mental health system – one of the great successes of MIND's campaign was the way in which it defined and addressed the multiplicity of factors which have conspired to create the present difficulties. What I wish to emphasise and illustrate is the often unrealised potential locked up in the mental health nursing workforce. It is essential that we consistently achieve this type of added value in the future from our existing nursing resources.

We are being asked why nursing is in a robust position to be able to contribute to future service provision. I believe that the answer to this lies in the nature of the role and relationship between nurses and users, and the way that this can be used to address many of the factors involved in the current reported failures of treatment.

In 1993, MIND (Rogers et al, 1993) published a survey of users' experiences with mental health services, entitled *Experiencing Psychiatry.* It provides one of the most comprehensive reviews of how users feel about the services and staff that they encounter. Given the problems our services have been facing it comes as little surprise that the survey often paints quite an unhappy picture of mental healthcare that is frequently perceived to be unhelpful and on occasions, actively antitherapeutic. One of the more positive experiences on an otherwise bleak landscape was the reported perception of nurses as by far and away the most helpful and responsive of the professionals encountered by users during the course of their contact with mental health services. If this is the experience of users of nursing over a period during which the profession has been relatively modestly terrific in terms of involving users, it is not unreasonable to suggest that terrific gains could be achieved from fostering more proactive collaborative and constructive relationships with people who use our services.

These gains are going to be increasingly important to providers. A growing body of evidence is concluding that we desperately need to understand more about the factors involved in failure of treatment and the dimensions of client dissatisfaction within this. It is clear that all too frequently users and staff have different expectations. There is sometimes too little in the way of preparing the user for treatment. Users report inadequate provision of information and are sometimes not engaged in properly informed discussions about the limitations of mental health services and the uncertainty of the solutions that we work with.

Nursing sourced initiatives need to be routinely adopted into local strategies for nursing and service provision. Given the significance to providers of people with major mental health problems such as schizophrenia, let us start at that point. Despite some interesting work on causation in the areas of genetics and biochemical origins of schizophrenia, medical research is not promising to cross any major thresholds in terms of delivering new treatment regimes. The escalating need to provide services for those with serious mental health problems over a period characterised by rapid de-institutionalisation will continue to focus attention on the development of targeted services, such as those developed in the United States, committed to exploiting strategies aimed at keeping users out of hospital. In response to this, mental health nurses, especially nurses working in the community, are moving from assuming a multiplicity of roles towards becoming more skilled in psychopharmacology, social support and the prevention of relapse.

New models of training nurses have been developed to support these endeavours. The Thorn nursing project, for example, based on training centres at the Institute of Psychiatry and at Manchester University enables mental health nurses working in the community and in residential settings to enhance their knowledge and clinical skills in a focused way on case management and family work, problem solving, advocacy and assertive outreach strategies.

In other services mental health nurses have comprehensively addressed, with users, the constellation of issues associated with compliance with medication. Real gains in user choice, informed consent and treatment options have been realised alongside more effective monitoring of treatment and greater engagement with the wider range of services and support mechanisms which we know are needed to minimise relapse.

Challenges with other key client groups also provide fertile ground for exploiting nursing initiatives. Services for mentally disordered offenders, for example, have been made a first order priority for the NHS. This requires NHS authorities to work with personal social services and criminal justice agencies to develop strategic and purchasing plans for services for mentally disordered offenders. The way in which the nursing role has been developed with respect to the prompt identification and assessment of offenders thought to be suffering from mental health problems, and diversion from the criminal justice system, both as closely as possible to the point of arrest and from court, needs to be replicated much more intensively across the United Kingdom, as do some of the strategies currently being employed by forensic community psychiatric nurses to manage people with a history of dangerousness in the community.

These initiatives have been enhanced further by a diverse number of nursing development units. These can offer alternative models of service provision and provide users with real choice over treatment options where choice has not been provided before. They have the potential to enhance the volume of service provided without always increasing costs, and can reduce the stigma associated with more conventional treatment models. They can offer better access and flexible, out of hours contact points. In, for example, areas as diverse as eating disorders, substance misuse, postnatal depression and self-harming behaviour nurses are pioneering nursing-led treatment regimes which really merit serious scrutiny and evaluation. Sometimes these involve acknowledging a more peripheral role for medicine in the mental health area.

Without doubt they will involve taking risks but for Chief Executives and boards and mental health nurses prepared to experiment, they have the potential to extend the current relatively meagre portfolio of service options to an audience of purchasers and users and GPs who are eager to see something different.

These issues have recently been the subject of *Working in Partnership*, the report of the Mental Health Nursing Review Team (Department of Health, 1994). This volume, *Perspectives in Mental Health Nursing*, develops in more detail some of the themes deriving from the review. It demonstrates how mental health nurses are rising to the challenges confronting purchasers and providers and confirms and consolidates their position as protagonists within progressive mental health services.

REFERENCES

Department of Health (1994) *Working in Partnership*. Report of the Mental Health Nursing Review Team. London: HMSO.
MIND (1992) *Stress on Women*. Policy paper on women and mental health. London: MIND.
Rogers A, Pilgrim D and Lacey R (1993) *Experiencing Psychiatry*. London: MIND.

Introduction

JOHN TAIT

CHALLENGES AND OPPORTUNITIES FOLLOWING THE REVIEW OF MENTAL HEALTH NURSING

Nurses working in the field of mental health have never been slow to accept challenges and to initiate changes and progress whenever these are necessary. We need to remember that our practice is part of a continuum. Change and progress may not always be easily effected. Nurses have sometimes been responsible for poor standards of care but in many instances it has been caring and committed nurses who first exposed malpractice and maltreatment which led to some of the major inquiries, the outcome of which led to significant improvements in the care of people with mental illness and a concentration on their special needs, which in turn has resulted in the development of specialist post-registration clinical courses. However, to meet those challenges and grasp the opportunities presented by the changes we will need clear direction, wise counsel and strong leadership if we are to continue to develop our knowledge and skills and ensure that the needs of the people who use our services are met. All these issues are addressed in *Working in Partnership*, the Report of the Mental Health Nursing Review Team published in April 1994.

The last official review of mental health nursing, *Psychiatric Nursing – Today and Tomorrow*, took place in 1968 and focused particularly on inpatient psychiatric nursing. We have come a long way since then. Our voice is much stronger, both in influencing national policy and in leading and managing mental health services.

Furthermore, a great deal has happened since the Secretary of State for Health announced her intention to set up a review of mental health nursing in April 1992. The reasons why a review was needed and the changes that have taken place in mental health service provision during the course of the review are worth noting, for they bear considerable significance when we examine how the Report's recommendations can be taken forward.

1

Since the 1968 review there has been a fundamental shift as part of government policy in the prevailing attitudes and philosophies of care, with a drive towards community-based services with admission to hospital only being used when absolutely necessary.

The work on the present review began in September 1992, under the chairmanship of Professor Tony Butterworth, and was completed in December 1993. The terms of reference were:

> **In light of developments in the provision of services for people with mental illness to identify the future requirements for skilled nursing care.**

Representatives from a wide range of interests within the field of mental health, including people who use services and voluntary agencies, took an active part in the review exercise and it is worth noting that despite these widely differing backgrounds they found themselves in broad agreement not only on the need for change, but also on the direction of that change.

The review process met with widespread support from people who use services, their carers and voluntary bodies, as well as statutory and professional organisations. It provided an opportunity to consider and respond to questions raised by service providers, researchers and the profession at large on a wide range of issues, including issues relating to the main focus of work for mental health nurses and the future direction of the profession.

Publication of the review not only gives mental health nursing an opportunity to examine the conclusions reached by Professor Butterworth and his team and to consider how recommendations can be taken forward, but it also marks the beginning of a new and exciting phase in the development of mental health nursing. The report sets out a number of key principles which underpin mental health nursing practice. These are:

- The principle of choice for people who use services and their carers needs to be fully established as a basis for the practice of mental health nursing.
- The work of mental health nurses rests on their relationship with people who use mental health services and that this relationship should have value to both partners.
- It is a fundamental right that 'people who use mental health services can expect to receive skilled, sensitive, professional support from competent mental health nurses'.

All the recommendations are based on the principle that mental health nursing should re-examine every aspect of its policy and practice in the light of the needs of people who use services. Everything mental health nurses do should in some way improve the way in which the needs of people who use services are met. The focus of the report is therefore on partnerships with people who use services and on collaboration with other nurses, disciplines and agencies working in mental health.

Throughout the period of the review, other important work was under way at national level, including the *Health of the Nation Mental Illness Key Area Handbook* and the Secretary of State's 10-point plan for achieving safe community care.

Furthermore, during this time, there was much activity under way in the context of the development of local mental health strategies and, given the wide representation on the review team, these are reflected in the final report. It builds on the work from 1968 and clearly indicates who has the lead action for carrying forward the recommendations. This includes not only mental health nurses, purchasers and providers of education and mental health services, but the NHS Executive and the wider Department of Health.

In the foreword to the report, the then Secretary of State for Health, Virginia Bottomley, welcoming the report as an excellent pointer to ways of ensuring that we have a well qualified and motivated mental health nursing workforce, states that:

> Mental health nurses have a pivotal role to play in the health care team and will need to be properly equipped with the skills to do so. They need the skills to care for people with acute and enduring mental illness. They need to be able to assess, plan, implement and evaluate care. Their profession needs to act both as practitioners and key workers in varied and diverse health care teams. Their work requires them to move confidently between hospital and community settings and to respond quickly and creatively to the rapidly changing demands of the service and its users.

The Review of Mental Health Nursing, therefore, sets out a strategy which will take us into the next century. Nurses, with other colleagues in the care team and with users of the service, need to work together to implement it. The opportunities and challenges that it offers are tremendous, not only because mental health nursing will be enhanced, but also – and above all – the quality of care to people with mental illness will be further improved, which is what nursing should be all about. I welcome this publication as another step forward in this process.

REFERENCES

Department of Health (1994) *Working in Partnership. Report of the Mental Health Nursing Review Team*. London: HMSO.

Ministry of Health, Central Health Services Council (1968) *Psychiatric Nursing Today and Tomorrow. Standing Mental Health and Standing Nursing Advisory Committees*. London: HMSO.

CHAPTER 1

Working With Service Users

PETER CAMPBELL

The ideal of user-centred services has become fundamental to the provision of mental health care. In the United Kingdom in 1994, it would be hard to imagine a local mental health service which does not make some attempt both to increase the control of individual service users over their own care and treatment and to involve service users collectively in the planning, managing and monitoring of services. Whatever the quality of that work, it now has to be done and to be seen to be done. This is a relatively recent imperative which, despite the long-standing work of mental health nurses and other professional groups to empower service users, has immense potential for positive change. It is important to understand the major elements that have combined to produce the current emphasis on user involvement in mental health services.

THE GROWTH OF THE USER MOVEMENT

One element in the change of climate within services has been the development of 'the user movement' – the growth at local, regional and national level of independent organisations of people who are using or have used mental health services working, often in very diverse ways, to effect transformations not only in the provision of care but in social attitudes and practices on a wider level. Such action is at once comparatively novel and based on a long tradition of protest. It is possible to argue that psychiatry, by the very nature of its field of operation, will always provoke protest from its recipients and to point to instances of organised opposition from the mad to systems of care in centuries preceding the invention of psychiatry. Certainly the Alleged Lunatics Friend Society, influential in the mid-nineteenth century, was a clear forerunner of current self-advocacy groups. Nevertheless, the rapid growth of user action and the increasing openness of the mental health system to the contribution of service users is very much a phenomenon of the last 10 years.

In 1983, the year of the introduction of the last Mental Health Act in England and Wales, there were only half a dozen independent user action groups in existence. If service users were at all involved in the discussions that developed the Mental

Health Act, and it would be hard to argue that many service users were mean-ingfully involved, their voices would have been heard largely through voluntary organisations which spoke on their behalf. In 1994 the situation is radically different. There are between 200 and 300 local groups. Wales and Scotland each have national user networks. There are two networking organisations – the United Kingdom Advocacy Network and Survivors Speak Out – which cover the entire United Kingdom. National MIND, the largest mental health volun-tary organisation in England and Wales, has its own advisory network – MINDLINK – with 700 members. The two most recent debates on major changes to the Mental Health Act – for example, the proposals for Community Supervision Orders in 1993 (Department of Health, 1993) – have both signifi-cantly included, and been influenced by, contributions from the user movement. The landscape has clearly changed. It is no longer possible to think in terms of the organised armies of interest groups – the government civil servants, the Royal Colleges, the unions and associations of caring profes-sionals, the voluntary organisations – and the common rabble of service users, essentially a collection of disparate and passive individuals on whom the armies conduct their manoeuvres. Now an increasing number of that rabble are organised and operating as an interest group that must be respected in its own right.

The arrival of a newly organised interest group at local or national level brings inevitable problems. Attempts to involve and empower individual service users must be seen in the context of these difficulties. Thus, while at first sight it may seem a relatively straightforward task to give individuals more control over their own care and treatment, the objective of involving service users in the planning, managing and monitoring of services which may determine the successful crea-tion of a culture of individual empowerment remains more complicated and arduous. One major difficulty is the technical one of how you actually involve service users in these activities. This has not happened before. The majority of service users have had little or no experience of sitting on committees, of wading through reams of minutes and reports at short notice. They are not familiar with the mental health system from a provider's or planner's perspective; they do not understand how it works or how different pieces of the system relate to one another. The language and procedures mental health professionals employ often mystify and alienate.

None of these problems are insuperable, but they do require serious considera-tion. Nor should the particular difficulties of mental health service users be over-emphasised. Involving ordinary people, non-experts, in any planning and man-agement process is going to be difficult. In the initial stages there may be conflict. It will probably be necessary to start doing things slightly differently and this may require more time and energy, perhaps even more money. Nevertheless, it is already evident that successful involvement can be achieved if sufficient sup-port, information and preparation time is given to user representatives and if, in particular, systems of consultation are made as flexible and as accessible as possible – for example, using a full range of mechanisms: not just user representation on planning groups but attendance by planners and managers at users' own forums and the sensitive use of surveys and questionnaires.

Another difficulty is the criteria for involvement. In the last 2 or 3 years the main argument seems to have moved on from 'Why involve users?' to 'Which users do we involve and listen to?' There is still much uneasiness about the presence of independent and organised groups of service users. Some of this feeling may be attributable to the awkward remnants of outdated expectations of what the so-called mentally-ill should be doing with their lives. Perhaps it is somehow cheating for the psychotics to get organised. On the other hand there are legitimate concerns, particularly around representativeness. Many service providers feel that user organisations are unrepresentative, that they voice the wishes of the most articulate, the most radical, the least 'ill'. While user organisations are usually clear and open about whom they do and do not speak for, service providers often seem to be in an ambivalent position, grateful to have user groups who are keen to respond to their invitations to involvement, yet not liking some of what they hear and uncertain whether any of it fairly represents the views of all service users. In this situation what is needed is some honesty and some action. Just how important is representativeness and what exactly is required? If providers do require representativeness and demand it in their consultations, they should be explicit about their conditions and the justification for them. They should then release the resources for user and other organisations to try and meet their conditions. It should not be assumed that user groups do not wish to be representative. On the contrary, the history of the last 10 years makes it clear that user organisations are keen to give a voice to the most vulnerable and alienated individuals. If, on the other hand, providers are unwilling or unable to secure the resources to enable a more comprehensive involvement, they should acknowledge where the problem truly lies, give up their reservations about user organisations and engage wholeheartedly in the consultations that remain practicable.

When considering the impact of the user movement on the development of user involvement in mental health services, it is essential to remember that the work of user organisations goes beyond the mental health service system itself. Service users are not just consumers of health care. They are also citizens in a society that routinely discriminates against them. Many service users now talk of empowerment. This is an empowerment that goes much further than merely being involved in their own care and treatment or in the planning and provision of services. It touches on every aspect of their life inside and outside services, addressing both their status as citizens and the way their personal experience and behaviour has been misunderstood and devalued. It may be possible for people who work in the mental health system to separate their professional responsibilities from the rest of their lives and make minimal connections between them. For those of us on the receiving end, separations of this kind are neither possible nor desired. Unless these wider personal and political objectives are acknowledged, there is a real danger that the respective agendas will diverge completely or, more likely, that the agendas of mental health professionals will capture and control the agenda of the user movement. Empowerment and user involvement are different things. Empowerment demands the opportunity to be flexible, to develop and change agendas, to decide what you most want to be involved in. User organisations and individual service users must be given the space to define and pursue these goals.

INFORMATION AND ADVOCACY

Despite the difficulties outlined above, the involvement of service users has begun to effect positive change in the way services are delivered. One important area of improvement has been the provision and delivery of information. Clearly, information must play a key role in any attempt to give individuals increased control over what is happening to them, what is being done to them. In mental health services, where a person's freedom may be curtailed under the Mental Health Act and treatments are often controversial, information becomes even more important. Over the last 10 years the amount of information available to service users has certainly increased. Hospital wards will now usually have properly maintained notice boards. Some will even display leaflets explaining drug and other treatments. It has become unusual for people not to be given information on their rights when they are detained under the Mental Health Act. At the same time expectations have increased that nurses will spend considerable time giving and explaining information. For many service users information-giving and caring have taken on an equal importance.

In a number of areas (e.g. Nottingham, Parkside in North West London, Lambeth in South West London) efforts have been made to improve the quality of information by directly involving service users in writing leaflets. In Nottingham people being discharged into the community can choose a pack of information from a resource developed in conjunction with Nottingham Advocacy Group (a user-led organisation) and local service users. Lambeth Link have produced a self-assessment form to help people identify their wants and needs when care programmes are being planned. In other parts of the country service users have been involved in drafting general information leaflets for newly admitted patients. Through collaborative working it is becoming increasingly possible not only to provide more information but to make sure that it is better quality information that makes more sense to its recipients.

Such information is particularly necessary in regard to psychiatric treatments. Although there is now more openness about treatments, significant numbers of users still remain ignorant of the full range of positive and negative effects of treatments. National MIND's recent discussion document *Safe and Effective* (Cobb, 1993) illustrates the major concerns that still remain. One example of the basic confusion that exists is that some users misunderstand completely the difference between antipsychotic and anticholinergic medications. Collaboration on writing leaflets about treatments can be complicated as the balance in including information on positive and negative effects is often very difficult to agree, but the effort is worthwhile. Clear and realistic information is essential. Nurses must face up to the challenge of themselves knowing enough about treatments to give information on demand. They should become proactive in disseminating information to those in their care. It is no longer acceptable for questions about treatments to be sidestepped or for mental health workers to refer people to the local reference library for more details and to still pretend they are providing a good service.

The provision of independent advocacy is increasingly being seen as a necessary element in good quality mental health services. The intrinsic nature of institutional care systems and the disabling effects of emotional distress often combine to prevent service users from making their wishes known and inhibit them from effectively pursuing these with care providers. This is particularly true when there are disagreements over a course of action. Independent advocacy can moderate the imbalance of power between the giver and recipient of care. Even if the outcome of a particular discussion does not correspond to the service user's wishes (and this may be a fairly common event), the fact that the individual has been able to be fully involved in the decision-making process and has had the best assistance in putting forward their case can have a significant impact on the degree of satisfaction or dissatisfaction felt afterwards.

There is currently some confusion around what advocacy in mental health services means. This is partly because there are a number of types of advocacy being offered: legal advocacy, citizen advocacy, peer advocacy, individual or collective advocacy, crisis advocacy, long-term advocacy. The situation is further complicated by the fact that the term advocacy may be used in a more general sense to cover a wide range of activities including campaigning and lobbying and even the provision of innovative services (exemplary advocacy). It is important that advocacy should be clearly defined and that nurses and other mental health workers become better informed about the theory and practice that lie behind different advocacy projects.

At the heart of all ideas of advocacy should be the individual independent advocacy relationship where an advocate, whatever their particular skills and qualifications, takes up the cause of another and carries it forward through speech and action as if it were their own cause. Individual advocacy does not involve persuading your 'client' to accept a particular course of action – helping the doctors 'make them see sense', for example. It does mean helping people to decide a course of action and then supporting them to the utmost to carry it through. Equally important for many service users is the belief that self-advocacy is the best form of advocacy, so advocates should always work in a way that enables individuals to speak out and act on their own behalf rather than becoming a 'case' that is taken over by the advocate. With the right support, advice and information many people can do it themselves.

Nurses are often suspicious about working alongside advocates and feel their professional role is being undermined. Like other mental health workers, their training has included an emphasis on working as 'the patient's advocate' (professional advocacy). They have been taught to listen to patients and to represent their wishes to other mental health workers in the caring team — for example, in multidisciplinary ward rounds or care-planning meetings. Such advocacy is essential and should not be devalued. Nevertheless, it does have limitations and it is these that the new advocacy services are attempting to address.

Advocacy by mental health workers can never be fully independent. Conflicts of interest are bound to arise. It is hard to see how an employee of a health authority can freely advocate for someone who is making a complaint against that authority. How far can a nurse go in pursuing a change of treatment for a patient with their consultant psychiatrist? Many service users now feel that independence is an essential element in any advocacy service.

One of the major advantages of having an independent advocacy service is that it should be able to provide much more time and expertise to users than mental health workers can contribute alongside their other commitments. A useful illustration is that of crisis advocacy during the assessment of an informal admission for compulsory detention under Section 5.3 of the Mental Health Act. In this situation it is likely that the advocate would be involved in a meeting prior to the assessment, would be present at all the assessment interviews and would meet with the person again at the end of the process. These meetings might stretch over 72 hours or might all take place on one day. It is quite unlikely that any mental health worker could combine such intensive advocacy work with their other duties.

Independent individual advocacy should be welcomed as a complement to the nurse–client relationship. While nurses will have to re-think some of their approaches to patient care and may have to adapt the boundaries of their responsibilities, the sensitivity of services to the wishes of its recipients should improve. Although advocates will become involved in conflict situations, their function is to help resolve conflict, not to incite it. While it remains clear that their brief is to work with service users and to promote their interests, they are not adversaries working against nurses. Independent advocacy projects remain a novelty in mental health services and will inevitably be approached with wariness by many mental health workers. Nevertheless, with adequate pre-planning and properly agreed guidelines, they can become collaborative schemes that signifi-cantly increase the power of individual service users.

PATIENT COUNCILS

Advocacy projects that seek to give individual service users a greater say over their own care are now often accompanied by patient councils which enable users to influence collectively the service they are receiving. Nottingham, where the first patient council in the United Kingdom was established in 1986, now has a well developed system of collective and individual advocacy and representation that includes patient councils in two hospitals, a legal advocate, a citizen advocacy scheme and user groups attached to sector teams in the com-munity. In hospital settings, patient council schemes usually comprise user only meetings on hospital wards with representatives from the wards attending a regular hospital-wide council meeting to which senior management are invited. Issues arising from ward meetings will be resolved at that level if possi-ble with difficult issues or ones that affect the hospital generally being dealt with at the full patient councils. Patient councils will often be involved in comment-ing on policy and planning changes and can be effective in devising better information systems for service users.

The development of patient councils is a long and complicated process. It is possible that a well-developed system, such as the Nottingham example, may be the exception rather than the rule. In other places, a unit may have a patient council but no individual advocacy service or vice versa. Some hospitals may have user-only meetings on certain wards that do not have a regular connection to a hospital-wide council. Patient council schemes are more likely to develop piecemeal than to arrive rapidly at a comprehensive structure.

Whatever their stage of development, every patient council presents major chal-lenges to mental health workers. Giving greater power to service users necessarily means that service providers must give up or at least share some of their power. New boundaries must be negotiated. The idea that inpatients should be encouraged to meet together on their own to discuss their care and treatment is seen initially as a threat by many nurses. As with individual advo-cates, patient council facilitators will often be suspected of being adversaries, coming onto hospital wards to stir up inpatients or to propagate their own radical views on psychiatry.

In the majority of cases, such fears will prove unfounded and the value of patient councils in enabling nursing staff to achieve better care will be recognised. Nevertheless, important changes in attitudes and practices are necessary. If patient councils are to succeed, nurses will need support and training to work with service users. In particular, the preconception that service users are pre-eminently recipients, recipients of care, treatment, advice, food and succour and are not also the possessors of valuable insights, knowledge and information must be changed. Expertise does not lie exclusively with the providers of care. Advocacy, information systems and patient councils are valuable mechanisms for adjusting the imbalance of power between the carer and the cared for. However, ultimately these mechanisms will only succeed if nurses accept that reciprocity is the key to therapeutic intervention.

THE CARING RELATIONSHIP

The personal relationship between mental health workers and service users is fundamental to mental health care. The quality of this relationship is particularly significant for nurses who are likely to be the service providers in the most consistent and frequent contact with users. A recent survey of service users' experiences entitled *Experiencing Psychiatry – Users' Views of Services* (Rogers et al, 1993) supports anecdotal impressions that nurses are often seen as the most helpful of mental health professionals and that general satisfaction with mental health nurses is high. Nevertheless, it is important to recognise that 40 per cent of those interviewed in the survey expressed dissatisfaction with nursing and to acknowledge the detailed criticisms service users are now making.

The nursing relationship should be one founded on a relative equality of power where the objective is to restore the service user's autonomy or self-control. Information giving and advocacy are important aspects of this relationship and recent progress in these areas has already been indicated, but more basic questions need to be addressed. In the first place it cannot be assumed that meaningful relationships are always established between nurse and service user. It is far from certain that most mental health nurses spend significant amounts of time with patients. Despite the development of the key worker system or the named nurse approach, the complaint: 'there is no one to talk to me and no one to listen to me' remains the most common single criticism of mental health services. It is still possible – and in the light of current trends in staffing psychiatric wards it may become increasingly possible – for people to go through crisis, admission and immediate recovery without being given the opportunity to discuss their predicament with a nurse or other mental health worker. Moreover, while nurse – patient ratios inevitably place a limit on creative interaction, the problem is not just one of numbers. One of the most common complaints about nurses on psychiatric wards is that they spend most of their time in the nursing office and there are new concerns that the key worker system may encourage this by creating 'nursing by appointment'. For many users, the psychiatric ward has become a barren environment, more a warehouse in which they await delivery back to the community than a therapeutic space where creative interactions take place.

Individual nurses and the profession as a whole must decide what priority they give to spending time with their patients, to being with them on a person to person basis. On one hand we are given to understand that increasing numbers of mental health nurses are demanding and being given more counselling skills. On the other hand many service users say they spend less and less time with nurses. This is a discrepancy that needs urgent attention.

It is essential that nurses conduct a detailed examination of their day to day practice in the light of service users' response to it. Many nursing practices in hospitals are not open to public scrutiny or even the scrutiny of other mental health professionals. However, service users who are on the receiving end of nursing practices are both aware of its effects and capable, if given the opportunity, of presenting considered reactions. Thus it could be of great benefit if nurses were to consult service users over basic issues affecting the quality of care at the most practical level. For example, why is it necessary to keep people who cannot sleep at night lying in their beds? Does it matter if medication is dispensed at mealtimes from the middle of the dining room floor? Is it appropriate for mealtimes to last only 15 minutes? Is it ever acceptable to threaten people? When day to day practice is examined from the service users' point of view, it frequently becomes clear not only that certain procedures do not make therapeutic sense but that relatively minor changes in daily procedures can make major differences to levels of satisfaction among service users. Even today, most psychiatric wards would benefit from detailed scrutiny of practice and procedure shift by shift on the basis of the following sorts of question. Is it necessary? Is this desirable? How do service users feel about this?

Mental health nurses need to be aware how the organisation of the therapeutic environment in which they work can place barriers between them and service users. One significant obstacle is the compulsory element in mental health care. It is not always clear that mental health nurses, even well qualified and experienced nurses, are sensitive to the full impact of compulsion on the way inpatient care is perceived by its recipients. Even if inpatients are not detained on a section of the Mental Health Act and thus not directly subject to compulsory powers, they are aware of its existence and availability and know it could be used against them. As a result, many service users would claim that there is no such thing as informal status for an inpatient and that freedom is not a very real feature of the caring environment. Mental health nurses must be aware of these perceptions and realise their implications for the caring relationship. On one hand, they need to have a good knowledge of the Mental Health Act and be honest and realistic about its powers when informing and advising inpatients. On the other hand they should always work to minimise the effects of the imbalance of power between carer and cared for and to counteract the 'compulsory atmosphere' of the psychiatric ward.

Such detailed considerations should be conducted in the context of wider questions about the role of the mental health nurse. Current concerns within the profession itself must be related to what service users feel about the nurse's role. Sharma et al (1992) cite research evidence suggesting significant differences in the value nurses and service users attach to particular forms of psychiatric intervention. Such findings call for imaginative responses not for new methods of educating service users to accept what they are currently offered. There is also growing uncertainty about which aspects of mental health nurses' many functions users most value. These questions have not yet been adequately researched, but it does appear that many service users place higher value on 'human caring qualities' than 'specialised and technical skills'. People will often talk of preferring an 'untrained nurse' to the trained experts who 'only carry out doctors' orders'. If we are truly entering an era when services are more closely tailored to the wants and needs of recipients, it must now be the time to start investigating these preferences in detail and discovering their implications for the training and organisation of mental health nurses.

At the same time it seems that many users would like a higher quality of physical care from mental health nurses and are most appreciative of nurses who do not prevent them from doing things that other mental health workers may not allow – creative non-intervention. When such responses are considered, alongside the continuing impression that what many service users living in the community want is a care worker who will not only talk to them about their health but will help them do the shopping or redecorate their flat, the challenge to the nursing profession becomes very real. Exactly what is the special contribution of the nurse? It is in the interests of both mental health nurses and mental health users that the favourable responses uncovered by the Experiencing Psychiatry Survey are most closely defined.

Whatever the range of support service users seek from nurses in the community or in hospital settings, the value placed on the personal relationship reigns supreme. Any change in the technical accomplishment of nurses should be accompanied by an increased sensitivity to the nature of the distress that service users experience. It is not sufficient for mental health nurses to accept unchallenged the traditional explanations of the differences between those diagnosed as having mental illnesses and other people. These differences need constant examination and review, in particular in the light of what service users say about themselves and their lives.

One of the most important aspects of the 'user movement' in the last 10 years is the work it has done to bring people together to discuss and revalue their own experience of madness. The Self-Harm Conference 1990 (see *Self Harm: Perspectives from Personal Experience*, Survivors Speak Out, 1994) and the Eating Distress Conference 1992 (see *Eating Distress: Perspectives from Personal Experiences*, Survivors Speak Out, 1992) are good examples of this. The Hearing Voices Network (Romme and Escher, 1993) is a notable example of a user-led initiative which has developed important self-help and educational activities. If nursing practice is to empower its recipients it must acknowledge the mad person's search for meaning and start to engage with the new understandings of the mad. This is the essence of any new caring partnership. One reason for the barren feel of some admission wards may be the lack of imagination of nurses when faced by mental distress. Unless we become open to the full dimensions of such distress, the spiritual, psychological and moral potentials as well as the medical ones, we will all remain captives of madness. If nurses actually accept that service users are significantly different, and different only in negative ways, can they make more than a superficial contribution to recovery? The caring relationship must be based on the belief that we are essentially the same, not different, that the understandings of the recipient are of central importance and not discredited by diagnosis and that we are working towards goals that are both common and openly agreed.

CONCLUSION – WORKING WITH USERS

In recent years the relationship between service users and mental health services has begun a major change. At least in the rhetoric, users individually and collectively are centre stage, at the starting point of their own care and the design and planning of the service system as a whole. In this chapter I have outlined some of the problems and possibilities this change of focus has revealed. At this relatively early stage it is unclear how dramatic and far-reaching the changes will be. User organisations are already aware of the system's resistance to new services that seriously challenge the traditional approaches – for example, the difficulty in meeting the widespread demand for 24-hour non-medical crisis services. Equally, some service users now complain that although they or their representatives are involved in planning structures, their control over their own care and treatment has scarcely improved.

This goes to the heart of the problem. New ways of working with service users demand a change in attitudes and culture. Changing structures will not be enough. In this respect mental health nurses, like other front-line workers, play a key role. They are in prolonged and intimate contact with people in distress. Without changes in practice at this level many of the other changes may be rendered meaningless. On the other hand there is evidence that many of the things service users want are also the things mental health nurses want to provide. The caring relationship is close enough for us to believe that caring alliances can be formed. The time is right to encourage greater dialogue between nurses and service users, both at an individual and collective level. The benefits of a newly negotiated relationship – benefits for both partners – are too great to be ignored.

REFERENCES

Cobb A (1993) *Safe and Effective*. London: MIND.

Department of Health (1993) *Legal Powers on the Care of Mentally Ill People in the Community.* London: Department of Health.

Rogers A, Pilgrim D and Lacey R (1993) *Experiencing Psychiatry – Users' Views of Services.* London: MIND.

Romme M and Escher S (1993) *Accepting Voices*. London: MIND.

Sharma T, Carson J and Berry C (1992) Patients' voices. *Health Service Journal* **102**(5285): 20–21.

Survivors Speak Out (1992) *Eating Distress – Perspectives from Personal Experiences*. London: Survivors Speak Out.

Survivors Speak Out (1994) *Self Harm: Perspectives from Personal Experience*. London: Survivors Speak Out.

CHAPTER 2

Mental Health Nursing Development Units

ANTONY SHEEHAN

INTRODUCTION

A 'beleaguered Health Secretary' was how Janet Snell (1991) described William Waldegrave in 1991, after his announcement at the Royal College of Nursing Congress in Harrogate, that an extra £3.2 million was to be given to nursing development units (NDUs). Beleaguered, perhaps, because of NHS reforms and other proverbial thorns in his side such as clinical grading, which continued to cause him pain. Some solace was found for William that year at Harrogate; perhaps it is only appropriate that a profession in part focused on helping with others' pain should help the Minister with his.

Professor June Clark, in a tempered, uneasy welcome to the announcement, declared that the Minister appeared to show 'more affinity for nursing' than his predecessors. I think she was probably right. How did this affinity come about? Well, through the power and influence only the likes of which a force such as the profession of nursing can bring to bear. In a sense, a movement had begun. If expansion in numbers and having a discrete but robust influence on positive practice can be deemed to be a movement, then nursing development units had become such.

The history of NDUs reads, in its early chapters, more like a spy novel, full of intrigue, controversy and behind-closed-doors discussions. Beeson ward at Oxford's Radcliffe Hospital was one of the original leading lights (Pearson et al, 1992). It was, in a sense, a victim of its own success, proving that a unit which was nurse-led, and relied almost purely on nursing interventions, could show the way. It seemed that more people got much better, more quickly and more cheaply. Success on all fronts, it would appear, resounding applause from all quarters, one would assume, but no: a shocked and cynical establishment, in wanting to protect its tradition, closed ranks and the unit was closed down, some say because of a bitter reprisal against the nursing profession taking and making the very best of such a unique opportunity. Perhaps the time was not right, however; perhaps we needed that extra 10 years of influence being brought to bear by such charismatic and innovative nurse leaders as Alan Pearson (1984), Jane Salvage (1989) and Steve Wright (1989a), to place nursing in general, and nursing development units in particular, firmly on the political agenda.

Steve Wright was one of the country's first consultant nurses. Tameside NDU was set up in 1981 and grew from a single ward unit to include more wards and a day hospital becoming, to date, the largest and most successful nursing development unit in the United Kingdom (Wright, 1989b). It was on this unit that the Minister, 'with an affinity' for nursing, clearly had demonstrated to him the value of nursing and what nurses could do.

Turning points in attitude and perception often happen in but a moment. Steve Wright describes the visit of Mr Waldegrave to Tameside NDU as a real turning point, but it seems that it was just one older lady who made the real difference. On the usual political walkabout, the Minister stopped at this lady's bedside. He conversed with her for a while. He said that he had heard that they were practising a named nurse system on the ward, and had been told by the 'professionals' that this was really helpful. He asked the woman if she knew who her named nurse was. At that moment a silence seemed to befall the scene; nursing staff fidgeted as they anxiously awaited the lady's answer. They need not have been concerned. Not only did she know who her named nurse was, but what that person's role was, and why the system was such a good idea. A coming of age had occurred. A politician had been so strongly influenced by nursing and nursing development units, and their contribution to such initiatives as primary nursing, the named nurse, and the Patient's Charter that he decided to put his money where his rhetoric was.

WHAT ARE NDUS?

Defining what an NDU actually is brings much contention among those who engage in the debate. The King's Fund (1993) suggest that NDUs are clinical sites where nurses are striving to develop the service they offer to patients or clients.

A unit has been defined loosely as a group of nurses working together within a defined clinical area such as a ward, clinic or indeed, a patient's home: More than this practical definition, however, is the philosophical underpinning of nursing development units – that is, to develop nursing; these units should be developing nurses, and be creative in so doing. Nurses constitute the largest number of health care workers. It is inevitable, therefore, that improvements in nursing will have a greater impact on health care than introducing change in any other single discipline.

NDUs exist to promote and develop professional practice as a means of improving nursing, midwifery and health visiting. Common themes among all NDUs include increasing patient involvement in their own care, encouraging nurse leadership, developing nursing staff themselves and exploring the contribution of nursing care to health.

The King's Fund became involved with the NDU initiative in 1989, when funding from the Sainsbury's Trust enabled the setting up of four new NDUs. In 1991 they were given ministerial charge of the £3.2 million grant for 30 new NDUs. They now play an essential role in providing the support for new and existing NDUs and crucially will begin to report to the Department of Health in 1995, as to the specific outcomes and value of the units.

In choosing which units should receive major grant status, the King's Fund Nursing Developments Programme identified the following key characteristics as necessary criteria for a unit to be defined as a nursing development initiative (King's Fund Centre, 1993).

A nursing development unit should

- be a defined clinical area where care is given directly to patients/clients, or be a defined nursing team;
- have a clearly identified clinical nursing leader, who has day to day responsibility and authority for clinical practice within the unit. This leader should have a democratic management style, and act as a major change agent in the unit;
- have a philosophy of care which is developed collectively, and which is underpinned by a shared vision of high quality nursing practice, and which demonstrates the value of equity and quality in care;
- use an approach that increases the involvement of patients/clients in decision-making regarding their own care,
- be a place where staff accept change as a way of life, and take a proactive, dynamic, challenging and planned approach to the management of change; NDU nurses experiment constantly to improve practice and develop themselves;
- require all nursing staff within the unit to be involved with and have ownership of the ongoing development of clinical practice: this depends on a high level of individual practitioner autonomy;
- adopt strategies and development programmes aimed at empowering individual nurses;
- place a strong emphasis on staff professional development, regardless of grade or qualification;
- have already established, or be in the process of planning reliable methods of evaluating the efficiency and effectiveness of nursing care;
- Share knowledge of new ways of practice; and

- Encourage unit staff to develop research-based practice.

Vaughan (1992) describes nurses working in NDUs as often challenging the norms of practice, and in so doing, leaving their work open to challenge, critical scrutiny and evaluation.

Clearly, then, elements of risk taking are apparent for nurses working in NDUs. However, for any group still striving towards (and arguing among itself about) professionalism, risk taking is an inevitable feature of such developments.

The above characteristics, when associated with any area of nursing practice, must be seen as rewarding; in addition, they bring with them a number of responsibilities. Where development is taking place there is a need for accountability. Clearly, then, part of central government's hidden agenda is to establish whether the nursing profession is up to the task in hand.

Nurses practising in NDUs have a clear vision of the potential for nursing. They see clinical excellence and questioning, enquiry, research, teaching and consultancy as part of everyday life. Change is not only accepted, but expected.

NDUS AND MENTAL HEALTH NURSING

In the initial momentum of the nursing development unit movement there were no NDUs based in mental health care settings. Perhaps this was inevitable, as those initial nurse leaders were all general trained nurses. The last round of bids to the King's Fund changed all that, and several mental health units were recognised and supported for their excellence in nursing practice and their contribution to mental health nursing care.

It would be helpful, I think, to describe some of the work in progress in the units, but first I would want to take a personal perspective of the importance of NDUs within a mental health focused provider unit.

Facilitating an NDU within a mental health setting is full of trials, tribulations and traumas. Most of all, however, there are wonderful advantages of having such an initiative, and making good use of any statutory health care settings' most important major resource – nurses. Personal experience of mental health nursing developments has been within the context of day care provision, enabling accessible responsive services to clients with a broad range of mental health concerns. The Nursing Development Unit at St George's Hospital, Stafford, which relates to this personal experience was, prior to the effort put into achieving an NDU status, a fairly traditional day hospital setting, which was restricted in terms of referral routes and limited in terms of the options it could offer to its patients.

A groundswell of dissatisfaction led to an audit of skills available throughout the hospital, in order to ascertain how the service options available to clients of the day service could be broadened. Astonishingly, nurses from all areas came forward with qualifications, experiences and areas of interest based on research which they could not fully pursue due to the restrictions of the jobs in which they were placed.

Nurses with diplomas in hypnotherapy, staff with degrees in art and postgraduate qualifications in art therapy all came forward offering their services. The anomaly of not using these skills was worsened by the fact that much of the training had, in some way or another, been paid for by the organisation – an indictment indeed.

The first component, then, of the proposal for the NDU at St George's Hospital was to explore the potential of 'sessional working'. This describes a process by which skills or interests should be pursued under the auspices of the NDU. Literally overnight, options available to clients doubled. Nurses were happy, finally, to be able to use their skills to their best potential; clients were happy to get a much broadened and accessible service to meet their needs.

Having then begun to address the problem of limited patient care, it became apparent that the next issue was to consider the limited referral routes to this broader range of skills (previously it had been through consultant psychiatrists only). National recognition, which influenced local management support, enabled the unit to open up its referral routes so that any individual or group could refer. Nurses were now receiving, assessing, treating and discharging their own patients, using discrete interventions which formed part of their professional armoury.

To use nursing skills on a sessional basis to enhance the care provision in a provider unit is a unique venture. Often the 'specialist' skills of others (doctors, social workers, psychologists, etc.) are drawn upon to support a ward or department. Only if a nurse has a defined clinical specialist role are they considered a resource. The NDU at St George's, Stafford recognised the wealth of experience, knowledge and skill from the wards and departments.

Referrals are received in the unit and processed through one administrative system. Often clients can be supported through the core programme within the day unit. However, where there is no suitable mechanism on offer within the programme staff can call upon the considerable resource of the sessional nurses, of which there are more than 30, each with different areas of interest ranging from the skills-based areas such as hypnotherapy to issues-based areas such as bereavement.

This sessional back-up has allowed the NDU to offer a substantial service that is working towards being client-led rather than simply reliant on whatever is available within a restricted programme.

The process of sessional working at Stafford NDU can be seen as a 'nurturing' process enabling the development of new, nurse-led initiatives. Perhaps the finest example of the success of this process is the initiation of a nurse-led service for adults who had suffered childhood sexual abuse. A unique opportunity became apparent for nurses who had studied the psychosocial impact of sexual abuse in great depth to offer support to clients who were disclosing the traumas of their experiences. Such was the resultant demand for this service that the Chief Executive was lobbied to formalise it. He did, and the NDU's first major development was achieved.

It is anticipated that the process of sessional working, which could be appropriate in a number of nursing settings, not just mental health care, will facilitate the birth of more nurse-led services based on client identified need. Despite the apparent positive nature of such developments for all concerned, there were those who were less than happy with these nurse-led initiatives. Fears were abundant, accusations were many – 'it is a cheap service', 'it doesn't have any research underpinning', 'it is dangerous!' These important accusations needed addressing, and proving credibility was the key.

For any NDU, particularly those working with potentially vulnerable clients such as those with mental health concerns, it is essential that a context for service provision should be maintained, and this context should include elements such as:

- excellence in training, so that services are only offered by practitioners skilled enough to provide them;
- clinical supervision, so that practitioners are fully supported in their clinical work, and have a mechanism by which they can check out what they are doing;
- evidence of research and evaluation-based practice, so that interventions can be firmly substantiated; and
- an acknowledgement of professional limitations and the role of colleagues.

These are the features which combine to provide a credible backdrop to nursing clinical practice.

The Nursing Development Unit at Stafford began to meet three important agendas within the context of mental health care; first, the professional agenda in terms of clinical development and the facility to practise skills autonomously but within a supportive context. Secondly, the purchaser agenda was being met by providing an innovative service, based on quality and equity meeting defined local needs. Thirdly, and most importantly, there was a meeting of client needs in providing an accessible, responsive service without having long to wait.

These three agendas – the professional, the purchaser and the client – would seem to constitute the total service in this brave new world of NHS reform. The model adopted at St George's Hospital, Stafford, also contributed to the national agendas, including the Health of the Nation Document (1992a) and Patient's Charter (1992b). Notably, from this tripartite analysis of the total service, managers were absent. This illustrates, perhaps, where the power now really lies, and the opportunities that are there to become part of a powerful movement for change. Some would argue that it is right and proper that managers, particularly, should be absent as their role, although important, is only an enabling one. Some would go further and say that it is nurse managers who have held the nursing profession back for so long, and it is only fair now that practitioners are taking the lead.

Nurse, or any other, managers aside, innovations are occurring in the mental health nursing developing units the length and breadth of the country.

Cartmel Ward, Prestwich Hospital, Manchester

This NDU in a traditional mental health unit is using information technology to have a major impact on the unit and the service it provides to its rehabilitation type clients. The overall philosophy is to assist residents in well-being and a sense of belonging and dignity through the medium of human relationships. An investment in the future of nurses and nursing is an investment in the future of their residents. The information technology project, as well as in-house training and contextual support (including clinical supervision) is focused on facilitating this investment.

Department of Psychiatry, Psychiatric Day Hospital, Tameside, Glossop Health Authority

As with the NDU at St George's Hospital, Stafford this unit is based in a psychiatric day hospital provision, and again clinical supervision forms a key and important aspect of this NDU.

As nursing roles develop in more specialised areas of care and the acquisition of sophisticated practitioner skills becomes apparent, the need for nurses to receive regular supervision is seen as essential within the unit. As part of this project, Tameside Psychiatric NDU has commissioned a post, the prime function of which is responsibility for researching and developing various models of clinical supervision for nurses working within different settings. Other particular posts that have come about as a result of the NDU initiation have been those of liaison nurses who have been trained to coordinate services on offer, and to act as link personnel between community, hospital and day services.

The Anorexia Nervosa Unit, St George's Hospital, London

The clinical nurse specialist in anorexia nervosa at St George's Hospital was awarded a nursing development unit grant to develop practice for the benefit of those who experience anorexia nervosa. This unit will provide treatment in a non-institutionalised community setting. As well as treating patients, one of the NDU's aims is to establish teaching and training programmes for nurses and other professionals working with clients suffering from anorexia nervosa. It will also undertake research into the treatments offered, the role of the specialist nurse practitioner in mental health and the development of the NDU itself.

Maudsley Hospital, Camberwell, London

As an acute admission ward for adults with mental health problems, this ward at the Maudsley Hospital aims to evaluate nursing practice development through the use of a comprehensive discharge package. They aim to increase remission periods and improve patient satisfaction, and so lead to cost effectiveness and quality.

Innovations include extending nursing services to both pre- and post-discharge patients; in so doing, they are more consumer-led. These services include discharge groups, patient information groups, drama groups, nursing outpatient clinics and community visits.

V and W wards, Leeds Community and Mental Health Unit, Elderly Psychiatry

These two wards at Seacroft Hospital together form a small unit providing a comprehensive acute service to the over-65-year-old population of south and east Leeds. The staff are exploring the boundaries of nursing in an environment that promotes the right of every individual to make decisions and exercise choice. This is the crucial area that binds together several areas of research study and investigation. It is envisaged that this research will be integrated into everyday nursing care.

Anston Ward, Rampton Hospital, Nottinghamshire

Rampton Hospital is run under the auspices of the Special Hospitals Service and provides a service for detained mentally disordered patients who require treatment under conditions of special security. Key objectives for the Rampton NDU include training and learning opportunities, the promotion of the concept of named nursing, providing greater and more comprehensive information to patients and those who are significant in their lives, enabling choice about individual health matters and evaluation of progress of nursing development, including standards of care and promotion of the role that nurses have to play in this important speciality. (Extracts adapted from King's Fund Nursing Development Unit Newsletter.)

Clearly, it can be seen that the breadth and excellence in terms of nursing developments available within mental health units, is indeed substantial.

One thing seems to bind all the projects together: the subject of empowerment. Empowerment is important to the nursing profession (Styles, 1993); crucially however, we know that we cannot empower our clients, those clients who we see daily, the most marginalised and disenfranchised in society, if we do not empower the staff who work with them. Empowerment of staff is a key function of any nursing development unit (Wright, 1989b).

Why are nursing development units so important in mental health settings? Well, mental health nurses provide the sustaining and encouraging support that most of our clients need. They are the biggest, and I think the best qualified resource of any manager attempting to give direction to a mental health unit. Mental health nurses are those clinicians who are honoured by the very personal traumas, emotions, symptoms and feelings their patients share with them. They are the clinicians who, in return, bestow the gift of support to their clients, support in terms of assisting clients in adapting and managing their lives (Sheehan, 1993).

Chief executives and unit general managers of mental health provider units now see those NDUs that have become ensconced in the culture of their organisation as essential. Not only do NDUs in mental health care provide a service, but they also sustain staff and assist managers in challenging tradition and creating change – issues that are relevant on all managers' agendas.

They are stating simply that mental health nurses delight in: the simplicity and uniqueness of what they contribute to patient care. They are making a stand for those skills, encouraging practitioners to own them and encouraging our articulate and intelligent voices from the grass roots. They are taking hold of an opportunity, they are acknowledging that it is the care of the mental health nurse that protects, maintains, sustains, encourages and gives hope. However, it is not in an emotional way that those who are leading NDUs in mental health care are approaching these issues – it is with professionalism and sound research-based practice.

Those managers of mental health units who neglect their main staffing resource (RMNs) and do not allow the reins, if not to run free at least to become a little more slack, would be committing a grave error. Mental health nurses can and do take responsibility professionally for clients. In a sense, they have a more legitimate claim to leadership than any other colleague working in the mental health care context who may merely be acting as a gatekeeper to the actual treatment services that mental health nurses provide.

To use a comparison with midwifery, it is now accepted that the majority of births are supported by midwives. Not all expectant mothers either need or want to be attended by a consultant obstetrician at the time of birth. In much the same way only a small proportion of people with mental health concerns need to see a consultant psychiatrist (Sheehan, 1993).

Services need to move away from the acceptance of everyone coming into mental health care systems needing the total package: the beds, the meals, the doctors, etc. Services must become much more focused in their care. Mental health nursing can do this, and to ignore this potential would be foolhardy. Mental health nursing development units make common sense. They are value for money, they are making the most of what mental health units have, they are meeting national as well as local agendas, and they are breaking with tradition without throwing proverbial babies out with bath water. Above and beyond all this, they provide a service that is second to none for their consumers.

More than 10 years have passed since the first nursing development units were established. With dramatic changes in health service provision, the need to evaluate nurses' contribution critically is even more paramount. In no other area of health care provision has there been greater change than in mental health care. As well as having to cope with NHS reforms, mental health has also had to provide leadership into the community. Mental health nurses will be leading this initiative, along with all the others in the past. NDUs provide a focus for examination of this leadership role; they provide a focus and a mechanism that can highlight what mental health nurses can do.

NDUs are a small but crucial contribution to this much wider drive to recognise and develop the potential of nursing. Challenging times lie ahead, but it is up to nurses, particularly in mental health care, to seize this opportunity to ensure that they can control their contribution because if they do not, other people will. The mental health nursing development unit at St George's Hospital, Stafford is a prime example of how mental health nurses can provide a real alternative to mainstream psychiatry. The staff are indeed defining their own role.

The unit advocates an acknowledgment of the simplicity of mental health nursing practice and its uniqueness as a profession which has containing, sustaining and maintaining value and belief in quality substantial training to support clinical practice (Dodd and Sheehan, 1993). Nurses in this particular unit are not defining themselves according to other disciplines' parameters; they are finding their own boundaries and taking seriously crucial issues such as clinical supervision and research- and evaluation-based practice. The nursing development unit provides what mental health nurses require to exemplify true leadership. The three key components are:

Professionalism, facilitating balanced and objective decision-making practice. Professionalism also provides a supportive network encouraging research and sharing innovation.

A *skills base* borne out of effective training and clinical awareness, the skills being the necessary vehicle to deliver patient care.

A *humanity* which is evident in the unit and allows a glimpse of the person beneath the professional mask.

Any imbalance of this context for mental health nursing in the nursing development unit causes a loss of focus in terms of care. The support of the nursing development unit structure ensures a retention of this focus.

At this time leaders in mental health nursing are attempting to describe those common denominators which define our practice. Their task is made more difficult by the diversity of those roles which make up what certainly could *not* be described as a homogeneous professional grouping. Mental health nursing is a unique profession. Its diversity helps to make it so. What also helps to make it unique is the simplicity of delivery of its skills, and how the delivery dovetails with patients' and clients' needs. How people are defined, for example schizophrenic, addicted, old and demented, depressed or anxious, matters little. What is important are the common needs, to be heard, to feel secure, to be valued, to be offered hope, to be sustained, to be allowed to grow and to be helped to live. Clients or patients do delight in the simplicity of what we as mental health nurses do.

> It is in simplicity
> That most pleasure is gained
> and depths attained. (English, 1993)

So why can't we too delight in and be proud of how we work? Emotion does not necessarily need to be therapied. It may, however, need to be expressed and understood, with the individual feeling supported. It really is a simple equation with the answer being a relationship: a mental health nursing relationship.

NURSING DEVELOPMENT UNITS – THE WAY FORWARD

Much of current mental health care lays great emphasis on the assessment, diagnosis and treatment of mental illness, which is best provided allegedly in a traditional medical context. Medical and paramedical therapies are seen as having the central role in resolving these 'biological crises'. Nursing is often sidelined into the supporting role, involved in some treatments but primarily 'caring' for the patient with attention to comfort and hygiene needs, while the 'curing' work of the doctors and others takes effect.

Nursing development units are part of the current movement in nursing which is re-examining the role and function of nurses and nursing. NDUs are centres of clinical nursing, where nurses collaborate to re-examine their practices, develop themselves and their roles and accept a continued, planned process of change. Some NDUs may possess 'nursing beds' (where nurses can admit and discharge patients). However, all are involved in promoting patient-centred methods of care, often with high level involvement of patients and relatives. Examples of this are self-medication schemes, developing care management, primary nursing and access to case records. NDUs may be in the hospital or the community, in the public or the private sector. All focus on the explicit development of nursing to fulfil its potential in the multidisciplinary team. They are underpinned by the notion that nursing is a therapeutic force in its own right, with overall benefits to patients and all involved in health care when its potential is fully realised and exploited.

The setting-up of NDUs or, indeed, any sort of nursing development project, is not without controversy or conflict. When nurses change their roles and practices there is an impact on the multidisciplinary team and the wider organisation. The successful planning and management of change is a key feature on NDUs. Mental health nurses offer assistance to patients in learning to adapt and manage changes in their lives. Because of the NDU movement, they are now doing this for themselves.

NDUs are not alone in developing nursing, nor do they lay claim to always achieving excellence (although they all aspire to it). Similarly, the practice of therapeutic nursing can be achieved wherever nursing is taking place, although it is argued that it is best facilitated in specific nursing units. However, by contributing to the development of nursing practice, they assist in the overall reappraisal of the most effective ways of developing health care.

Mental health NDUs are meeting many agendas. They are an alternative which through evaluation and sharing of innovation will highlight a break from tradition with nurses truly leading the way. More mental health NDUs are necessary in what Rowden (1993) describes as 'the developing UK health agenda'. This agenda includes increased mental health problems. Medicine in its traditional form can only begin to work at the periphery of the agenda because of its curative foundation. It is mental health nurses who will provide the curative approaches necessary to impact on the agenda. Mental health NDUs are the nurseries that are nurturing these approaches.

In mental health NDUs throughout the country nurses are developing while they work with their patients. As Garbett (1992) sugggests, opportunities are indeed inherent in clinical practice for professional growth. There can be no stronger message to nurse managers and educators from practitioners about where nursing development should start.

REFERENCES

Department of Health (1992a). *Health of the Nation Document*. London: HMSO.

Department of Health (1992b). *Patient's Charter Document*. London: HMSO.

Dodd T and Sheehan A (1993) *Mental Health Nursing – A tin of beans, no can of worms*. Unpublished Report: Stafford: The Foundation of Mid Staffs NHS Trust.

English P (1993) In: Dodd T and English P (eds) *Client Perspectives*. Unpublished. Stafford NDU, The Foundation of Mid Staffs NHS Trust.

Garbett R (1992) Attested development. *Nursing Times* **88**(35): 40–42.

King's Fund Centre (1993) *Nursing Developments Newsletter*, special edn Neal K (ed) London: NDU Key Characteristics.

Pearson A (1984) The Burford experience. *Nursing Mirror* **159**(22): 32–35.

Pearson A, Durand I and Punton S (1992) *Nursing Beds and Evaluation of the Effects of Therapeutic Nursing*. London: Scutari Press.

Rowden R (1993) From a speech to the Celebrating Nursing Conference. University of Manchester: King's Fund Centre/TENDA Conference.

Salvage J (1989) Nursing developments. *Nursing Standard* **3**(35): 25–26.

Sheehan A (1993) Protecting the skills of mental health nursing (Editorial). *British Journal of Nursing* **2**(11): 557.

Snell J (1991) No brakes on reform says Waldegrave. *Nursing Times* **87**(21): 5.

Styles G (1993) Empowerment and Nursing. From a speech made to Royal College of Nursing Annual General Meeting, St David's Hall, Cardiff, 20 October.

Vaughan B (1992) The pursuit of excellence. *Nursing Times* **88**(31): 26–28.

Wright SG (1989a) *Changing Nursing Practice*. London: Arnold Press.

Wright SG (1989b) Defining a nursing development unit. *Nursing Standard* **4**(7): 29–31.

CHAPTER 3

Case Management

KEVIN GOURNAY

INTRODUCTION

This chapter concerns an approach that is arguably one of the most important in the range of contemporary developments in the care and treatment of people with serious mental health problems. As we shall see, case management offers considerable hope to the users of services and their carers. At the same time it provides a major challenge for mental health nursing in the 1990s. The current high profile of case management and its priority on the agendas of health service planners in the United Kingdom today is due to recent changes in government policy. However, as we shall see below, the seeds of the case management initiative are to be found in several places over the last 30 years.

Caring for People was published in 1990 as a White Paper on Community Care (Department of Health, 1990) and eventually the principles described in that paper became enshrined in the Community Care Act of 1990. The policy changes are aimed at clearly coordinated programmes of care in the community for people with serious mental health problems. The legislation has also meant that health agencies and local authorities have had to work together in order to ensure funding. While these changes are, in principle, to be welcomed, central funding problems have continued to cause major difficulties for the proper implementation of these policies. Furthermore, as we shall see below, there are other obstacles to providing a specialist and comprehensive service to people with serious mental health problems. For example, there are considerable difficulties in establishing and maintaining adequate training in case management skills and in many areas there is a paucity of truly well developed multidisciplinary working arrangements.

However, despite the many real difficulties of implementation, government policy guidance on case management is to be applauded because the objectives clearly summarise all the commonly accepted key features of effective community care. These objectives are as follows:

1. To meet individual care needs through the most effective use of resources.
2. To restore and maintain independence by enabling people to live in the community wherever possible.
3. To prevent or minimise the negative effects of disability, illness or mental distress in people of all ages.
4. To achieve equal opportunities for all.
5. To promote individual choices of determination and build on existing strengths and care resources.
6. To promote partnerships between users, carers and service providers in all sectors.

Furthermore, the three core processes of case management were defined as:

1. Assessment, which includes the support needs of carers.
2. Planning and agreeing preferred options for support with the involvement of users, carers and other relevant agencies.
3. Implementation, monitoring, review and revision.

Case management has been given a further priority within *The Health of the Nation* initiative. *The Health of the Nation* White Paper was originally published in July 1992 and then in the Spring of 1993 a Key Area Handbook on Mental Illness was produced by the Department of Health. This key area handbook defined various priority areas for action. With regard to case management, the handbook contains a great deal of detailed direction. It covers, in a comprehensive way, issues such as needs assessment, seeking the views of consumers, developing alliances between various agencies, agreeing targets for local areas, developing skills, improving information and, importantly, defining what monitoring arrangements should be in place.

THE ORIGINS OF CASE MANAGEMENT

The origins obviously lie in the community care movement which began in the post-war period. In the United Kingdom developments in community psychiatry occurred before the 1959 Mental Health Act. For example, the first community psychiatric nursing service was developed from Warlingham Park Hospital in Croydon in 1954 (Moore, 1961). Certainly the 1959 Mental Health Act provided an impetus for community based services and during the 1960s and 1970s the large psychiatric hospitals began to reduce their bed size. In the United States comparable changes were occurring. As with British hospitals, the state mental hospitals in the United States developed from 1850 into large institutions which Stein (1991) referred to as 'warehouses for human beings who have been discarded by society'. The process of reducing the size of the

population of mental hospitals began in 1955 and the period of deinstitutionali-
sation saw a reduction in the population from over half a million to just over
100 000. President Kennedy, in response to the process of deinstitutionalisa-
tion, began the process of setting up community mental health centres and the
early 1960s saw a time of great hope for the community care movement.
However, the staff in these centres changed the primary purpose of these centres
(i.e. caring for people with serious mental illness) and largely devoted themselves
to treating people without major mental health difficulties, such as general anxiety and life and relationship stress, with various (and usually ineffective) forms of
psychotherapy. The same process has of course occurred in this country and has
latterly been exemplified by very large numbers of community psychiatric nurses
targeting their efforts on people with minor mental health problems in primary
care (Gournay and Brooking, 1992, 1994). This process has been to the great
disadvantage of people with more serious mental health problems – schizophrenia in particular. Thus by the late 1970s many mentally ill people throughout the
western world were neglected by services and were encumbered by a range of
serious social and economic problems. It also goes without saying that the consequences for many families were devastating. In this setting, Dr Leonard Stein
and Dr Mary Ann Test pioneered a 'ward in the community' in Madison,
Wisconsin. In this programme, the nursing staff together with psychiatrists,
psychologists and social workers and some secretarial and administrative support staff, moved into a house in the community and administered care to
their population of patients. The house was a base from which the team worked
and all clients were seen in their natural setting.

Stein and Test recognised that people who suffered serious mental illness were
also disadvantaged by secondary impairment, including difficulty with interpersonal relationships, dependence on family or institution and deficiencies in
coping skills such as budgeting, using public transport, shopping, cooking,
etc. They recognised that in order to provide a suitable service to people, and
to stand any reasonable chance of long-term success, services needed to provide
a comprehensive package, ideally delivered by one person (case manager). Therefore, the role of the case manager included not only the management of
symptoms and the administration and monitoring of medication, but a whole
range of other functions that impacted directly on social function. After some
time piloting this approach Stein and Test (Stein and Test, 1980; Test and Stein,
1980) subjected this mode of care to a clinical trial, in which 65 patients were
treated using this method and 65 patients were treated with traditional hospital
care and routine outpatient follow-up. The majority of people referred to the
service had a diagnosis of schizophrenia and three-quarters of them were either
single, separated or divorced. Many of them had been in hospital with an average
of five prior admissions. The other key characteristic of the comprehensive programme was that it reached out actively to patients and did not allow them to
become passive dropouts of service (a function now known as Assertive Outreach). By the end of the first year of the study there were very large differences

between the two treatment conditions. In the comprehensive community pro-gramme (compared with the traditional hospital and follow-up condition), there were many fewer admissions (12 of 65 compared with 57 of 65). On other measures, the community group were much more advantaged. With regard to the costs of both modes of treatment, there was no difference between treating patients in the community in an intensive way and managing them in the traditional way. At the end of the 12 months the community care intervention ceased, but patients continued to be studied for a further 14 months. Test and Stein found that the gains made by the community group were lost quite quickly when they were returned to a traditional mode of care. Furthermore, many of the people who had previously been in the comprehensive programme of community care were being readmitted to hospital and had experienced a deterioration in their employment and social circumstances. This finding was very important because it highlighted the need for long term, and in some cases indefinite, management. Thus, for the first time, experimental data indicated that services for people with serious mental health problems should be seen as needing to be given over an indefinite period of time, albeit intermittently in some cases. The programme of care has been developed in this area of Madison over the last 16 years and this model of treatment has been extended internationally. However, it is worth focusing on what now happens in Madison as it provides a useful model for other services.

Currently all people with severe and persistent mental illness in the Dane County area of Madison are identified and every person in the system has a person identified who is responsible for that person's care and treatment (case manager). The services provided for this group include a mobile community treatment team which is targeted on people who are difficult to treat – for example, those who are unwilling to attend clinics and those who do not take their medication. The service is augmented by day treatment facilities and an outpatient clinic but also with a 7-day crisis intervention service which provides a 24-hour response. With regard to the funding of services, as Stein (1991) points out, the average expenditure on mental health services in the United States is divided between 70 per cent on inpatient services and 30 per cent on outpatient services. In the Madison service, 85 per cent is spent on the community service and only 15 per cent on the inpatient services. In addition, the service in Madison receives less money than the national average and, therefore, one could argue that in the long term, this reversal of funding leads to a huge cost benefit to the system.

As mentioned above, the Madison model of treatment has been extended internationally. Another service that has been running for more than a decade is the Boulder, Colorado treatment system. This, too, offers essentially community based programmes with some modifications of the system running in Madison. Like the Madison system, the Boulder system utilises the bulk of its funding for community programmes. Thus, the service which covers the 210 000 residents of the mixed urban and rural region of Boulder County only uses eight acute hospital beds. In addition, 10 Boulder residents are in long-term care in the state hospital and the service also uses a large house for 15 people who need short term 'community asylum' and more intensive medical treatment. Like Madison, the Boulder system covers virtually all people known to have a serious mental health problem and of these there are 550 people known to have major long standing problems, of whom about 80 are in contact with an intensive community support systems programme. This population comprises the most seriously ill group, who often exhibit an array of challenging behaviour and who in many areas would be looked after in the restrictive settings of psychiatric units or long-stay wards. This programme runs on a 7-day, 24-hour basis and uses an assertive case management system, thus keeping track of all people with serious mental illness and not allowing them to drop out. The 1992 annual report for the mental health centre of Boulder County reports that a sample of 25 seriously mentally ill adults improved progressively over the years that they were treated by the community support systems team. The proportion of this population with no inpatient admissions during a 2-year period improved from 4 per cent to 57 per cent. The proportion who were 'revolving door' patients decreased progressively from 28 per cent to 5 per cent. (For a more detailed review of the Boulder system, see Mosher and Burti, 1989).

Several other aspects of the Boulder system are interesting. The mental health services in Boulder employ very few nurses. Of a staff of 250 full-time equivalents, only 17 (6.1 full-time equivalents) are nurses. The majority of case managers and other mental health workers are people who have a first degree, not necessarily in a mental health area, who have received on-the-job training. The service employs about five full-time equivalent licensed psychologists and about 20 full-time equivalent certified social workers. However, in general the service relies on a group of mental health workers very different to that found in the United Kingdom. These workers receive considerable in-service training and many of them return to further full-time study. Thus, many of the staff of the programme have Masters degrees in counselling, psychology or other related disciplines. Another interesting feature of the Boulder system is their employment of consumers as case management aides (see below). At present, consumer case managers are employed in the intensive residential service and supervised housing, while consumers also take part in planning meetings. The Boulder system also uses a consumer clubhouse. The clubhouse system is one which has spread in the United States and consists of buildings that may be owned by the mental health service but in many respects the service functions autonomously. Clubhouses may be assisted in minor ways by mental health professionals but they are run by consumers for consumers and provide a range of activities during the day, evening and weekends and give practical help and advice regarding employment and housing. At present there is only one established British clubhouse (in Dartford, Kent) in the international clubhouse directory. This is a pity, as the clubhouse movement seems to provide another way in which consumers can become more responsible for the management of their problems and the rehabilitative process.

Another pioneering service in Sydney, Australia is worth describing in some detail as it represents an ideal model and it is also based on more than a decade of experience. Furthermore, the State of New South Wales has arguably one of the most advanced and developed case management public policies in the world. The services in Sydney owe their original stimulus for development to the Madison programme. The original research-based project on Sydney's North Shore (Hoult et al, 1984; Hoult, 1986) has acted as an initial building block for the development of a number of case management-based teams in other parts of the metropolis. The Inner City Service (ICS) is particularly interesting. The ICS has several teams. First, there is a team that responds to acute episodes by sending a mental health professional to see the client in the situation where the crisis has arisen. This worker, who is a designated case manager, may be a nurse, social worker or other health professional and this person makes an initial assessment of the difficulty. It may be that at this point specialist psychiatric help is required and therefore a psychiatric opinion may well be sought by the case manager. This, however, is not necessarily the case, as in the inner city many crises may evolve that are predominantly social in nature. Having said that, all workers on the team will be familiar with, and skilled in, screening procedures for mental illness and will be particularly skilled in discerning the various symptoms of mental illnesses.

The ICS covers an area of 60 000 people and this area of Sydney has high levels of social deprivation and homelessness. The incidence of serious mental illness in this area is four times that in the city as a whole. Assessment by the case manager from the acute service often reveals that the most important needs of the person are social rather than medical. The case managers, therefore, very often find themselves in positions where they need to help the client find accommodation and access to a range of agencies. The client, in turn, may well have a difficulty with these areas because of the sequelae of their mental health problem. Alongside the acute service, there is also a team that specifically services the homeless and which actively reaches out to all of the key voluntary and statutory agencies that have contact with the seriously mentally ill. Thus, for example, workers from the mental health service visit shelters for the homeless to access those in need. These workers also have excellent relationships with police and other members of the justice system and this ensures that, where possible, people with mental health problems who have come into contact with police and the courts are given appropriate access to services.

Various projects have been set up in various parts of the world, based to some degree on the Madison model. In the United Kingdom there have been two large research-based projects, both set up in London. The first was the Early Intervention Service set up in the Paddington area and the workings of this service are referred to in detail by Onyett (1992). The second London service was the Daily Living Programme. This was set up at the Maudsley Hospital in 1987 and essentially compared home-based treatment with standard hospital care for seriously mentally ill patients facing immediate admission (Muijen et al, 1992). The Daily Living Programme team consisted of seven psychiatric nurses, an occupational therapist, a social worker, a psychiatrist and secretarial and administrative support. The staff: patient ratio on the project was 1:10 and by comparison with traditional services the intensive community care provided considerable support and treatment. The components of the programme included continuous support for the duration of the 3-year project, coordinated care by a key worker (case manager) and crisis intervention that included brief hospital admission if required. The programme also included rehabilitation, including skills training where necessary, support for and education of relatives, employers, landlords and statutory and voluntary organisations, advocacy and, perhaps most importantly, the provision of 24-hour care 7 days a week with access to telephone contact with the case manager at night. At the end of the first 18 months of the study, 60 patients had been treated within the Daily Living Programme condition and 60 patients had been treated with traditional hospital care. The population came from one of the most deprived areas in London and contained one-third of Afro-Caribbeans, this being somewhat higher than the proportion of Afro-Caribbeans in the local population (20 per cent). As the authors reported, the Daily Living Programme reduced hospital use by 80 per cent. However, of some concern was the suicide of two patients in the Daily Living Programme and one patient who committed murder. Given the fact that these patients all presented with a serious acute mental illness these episodes, while deeply regrettable, were not outside the statistical expectation of such a population. The Maudsley Hospital service has provided an inspiration for other services to develop along the Daily Living Programme lines. Both the Early Intervention Service and the Daily Living Programme have spawned a number of clone services that provide intensive and effective programmes of community care for people with serious mental illness. In addition to these large research-based projects there have been several other innovations in the United Kingdom, which have not been based on research programmes but have been set up within the context of normal mental health service provision. Exemplary services are to be found in Lewisham in London and Sparkbrook in Birmingham and there are signs that many other local services are beginning to provide, within limited resources, excellent care and treatment for the very marginalised group of people with serious mental health problems.

Which client group?

Case management in general is targeted at vulnerable people with continuing physical and mental health problems. However, this chapter focuses only on people with mental health problems.

While it is generally agreed that the bulk of the case managers' workload should involve working with people with schizophrenia and long-term affective disorders, the current shortage of suitably trained case managers means that there will need to be some priority-setting with regard to which individuals should receive an intensive approach. Some recent research (Ford et al, 1993) has indicated that there are two major subgroups of clients who should be targeted. First, Ford and his colleagues describe a client group who have had a long institutional history and who have been discharged to situations of social isolation and who remain totally dependent on services because of poor daily living skills. The second group is characterised by frequent short admissions and a history of violence to themselves or others. The authors say that these people appear to be more akin to those referred to as 'revolving door' cases rather than long-stay patients. Eighty-five per cent of the study sample had a diagnosis of psychotic disorder and in general they had been in contact with psychiatric services over a long period of time (a mean of 22 years). Twenty-five per cent of the sample had been inpatients for more than 1 year. The poverty of the population's social life was profound; only 16 per cent were married and 45 per cent had no social contacts outside mental health services. Only two of the 234 clients studied were in any kind of competitive employment. Onyett (1992) describes some of the dilemmas faced in allocating case management services and while accepting that case management should in theory be offered to a wide range of clients, acknowledges that for many clients case management may become an indefinite arrangement and thus finite resources need to be targeted on this high priority population. Indeed, in the original study in Madison, Wisconsin, Stein (1991) reported that when the experimental case management model was withdrawn after 1 year to be replaced by traditional services, the clinical and social status of clients deteriorated. In the light of research carried out nationally and internationally and because of the finite nature of services, it is therefore essential that all services monitor the local effectiveness of case management and attempt to ensure that the most needy groups are receiving adequate resources.

MODELS OF MENTAL ILLNESS

One of the major debates in mental health in the last three decades has been the somewhat time-wasting controversy regarding the cause of mental illnesses. In particular, as referred to elsewhere in this chapter, in the late 1960s there was a prevailing theory that schizophrenia was largely caused by faulty family interaction and indeed, the whole concept of schizophrenia has been questioned (see, for example, Laing and Esterson, 1964; Szasz, 1987). However, the contemporary and informed view of the causation of schizophrenia (and indeed the major affective disorders) is that there are many factors implicated and these include genetic defects which lead to various biochemical abnormalities. In addition, there is now considerable evidence of structural differences in the brains of some people with schizophrenia. Nevertheless, there are clear social and psychological factors that seem to be responsible for the triggering and maintenance of the syndrome and we know, for example, that the long-term outcome of people with schizophrenia is far worse in western industrialised society than in the developing countries. This is almost certainly connected with poorer family and social support structures in the the so-called civilised western societies (Lin and Kleinmann, 1988). Therefore, in summary, the current thinking is that schizophrenia is a predominantly biological disorder with many different social and psychological factors affecting its course and that there may be a considerable variation in the way all these factors exist in different cases (for a review of the area see Gournay, 1993).

Perhaps a more practical way of looking at schizophrenia and probably mental health problems in general is to use what has been called the 'stress vulnerability model'. This model comes from the work of Zubin and Spring (1977) and argues that there is a vulnerability to mental health problems that is essentially biological and stems from genetic aberrations but that this biological predisposition will only be triggered into a full syndrome by various stresses from the environment (e.g. interpersonal problems, occupational changes, adverse life events). Furthermore, the model postulates that the way in which the individual deals with this depends on their coping resources. Obviously, coping resources are made up of many factors ranging from the presence or absence of material resources such as money, adequate housing and so on through to the more complex cognitive and interpersonal coping resources. The model allows the practitioner to conceptualise the person's mental health difficulties without becoming drawn into time-consuming debates about the minutiae of causation. The model also allows for accepting that the individual is shaped by a whole range of social and psychological factors that determine individuality and which may or may not be of central importance in the development and maintenance of illness. For example, any clinician will know that some people with schizophrenia have life histories that are full of loss, separation and emotional deprivation while, conversely, other people with schizophrenia seem to be born into entirely happy and well-adjusted families and these people are characterised by an absence of any obvious psychological or emotional determinants of their illness.

THE CENTRAL TASKS AND PRINCIPLES OF CASE MANAGEMENT

(Onyett 1992) defines the five core tasks of case management as:

1. Assessment
2. Planning
3. Implementation
4. Monitoring
5. Reviewing

As such, these tasks can also be defined as the central aspects of any soundly based psychological therapy. However, in the setting of work with people with serious mental health problems, these tasks are accomplished within the context of other factors. Some of these factors are (in no order of priority):

(a) seeing problems and solutions as having a mixture of psychological, social and biological components (i.e. the biopsychosocial model);

(b) identifying the strengths of the individual and building on these, rather than adopting a primary focus on deficits;

(c) listening to the views and expressed needs of the user of service and their family and collaborating with them to achieve their social, occupational and domestic goals;

(d) applying case management in any setting that is appropriate to the needs of the user;

(e) assertively building reciprocal relationships with the appropriate voluntary and statutory authorities and acting as an advocate where necessary;

(f) taking a central and practical role in training and assistance with daily living skills;

(g) being proactive in the detection of relapse and, in a wider sense, in the detection of illness in particularly vulnerable groups; and

(h) using research-based interventions to deal with symptoms and using relevant interventions to increase and sustain social function.

ASSERTIVE CASE MANAGEMENT

Assertive case management is an umbrella description of approaches to the problem based on the idea that mental health professionals need to respond aggressively to mental health problems and in so doing actively seek out people who are in need of services, either by detecting people with serious mental illness, or by preventing people from dropping out of services. In this regard, mental health nurses may well need to adopt a different approach to mental health problems. It is fair to say that one side effect of a more liberal approach to treatment of people with mental health problems has been to allow more decision-making by sufferers. While this is a very noble principle which should be vigorously pursued it can, if accepted totally, lead to people with serious mental illnesses who lack insight, losing touch with services and abandoning treatment. While there is obviously a danger of encroaching upon people's civil liberties, there is also a need for mental health professionals to bear in mind their responsibility for protecting those who are unable, by reason of their illness, to protect themselves. By definition, major mental illnesses affect people's motivation, distort the processes involving reality and judgement and many sufferers are literally unable to fend for themselves. Assertive case management recognises this and thus the role of the case manager, in addition to the principles described above, needs to incorporate an approach which is proactive rather than reactive.

ASSESSMENT

The assessment of an individual with a serious mental health problem presents a huge challenge. This assessment process is only the beginning of a relationship with a service and, indeed, with an individual mental health professional working within that service, this relationship may carry on for many years. Obviously therefore the assessment needs to involve a process of engagement and relationship-building which should be done over a period of time rather than on one occasion. Ideally, assessment should be carried out in the client's home and with access to family members and friends. However, where possible and without being intrusive, it is always good to try to see the client in other settings, for example to visit them in their day centre or to have coffee or a snack with them in their locality. This will not only help the person feel more relaxed and on their 'own territory' but will also allow naturalistic observation.

A very helpful and detailed description of the process of engagement and relationship-building is found in Onyett (1992) and is recommended to those working in this area.

It is very difficult to be precise about what information should be included in a case management assessment, but the following list drawn from the Camberwell Assessment of Need (Thornicroft, 1994) is a good summary:

Accommodation	Safety (to others)
Occupation	Money
Specific psychotic symptoms	Childcare
Psychological distress	Physical health
Information about condition and treatment	Alcohol
	Basic education
Non-prescribed drugs	Company
Food and meals	Telephone
Household skills	Public transport
Self-care	Benefits
Safety (to self)	Sexual relations

The case manager also needs to look at the services immediately available to the client and during the period of assessment needs to make contact with agencies who may have been in touch with the client in the past or who continue to have contact.

PLANNING

Once the assessment process is complete, the case manager needs to formulate a plan which incorporates all interventions and these include medication, psycho-social interventions (see below), money management (see below) and a clear plan of how the client's occupational, social, financial and other needs are to be met.

It cannot be over-emphasised that the planning task needs to be carried out in the spirit of mutual collaboration with the client and that the client's expressed needs drive the whole process. Very often, stability of symptoms can be achieved very successfully by skilled management of medication and this is, of course, aided by frequent contact with the case manager. In many of the American services there seems to be much less need to give long-acting injections of neuroleptic agents because medication can be given orally, if necessary by the case manager, and the dose carefully titrated so as to allow for giving the mini-mum possible medication to achieve the optimum therapeutic effect. Additionally, this has the advantage of reducing the level of side effects so com-monly found in populations of people on long-term high dose neuroleptic medication.

IMPLEMENTATION

Implementation of the case management plan is a process which takes place, in some cases, over an indefinite period of time and, of course, the way in which the plan is implemented is subject to frequent revision. Obviously in chapters such as this, it is impossible to look at all aspects of case management (but Onyett (1992) is a good example of a comprehensive description). Therefore, what fol-lows is a description of some of the psychological interventions that have been developed in recent years and that form such an important part of the approach to serious mental health problems.

PSYCHOSOCIAL INTERVENTIONS

A very important point has been made by several authors (e.g. Birchwood and Tarrier, 1992; Muijen et al, 1992) and this is that case management programmes must not rely solely on the administration of drugs and the brokering of financial and housing aid. The case management approach must also deliver other inter-ventions which focus on the illness itself and its accompaniments – both social and psychological.

As we shall see below, mental health nurses are very often the most appropriate professionals to deliver these interventions. In the international context, British mental health nurses have led all other non-medical professional and other nurses in proving themselves capable of effective clinical autonomy. This is exem-plified in the field of community psychiatric nursing and in a more specialist way in nurse behaviour therapy. It is not possible by reason of space to review these psychosocial interventions in detail (see Birchwood and Tarrier, 1992, for a comprehensive review). However, the central strategies are summarised below.

1. Family interventions.
2. Social skills training.
3. Early intervention.
4. Symptom modification.

Family interventions

The family interventions used today are very different to the family approaches of two decades ago. These approaches were based on the idea that schizophrenia was caused by factors in family structures and various (pathological) family interactions. These theories, which were propagated by the anti-psychiatry school (e.g. Laing and Esterson, 1964) were not based on any objective evidence and arguably these theories led to a process of blame and considerable guilt in the families of sufferers because, in effect, what was being said was that schizophrenia was caused by 'bad mothers'. This era therefore probably delayed the evolution of more appropriate psychological strategies based on objective, controlled evidence and also led many carers to mistrust mental health professionals.

Contemporary family approaches find their source in the seminal research work on expressed emotion (see Leff and Vaughn, 1985, for a detailed review). In essence, expressed emotion comprises a group of behaviours seen in relatives and carers of people with schizophrenia. These behaviours are principally critical comments, hostility, over-involvement and a large amount of face to face contact. The original work and subsequent research studies have shown that the presence of these behaviours has a relationship with increased risk of relapse. However, the relationship is not a direct, simple one and therefore the presence of high negative expressed emotion can only be considered as part of the process of symptom maintenance and relapse. Therefore contemporary approaches with families need to be more comprehensive than simply aiming for a reduction of expressed emotion. As with any sound case management approach, any family intervention must be based on a comprehensive family assessment that should include the family strengths as well as any deficits. This approach therefore starts from the position that one wants to build on existing family structures and reinforce positive family behaviour. Additionally, there is a considerable body of research evidence showing that families require detailed education about serious mental health problems and that families need to acquire the ability to recognise symptoms of relapse. Furthermore, families also need skills in stress management and coping responses because the burden of trying to look after someone with a serious mental illness can obviously overwhelm the family and other carers. Family assessment should therefore lead to the setting of positive goals so that both the person with the problem and the family can work towards targets, supported in their endeavours by the case manager.

The family approach has been used extensively within the service in Buckingham (Falloon and Graham-Hole, 1991) and within this service (which relies heavily on mental health nurses) there is an emphasis on mental health teams based in primary care operating a case management model, but with the emphasis on augmenting and supporting already existing family support structures. In an exciting innovation specific to mental health nursing, Brooker et al (1992) have developed a specific package in family interventions for community psychiatric nurses. This comprises educating relatives and carers and helping the family by training in stress management and coping skills. The results of Brooker et al's pilot study indicate a benefit to families receiving this mode of intervention (as with other similar studies) but more importantly show that training can be delivered effectively and fairly briefly to CPNs with no previous training in this area.

In Australia mental health nurses have been trained to deliver family interventions since 1989 and, in particular, the University of Wollongong (about 60 miles south of Sydney) runs an excellent programme for nurses that includes a substantial training in cognitive behavioural family interventions.

Social skills training

This approach is one of the oldest of the behavioural interventions and has been successfully applied in various populations of people over the last two decades. Social skills training has also been widely used by nurses in various mental health settings (e.g. Hargie and McCarten, 1986) and has been a central approach of nurse behaviour therapists since nurse therapy training commenced in 1972 (Newell and Gournay, 1994). Traditionally, social skills programmes are carried out in groups and use role-play, feedback and the modelling of appropriate verbal and non-verbal behaviours. Generally speaking, the problems targeted by this approach have been inassertiveness, social anxiety and various social skills deficits – for example, poor eye contact or the inability to make appropriate approach behaviour to various social situations. In the last decade, social skills training has been applied increasingly to people with serious mental health problems and, in particular, to people with schizophrenia. Many sufferers have problems with apathy, lack of motivation and withdrawal from the spectrum of social situations and this leads to problems with establishing and maintaining all the necessary relationships involved in daily living, ranging from forming friendships to dealing with difficulties in obtaining accommodation and social security benefits. While the principles of social skills training with people with schizophrenia are similar to those used when dealing with people with social anxiety, the implementation of treatment programmes is generally very different. Because of the range and depth of problems encountered in psychosis and because of the sometimes severe problems with motivation, training needs to be carried out over a long period of time and tasks need to be broken down into smaller steps. For an excellent description of how social skills training may be applied with serious mental health problems, see Vaccaro and Roberts (1992). Social skills training needs, of course, to be embedded in comprehensive case management and it can be a useful adjunct to approaches that help the client to find work, social networks and accommodation. The case manager may well wish to refer the client to a social skills group run by a specialist nurse therapist or psychologist rather than carry out the training themselves. Nevertheless, the case manager still has an important function in helping with rehearsal of real life behaviour and modelling appropriate social skills. While the results of outcomes studies show benefit from this approach (Vaccaro and Roberts, 1992) it is not suitable for all clients and doubtless it is something which will deserve further attention from researchers in the future.

Unfortunately, most preregistration programmes in mental health nursing only cover this and other similar clinical skills acquisition in a superficial way. By contrast, nurse therapist programmes give literally hundreds of hours of skills training to the therapist trainees. While this intensity is not practical for most preregistration courses, nurse educators need to reconsider this vital area of omission urgently.

Early intervention

Serious mental health problems, particularly schizophrenia, are subject to high rates of relapse and we have known for some time that factors such as high levels of negative expressed emotion in the family (see above) and non-compliance with medication often precede such episodes. Therefore, in the last few years considerable research attention has been directed towards this phenomenon. The case manager obviously needs to be familiar with the principles of the intervention and there is now considerable information available regarding the various signs and symptoms which may occur before a relapse. For example, Birchwood et al (1992) describe anxiety, irritability, sleep problems, depression and withdrawal as being the most common symptoms preceding relapse. However, as a corollary to the recognition of these signs, the case manager needs to educate the family and other professionals regarding what symptoms to look for and, indeed, if there is a good relationship between the case manager and client, the client may very often be able to confide in the case manager before a full relapse occurs. Birchwood et al (1992) have described a systematic monitoring programme in which patient and either carer or case manager make regular observations of the absence or degree of certain signs and symptoms. Obviously, when such signs are observed, the case manager can intervene by organising re-evaluation of the medication and/or by increasing the level of support given to the patient and family. In addition, there may be some need to use problem orientated counselling to ameliorate the effects of various stressful events which may have recently occurred – for example, bereavement or job loss.

Early intervention is, of course, the stated aim of the programme run by Professor Peter Tyrer's team (the subject of Onyett's (1992) book) and in this programme, case management is delivered by CPNs. Early intervention is, however, an important principle for all CPNs working with serious mental health problems and yet this has never figured in any traditional CPN training programmes.

Symptom modification

This is a relatively new area of psychological intervention and may be helpful in the management of delusions and hallucinations which persist despite treatment with medication. Tarrier (1991, 1992) has described a range of behavioural and cognitive strategies which he and his collaborators call 'coping strategy enhancement'. This approach involves a detailed assessment and therapeutic approach which is founded on the principle of a therapeutic alliance between the therapist and client. Tarrier (1992) describes helping the client switch their attention from hallucinations, training the client to see the abnormal experience in a more rational light and to modify behavioural responses to the symptom so as to reduce its impact. Tarrier also describes the use of of the standard procedures used in behaviour therapy (e.g. deep muscle relaxation) and the use of strategies most commonly used in the cognitive therapy of depression. Tarrier (1992) reports some favourable outcomes of this approach but obviously longer-term evaluation using randomised controlled trials is still necessary.

While there is no evidence that nurses are currently using any of these innovations, such interventions could easily be implemented by trained nurse therapists. Additionally, there seems no reason why community psychiatric nurses should not, with a brief training programme, be able to deliver these treatments.

MONEY MANAGEMENT

The case manager often needs to help the client gain access to all the available financial benefits and needs to set up and maintain good relationships with the people in social security departments. It almost goes without saying that gaining access to appropriate benefits is difficult enough for most people and therefore people with serious mental health problems are often severely disadvantaged. Once a client has obtained the appropriate financial assistance, the case manager then may need to help the client acquire budgeting skills and continually monitor how well the client is doing. In the United States, the case manager often takes control over the client's money and, in many services, actually takes responsibility for paying various bills and giving the client money on a daily basis. This is often linked to the giving of medication and therefore in some services, the client does not receive any money until they have taken their medication. While this aspect of case management is obviously highly contentious for mental health workers in the United Kingdom, mental health workers in the United States seem to have little difficulty using their control over the client's finances to ensure compliance with treatment. However, what seems clear is that mental health nurses in the United Kingdom will, in future, need to become much more involved in patients' financial matters.

MONITORING AND REVIEWING

As with any good mental health intervention, case management should be subject to a rigorous process of monitoring and reviewing (or measurement and evaluation). The central principle of all evaluation in this area is the use of a number of valid and reliable measures of change that examine the global and the specific and that, when put together, form a comprehensive picture of the person's symptoms, function and overall quality of life. There is generally also a need to examine the impact of the person's illness on others. Where possible, measures of change should be instruments that have reliability and validity, although it is always reasonable to include measures that are specific to the individual. For example, asking the client to keep a diary of social interaction, noting what thoughts came into their mind on specific occasions or rating their anxiety on a simple 0–8 scale is very reasonable practice. Many services now use a diagnostic interview schedule as part of their assessment and increasingly these are computerised. A typical battery of measures would probably include a diagnostic interview, a self-report measure of depression, a rating of social function, a rating of living skills and perhaps a checklist of behaviours and attitudes. This battery of measures will need to be repeated at various intervals and certainly in every case within a 6-month period.

Apart from measuring mental health and social functioning on a formal basis using tried and reliable measures of change, each case should be subject to the formal process of review which includes a discussion with all the people involved in that client's care and treatment. Wherever possible, the case manager should obtain written summaries from all involved parties before a case review is held. In the author's experience in the United States and in Australia, case reviews on all clients with serious mental health problems are not only very feasible but form a central part of mental health service delivery. That being said, there is a tremendous variation regarding the use of formal measures of change and diagnostic interviews. However, the service in Wollongong in New South Wales is a model example for mental health nurses. In this service, nurses working in the rehabilitation section of the service with people with severe and long-standing mental health problems are responsible for administering computerised diagnostic interview schedules, measures of symptom and social function and other background social and demographic data. Therefore, other than the initial intake interview by the assessing psychiatrist, all the ongoing monitoring and reviewing is carried out by mental health nurses. There seems no reason why nurses in this country should not take a much greater part in regular evaluation using standard measures. However, this obviously will necessitate a significant 'cultural shift' from the current position, where mental health nurses see such measurement processes as outside either their remit or competence.

WHO MAKES THE BEST CASE MANAGER?

In the original studies in the United States and Australia, the majority of case managers were nurses. However, case managers are now drawn from all mental health professional groups and many services now employ people from other backgrounds. As mentioned above, case managers in the United States are often people who have a first degree and are then given specific case management training. Increasingly, in the United States, nurses are much less used as case managers and there are several reasons why this should be so. First, nurses tend to be rather expensive in salary terms and therefore budget-minded administrators began looking for alternatives. Secondly, nurses are often seen as bringing a traditional model of mental health care to services because of their background and many of the leaders in the case management movement see the traditional medically led approaches as anachronistic and encumbering. Furthermore, nurses are viewed as another aspect of this. Thirdly, many nurses who were previously employed in institutional settings have had great difficulty in adjusting to roles in community care and this phenomenon has caused service managers to rethink the employment of nurses who have had previous employment within traditional systems. Finally, traditional nurse training in the United States centres around physical care and thus much of the nursing background is seen as irrelevant.

Obviously, mental health nurses in the United Kingdom are in a much stronger position to play a central role as case manager, although some of the criticisms described above may be true for some mental health nurses. As we shall see below, the training of nurses in case management has already commenced. However, while these training initiatives are significant, there may be a move to train others as case managers. The greatest impetus for this may be in the shift of funding responsibilities to social services departments who may decide, as has been the case in learning disability services, to employ people in social work grades, often providing suitable people with no professional background in service training. There is considerable evidence that this shift away from nurse case managers is already taking place (as a glance at employment advertisements will show). Even in the area of medication giving, services in the United States have provided training in medication administration to non-nurse case managers, while using safeguards such as having a nurse audit medications or relying more on pharmacist-dispensed individual medication packs which are easily administered. Indeed, UK mental health nurses may not have a special claim in the area of medication. A recent study (Bennett, 1995) shows that CPNs' recognition of medication side effects is poor.

THE TRAINING OF NURSES IN CASE MANAGEMENT

As the most numerous group of professionals, mental health nurses have an obvious role to play in the delivery of case management. Nurses have already been trained as case managers on various research projects – for example, the Daily Living Programme at the Maudsley Hospital, the Early Intervention Service in Central London and on the Sainsbury Centre for Mental Health-based projects, also in London. In addition, a new and exciting initiative funded by the Sir Jules Thorn Trust is now in operation at the Institute of Psychiatry, London and the University of Manchester. This project is developing training in case management for nurses and eventually the aim is that every regional health authority in the United Kingdom will be able to offer such training. Encouragingly, this training does not stop short at service brokering and medication monitoring but includes family approaches and symptom modification. In addition to the Thorn initiative, the author has commenced (at Middlesex University in North London) the running of the first Masters programme which focuses specifically on the acquisition of case management and psychological intervention skills with people with serious mental health problems. This programme is part time and multidisciplinary in nature (although the majority of students are experienced mental health nurses). However, despite these initiatives, it will be some time before adequate numbers of nurse case managers are trained. The obvious solution is to incorporate case management skills training into undergraduate nursing programmes and to switch emphasis from other postgraduate courses to this area.

CONSUMERS AS CASE MANAGERS

The idea that consumers of service, and sufferers of chronic mental illness at that, could be trained as case managers seems revolutionary. However, as long ago as 1986 the Colorado Division of Mental Health began a pilot project to train and employ individuals with chronic mental illness to provide case management services to other mental health consumers (Sherman and Porter, 1991). This project was carefully evaluated and 2 years after the project, 15 of the 17 original course completers were still employed in roles best defined as those of case management aides, although several of these workers appeared to have progressed to positions of greater responsibility and autonomy. One apparent benefit of training was that the cohort only required 2 bed days of psychiatric hospitalisation between them in the 2 years following training.

The programme has been extended to various parts of the United States and any possible disadvantages are more than outweighed by the many benefits of the system. Sherman and Porter (1991) point out that consumer case managers may achieve a better rapport with other consumers, may gain cooperation with treatment more readily, may help produce positive attitude shifts in other professionals, may help to reduce stigma and, as indicated above, the training and job experience may enhance the consumer case manager's own mental health status.

However, despite the recent recognition of the importance of involving users in mental health care, innovations such as this are rare in the United Kingdom. Although the case management training project in Denver has been running for the last 9 years, it may be some years before such projects are run in this country and only then can we begin to claim any success of the user movement. Similarly, there needs to be much more involvement of users in planning services in the United Kingdom and all that can be said at the moment is that, compared with the United States, the user presence is but a token one.

CONCLUSION

This chapter began with the optimistic message that case management offers considerable hope to the users of mental health services and their carers. However, it is a new approach that is defined by different people in different ways and that incorporates a number of aspects yet to be tested by controlled experiment. Case management does, however, represent a major challenge for mental health nursing and in future case management and mental health nursing may, in the area of serious mental health problems, become synonymous.

REFERENCES

Bennett J (1995) CPNs and psychotropic medication. In Brooker C and White E (eds) *Community Psychiatric Nursing Research*, volume III. London: Chapman and Hall.

Birchwood M and Tarrier N (1992) *Innovations in the Psychological Management of Schizophrenia*. London: Wiley.

Birchwood M, McMillan F and Smith J (1992) Early signs of relapse in schizophrenia: maintaining methodology. In Kavanagh D (ed) *Schizophrenia: An Interdisciplinary Handbook*. London: Chapman and Hall.

Brooker C, Tarrier N, Barrowclough C, Butterworth C and Goldberg D (1992) Training community psychiatric nurses for psychosocial intervention. *British Journal of Psychiatry* **160**: 836–844.

Department of Health (1990) *Caring for People*. London: HMSO.

Department of Health (1992) *Health of the Nation*. London: HMSO.

Department of Health (1993) *Mental Illness: A Key Area Handbook*. London: HMSO.

Falloon IRH and Graham-Hole V (1991) Family care as an alternative to the mental hospital. In: Hall P and Brockington IF (eds) *The Closure of Mental hospitals*. London: Gaskell, Royal College of Psychiatrists.

Ford R, Beadsmoore A, Norton P, Cooke A, and Repper J (1993) Developing case management for the long term mentally ill. *Psychiatric Bulletin* **17**: 409–411.

Gournay KJM (1993) Trends in managing schizophrenia. *Nursing Standard* **7**(42): 31–36.

Gournay KJM and Brooking JI (1992) *An evaluation of the effectiveness of Community Psychiatric Nurses in treating patients with minor mental disorders in primary care*. London: Report to the Department of Health.

Gournay KJM and Brooking JI (1994) The CPN in primary care: an outcome study. *British Journal of Psychiatry* **165**: 231–238.

Hargie O and McCarten PJ (1986) *Social Skills Training and Psychiatric Nursing*. London: Croom Helm.

Hoult J (1986) Community care of the acutely mentally ill. *British Journal of Psychiatry* **149**: 137–144.

Hoult J, Rosen A and Reynolds I (1984) Community orientated treatment compared to psychiatric hospital orientated treatment. *Social Science Medicine* **18**: 1005–1010.

Laing RD and Esterson A (1964) *Sanity, Madness and the Family*. London: Tavistock.

Leff J and Vaughn C (1985) *Expressed Emotion in Families: Its significance for mental illness*. New York: Guilford Press.

Lin K and Kleinman AM (1988) Psychopathology and clinical course of schizophrenia: a cross-cultural perspective. *Schizophrenia Bulletin* **14**: 555–568.

Moore J (1961) A psychiatric out-patient nursing service. *Mental Health Bulletin* **20**: 51–54.

Mosher LR and Burti L (1989) *Community Mental Health*. New York: Norton.

Muijen M, Marks IM, Connolly J, Audini B and McNamee G (1992) The Daily Living Programme: preliminary comparison of community versus hospital based treatment for the seriously mentally ill facing admission. *British Journal of Psychiatry* **160**: 372–378.

Newell R and Gournay KJM (1994) British nurses in behavioural psychotherapy: A 20 year follow-up. *Journal of Advanced Nursing* **20**: 53–60.

Onyett S (1992) *Case Management in Mental Health*. London: Chapman and Hall.

Sherman PS and Porter R (1991) Mental health consumers as case management aides. *Hospital and Community Psychiatry* **42**(5): 494–498.

Stein L (1991) A systems approach to the treatment of people with chronic mental illness. In: Hall P and Brockington IF (eds) *The Closure of Mental Hospitals*. London: Gaskell, Royal College of Psychiatrists.

Stein LI and Test MA (1980) Alternative to mental hospital treatment. 1. Conceptual model, treatment programme and clinical evaluation. *Archives of General Psychiatry* **37**, 392–397.

Szasz T (1987) *Insanity: The Idea and its Consequences*. New York: Wiley.

Tarrier N (1991) Behavioural psychotherapy and schizophrenia. *Behavioural Psychotherapy* **19**(1): 121–130.

Tarrier N (1992) Management and modification of residual positive psychotic symptoms. In: Birchwood M. and Tarrier N (eds) *Innovations in the Psychological Management of Schizophrenia*. London: Wiley.

Test MA and Stein LI (1980) Alternative to mental hospital treatment. 3. Social cost. *Archives of General Psychiatry* **37**, 409–412.

Thornicroft G (1994) The NHS and Community Care Act 1990. *Psychiatric Bulletin* **18**(1): 13–17.

Vaccaro JV and Roberts L (1992) Teaching social and coping skills. In: Birchwood M and Tarrier N (eds) *Innovations in the Psychological Management of Schizophrenia*. London: Wiley.

Zubin J and Spring B (1977) Vulnerability: a new view of schizophrenia. *Journal of Abnormal Psychology* **86**: 260–266.

CHAPTER 4

Clinical Supervision and Mental Health Nursing

JEAN FAUGIER

INTRODUCTION

The review of Mental Health Nursing 'Working in Partnership' (Department of Health, 1994) strongly supported the policy statement of the Chief Nursing Officer, Mrs Yvonne Moores (*A Vision for the Future*, Department of Health, 1993), by calling for the rapid development and expansion of clinical supervision in mental health nursing.

Literature describing the implementation and practice of clinical supervision is fairly easy to find when it relates to professions such as psychotherapy, counselling and social work. However, until recently little of any substance had been published in the nursing literature and the absence of empirical data on clinical supervision remains widespread in all fields, particularly in nursing: in a majority of cases the term 'clinical supervision' has found its way into the vocabulary of mental health nursing without having any significant impact on the reality of practice or education.

In most cases, the word 'supervision' is automatically associated with a management relationship. Indeed, it is suggested by Hill (1989) that people at work tend to think of their supervisors as authoritarian and that the whole concept of supervision is linked conceptually to an authority figure. Watts (1987) states that:

> the generally held conception of supervision is of a lower management activity in which a group of workers is overseen by a supervisor for a variety of reasons such as ensuring timekeeping, processing pay entitlements, regulating rates of work, and monitoring the quality of work according to pre-set standards.

Literature from North America continues this theme, pointing to what is claimed to be a distinct difference in the understanding of clinical supervision between nurses and other disciplines involved in therapeutic input, especially in psychiatry:

> Many nurses have misconceptions about the nature of clinical supervision. They may be depriving themselves of one of the most valuable tools in existence for learning and refining skills of assessment and treatment of patients. (Platt-Koch, 1986).

In a full description of the use of clinical supervision, Platt-Koch also points to the lack of clear understanding of the nature of clinical supervision among nurses: 'To many nurses, supervision means observation by an administrative superior who inspects, directs, controls and evaluates the nurse's work.'

The conflicting needs and differing responsibilities of community nursing staff (school nurse and health visitors) and their managers were addressed by Kohner (1994) in relation to community nurses working with child protection issues. Work in this area found that a key issue in contributing to the development of nursing practice was the separation of managerial and clinical supervisory roles into twin spheres and different individuals. This increased the managers' ability to manage and provided staff with supervisors with up to date skills who possessed credibility in a difficult area of nursing practice.

The other assumption most common in nursing stems from a view of clinical supervision simply as a provision of support for a mental health nursing work-force suffering from stress or in danger of 'burn-out'. This misunderstanding is typified by the all-too-frequent belief that clinical supervision can be equated to an informal peer support group, the 'tea break/tear break' as described by Butter-worth and Faugier (1992). This is not to say, however, that such informal support for mental health nurses and their colleagues is not an important safety valve, particularly in the absence of any more formalised systems of supervision.

Until recently, very few models of clinical supervision were formalised at an organisational level. Such models have existed in mental health nursing more frequently in specialist settings, often based on a therapeutic community approach: thus, in some of the larger institutions and inpatient settings, group supervision was an approach sometimes found to be an integral part of nursing practice on more progressive wards and units. Clinical supervision in these settings was frequently delivered by nurses who had undergone training in other therapeutic approaches, often practitioners with backgrounds in psychodynamic therapy. In this sense, supervision was not seen as the right and responsibility of every mental health nurse, as Ivey (1977) pointed out: 'Supervision in the helping professions has too long been reserved for the master practitioner.'

Additionally, such supervision was more frequently aimed at the therapeutic 'milieu' and the nursing relationship with groups rather than the clinical supervision of individualised nursing care. There is no doubt that the demise of established models of clinical supervision in inpatient psychiatric settings is due to the inability of such models to adapt to a situation of individualised nursing care combined with much shorter periods of inpatient treatment. The search for alternative ways of structuring and implementing clinical supervision in mental health nursing has until recently always seemed to be overtaken by organisational changes.

Where the impact of individual responsibility for client care cannot be quite so effectively dispersed as it can in a ward setting (Menzies, 1961) mental health nurses such as those working in community settings have struggled to establish their own networks and models of supervision. Ferguson (1992) suggests that supervision arrangements are more fully developed for mental health nurses working in the community than they are for those working in inpatient settings; she goes on to cite White (1990) who reported that 75 per cent of community mental health nurses were in receipt of clinical supervision. Evidence to the ministerial review of mental health nursing (Department of Health, 1994) would suggest that this is a gross overestimate and mostly refers to a very informal peer support arrangement or a more administrative review of case work by a team leader/manager.

Extended clinical practice, greater autonomous practice and a greater degree of responsibility for decision-making have combined to increase awareness of the need for clinical supervision. In addition, the recent development of the internal market in the NHS and the changes in community care management brought about by the NHS and Community Care Act (DoH, 1990), combined with the implications of the Children Act (DoH, 1989), have all added to the demands on expertise felt by mental health nursing practitioners (Laurent, 1993). While some nurses do undoubtedly take the initiative and make their own arrangements for clinical supervision either as individuals, ward teams or community peer groups, it is interesting to note that, as Butterworth and Faugier (1992) point out, the strategies many nurses use to deal with the demands of clinical nursing and its inherent interpersonal relationship issues are not always enabling and remain frequently ill defined. Increasing numbers of nurses have found that the supervisory process, properly and responsibly facilitated, can, as Critchley (1987) indicates, assist in the refinement of their abilities to observe more precisely, to understand and describe more accurately and to assume less about their own and their clients' behaviours and needs.

Platt-Koch (1986) advocates regular formalised clinical supervision as the major method of learning and refining skill:

> One cannot learn how to interact therapeutically with a patient solely by reading a book. The nurse needs to practise therapeutic skills, have successes and failures, and learn from the inevitable mistakes. The key to

> learning is for the nurse to review the work with a senior clinician, one with more experience and enough skill to facilitate objective self evaluation by the nurse. Through this process of clinical supervision the nurse's strengths are acknowledged and professional weakness or learning needs are identified.

Stating that undertaking mental health nursing without adequate clinical supervision constitutes a disservice to the patient, Platt-Koch (1986) makes a similar point to Casement (1985) in noting that even the most seasoned professional will retain 'psychological blind spots' and need the relationship of supervision to understand fully the nature of interactions with patients. Casement (1985), while advocating the development of 'the internal supervisor' which involves the very high-level skill of examining one's own interactions and understandings critically and dynamically, also maintains that this can only be achieved with regular high quality external supervision. Similarly, Stuart and Sundeen (1983) argue that the need for supervision is never lost, regardless of the amount of experience a mental health nurse may have.

DEFINITION OF TERMS

Confusion has been significantly increased of late by the introduction of the terms 'mentor' and 'preceptor', originally coined in industrial settings in the United States (Collins and Scott, 1978). Mentorship and preceptorship schemes have developed momentum over the past decade and are particularly associated with nurse education and more specifically with Project 2000. The major objective of such schemes is to provide the support and educational input in the practice setting that was widely viewed as fundamental to the development and success of Project 2000.

Darling (1984), a pioneer of mentorship in the United States, has outlined what she perceives as the characteristics of 'good mentors'. These include the following roles:

- an *envisioner*: giving the learner a picture of what nursing can be like;
- a *standard prodder*: pushing the learner to achieve high standards; and
- a *challenger*: making the learner look more closely at her skills and the decisions she makes.

Also emphasising the educational aspects of 'mentorship', Puetz (1985) describes mentors as enhancing their protégés' skills and furthering their intellectual ability. The majority of nurse educators in the United Kingdom, having become deskilled through a lack of consistent practice, would not be able to fit into this definition and therefore cannot be seen as adequate mentors. Other writers, such as Burnard (1989), claim that if students are exposed to the skills involved in positive mentorship, especially active listening and empathy, they will be more inclined to employ similar therapeutic exchanges with patients. It remains the case, however, that in the majority of schemes mentorship is linked to academic achievement and success rather than the refinement of skill and the improvement of care.

Preceptorship is presented as a self-limited relationship aimed at facilitating the transition from student to newly qualified and confident practitioner. In many ways, the model postulated by the majority of writers closely resembles that employed in educational settings when newly qualified teachers are required to serve a probationary period before being accepted as a fully fledged practitioner. Much of the research work available in this field is American; it is therefore difficult to draw many lessons from its results that may be globally applicable to the situation in the United Kingdom. However, some studies (Allanbach and Jennings, 1990; Myrick and Awrey, 1988) conclude that, overall, preceptorship is a positive assistance in enabling students to move more readily into their new role as qualified practitioners.

Nurses working in community mental health have consistently adopted a somewhat broader definition of clinical supervision than those offered by generic nursing colleagues:

> Supervision is a dynamic, interpersonally focused experience which promotes the development of therapeutic proficiency. One of the primary reasons for all supervision is to ensure that the quality of therapeutic work with the client is of a consistently high standard in relation to the client's needs. Consequently, supervision must be acknowledged as a cornerstone of clinical practice. (CPNA, 1989)

Simms (1993) points to the evidence in recent literature of a consensus among social workers, counsellors and psychotherapists on the subject of supervision: although they arrived at it from a number of differing philosophical orientations, all agree that supervision is aimed primarily at protecting the client by ensuring that practitioners develop the highest level of skill and the most professional attitudes within the context of a trusting supportive professional relationship. Houston (1990) and Simms (1993) both argue for a move away from the obvious English understanding of the word supervision and for it to be broken down into its two component words, 'super' and 'vision'. In this context, supervision goes beyond the immediately obvious and describes an understanding of a situation from a number of differing perspectives.

Describing the manner in which various influences have shaped the view of supervision in psychotherapy, Wolberg (1988) claims that skilled supervisors must weave their way deftly through the sometimes very disparate needs of the supervisees, clients and institutions, until they can somehow fuse the various elements into a serviceable amalgam. While not discounting the earlier influences of psychoanalysis, supervision in psychotherapy is currently moving towards a more eclectic model whose primary function is not 'therapy' for the supervisee, but which concentrates instead on the educational and evaluative elements of the supervisory situation. Increasingly, supervision in psychotherapy is being viewed as an essential process for the acquisition of therapeutic skills, central to professional growth. Supervision is claimed by Dryden (1991) to concern the overall functioning in the clinical situation, which is unlikely to be assessed by concentrating solely on the unconscious of the supervisee; conversely, excluding the unconscious can only result in an incomplete assessment.

In the field of counselling, too, there has been an increasing emphasis on supervision which must ultimately influence client care rather than result in supervisees becoming more aware of their own psychological problems. In arguing that supervision in counselling should be mandatory and non-negotiable, Proctor (1991) makes the case that:

> supervision is non negotiable because the aim at its simplest is to equip practitioners to use counselling interactions skilfully and appropriately in their working situations. Personal supervision is the opportunity to share working practice in detail. Here it is possible to develop the ability to monitor one's work.

Other areas of supervision seen as vitally important in counselling are the receipt of direct personal feedback, the supply of appropriate guidance and information from a more experienced practitioner and the provision of a safe and challenging forum in which to examine issues of outcome and professional accountability.

Research into the effectiveness of supervision programmes in other disciplines, mainly counselling, psychotherapy and psychology, has concentrated on attempting to evaluate the developmental models of supervision most frequently utilised in the United States. This research, by Stoltenburg and Delworth (1987) and Holloway (1984), puts forward a tentative model by which it is possible to examine the various interactions/transactions of the supervisory relationship and its consequent impact on the supervisee. While research in this area is very difficult, time consuming and open to the usual criticisms levelled at process research, there is nevertheless a need to develop models capable of determining the factors which are prerequisite for clinical supervision as well as the various behaviour stages that supervisors and supervisees are likely to encounter. This would provide a stimulation and a guide to those undertaking further much-needed research.

THE SUPERVISORY RELATIONSHIP

It is important to examine the vehicle of delivery for clinical supervision, the relationship between supervisor and supervisee. Models of supervision tend to fall into three major categories:

- those that describe supervision in relation to the supervisory relationship and its main constituents;
- those that describe the elements of the main function or role of supervision; and
- developmental models that emphasise the process of the supervisory relationship.

Various commentators have suggested a three-function interactive model of supervision which is capable of easy application to nursing situations and experience. The three interactive functions are termed 'formative', 'restorative' and 'normative'.

The *formative* function of supervision is the educative process of developing the skills, understanding and abilities of the supervisees. This is achieved through reflection on, and exploration of, the supervisees' work with clients by a more experienced and qualified practitioner. Thus, a nurse might be helped by the supervisor to:

- understand the client better and move towards a greater understanding of individual needs;
- develop a greater degree of self-awareness and appreciation of how her interactions with the client are important in terms of a quality service; examine the nursing intervention and the outcomes and consequences of that intervention;
- explore other possible interventions or nursing input, ways of working with clients presenting similar challenges; and
- evaluate the way in which she interacts with the multidisciplinary team members to ensure the best quality care.

The *restorative* or supportive function is a way of responding to the way in which mental health nurses, engaged in intimate interactions with clients by the very nature of their work, necessarily allow themselves to be affected by the pain, distress and disability of the clients. The emotional stress that nurses experience is due to the very necessary empathy which a nurse–patient relationship requires, as well as constantly having to face situations of loss. If they are to maintain adequate emotions, stability and boundaries, it is essential that nurses become aware of how this has affected them so that they can understand, and deal with, any reactions. Failure to attend to these emotional issues leads ultimately to a workforce whose efficiency and ability to deal with concerns or critical incidents are very much reduced. Nurses are then likely to become over-identified with their clients, or to move away from them because of the level of emotional pain, or even to 'burn out' (Maslach and Jackson, 1982).

This is the crucial quality control element which is absolutely essential in all work with people. Even the most experienced mental health nurse will have inevitable blind spots, human failings, areas of vulnerability and woundedness from her internal and external world, prejudices of which she may remain blithely unaware. This aspect of the model emphasises the fact that when someone becomes a supervisor, he/she is duty bound to ensure that the highest professional standards of nursing are upheld and that the policies and procedures of the authority are followed.

With its educational, supportive and managerial elements this model combines the different functions of supervision and demonstrates how it can focus predominantly on one or other function at different times. However, the ultimate quality of nursing work demands that the supervisor should always consider them as interrelated and overlapping.

In an attempt to provide guidelines characteristic of a positive supervisory relationship, Faugier (1992) outlines the 'growth and support' model. Here, the role of the supervisor is to 'facilitate growth' and provide essential 'support' to the practice of clinical excellence. In order to achieve this, supervisors must be aware of the responsibilities they have towards supervisees and their clients. The main elements of this model are described below.

Generosity

This is an essential requirement for supervisors. They need to be generous with their time and to acknowledge the importance of clinical supervision by attributing time to it and insisting that it takes priority over all other activities, barring emergencies. It is also essential for the supervisor to be generous of spirit. Nurses who find it difficult to give either intellectually or emotionally within the supervisory relationship will be unsuccessful in providing the all-important inspiration to excellence. Supervision without praise or generosity can be a very punishing experience, leaving the supervisee confused and angry.

Rewarding

This aspect of the model emphasises that the supervisor will need to develop the ability to recognise and reward ability. The level of self-awareness of the supervisor is a prerequisite and the relevant authority must ensure that such training is undertaken prior to commencing the duties of supervisor. This may involve further self-awareness training for qualified practice nursing staff, tutorial staff and, of course, nurses in managerial positions. It is not appropriate for any supervisor to use the supervisory relationship to deal with unresolved feelings of inadequacy or insecurity. Moreover, such self-awareness in nursing should be on-going, and supervisors themselves should have access to either personal or group supervision in order to facilitate this process: Casement (1985) emphasises this element of self-development within the supervisor's role:

> Just as we can see our own errors more clearly in others, so too in supervising others. Here there are endless opportunities for a re-examination of one's work. Not infrequently, supervisors will be seeing reflections of their own difficulties. We do not always do as we teach others to do, but we can learn a lot by trying.

Although writing about psychotherapy, Bion (1975) coined the term which perhaps best exemplifies this process of continued self-awareness development necessary in the supervisor, when he claimed we should always be in a state of 'becoming'. Those nurses who, upon qualifying, feel that they know all they need to know, not only about nursing but also about themselves, should never be given the opportunity to stunt the growth of others through the medium of supervision.

Openness

In the course of supervising a process as complex and demanding as nursing, difficult and awkward times will occur frequently. Faugier (1992) argues that the supervisor must be open to the problems nurses face daily in dealing with the tapestry of emotional and physiological issues. The problems nurses face in their professional and personal life can easily become mirrored in the supervisory relationship. This aspect of supervision is termed the 'parallel process' by Eckstein and Wallenstein (1958), and refers to the analogy between the patient/ supervisee and the supervisor/supervisee relationships.

Traditionally, in the field of nursing, the person in the educational role such as a clinical supervisor is there to provide answers, to be all-knowing, whereas this model stresses the need for the supervisor to assist the supervisee in dealing with the uncertainty inherent in the business of nursing, by being 'open' to the feelings of the supervisee and therefore vicariously to those of the client.

Willingness to learn

Nursing organisation, although it has shaken off some of its hierarchical history, sometimes appears loaded against the development of continued learning. Sensitivity to position and seniority are handicaps that hamper the recognition of personal limitations and the ability to listen to others. Supervisors who fail to maintain an ability to continue learning throughout their careers are denying the very dynamic nature of nursing, and will be in constant fear of being engulfed by the oncoming tide of development represented by the person of their supervisees.

Thoughtful and thought provoking

The supervisees are in supervision to increase their knowledge of nursing, to acquire or improve skills, to move towards a qualification, or perhaps to aid promotion. The supervisor wishes to demonstrate competence as a senior clinical nurse while providing the right environment for supervision. The hospital, authority or service wishes to ensure that the client receives the best possible standard of nursing care and sees supervision as an important means of ensuring this. The supervisor must:

- 'lead from the front';
- retain access to actual practice material;
- observe as often as possible the practice situation;
- use data in the form of process material, recordings, and video material; and
- seek to stimulate thought by offering informed, theory-based links to the practice problems of supervisees.

Humanity

McFarlane (1982) described nursing as the art of caring. By its very nature, nursing is touched by the sorrows and joys of mankind in a very special way. Supervision must reflect the essential humanity of nursing, the ability to treat those we care for as valuable human beings in whose care we are privileged to be involved. Supervisors will reflect this in the manner in which they discuss clients, and in the way they handle issues of confidentiality, responsibility and ethics.

Sensitivity

Nursing is often difficult and frequently fails to make things 'all right' for the client. Supervisors need to be sensitive to the trials and frustrations that supervisees will display in supervision. It is necessary for the supervisor to respond in ways which acknowledge the level of work frequently expended by supervisees and the subsequent feelings of failure and guilt when it becomes obvious that much of the work was misguided or has failed to demonstrate the hoped-for results. This ability to value the nurse and her efforts can lead to an effective use of supervision for the purpose of exploring alternative strategies and interventions. It also makes it less likely for the nurse to feel that inability to meet standards should be hidden and covered up in a climate of failure and silence.

Uncompromising

An uncompromising rigour is also one of the most vital components a supervisor can bring to the overall process. The practice of nursing cannot be open to any compromise in the standards of care for individual patients and this should be reflected in the supervisory process. Through probing case work, peer group assessment, supervisor observation, individual presentation of nursing care plans and evaluations, the supervisor can maintain an environment in which warmth and understanding go hand in hand with clinical and intellectual rigour. In addition, supervisors must establish an atmosphere of uncompromising trust, confidentiality and professionalism. These issues, particularly that of maintaining professional boundaries, can be demonstrated by the relationships within supervision and act as a role model which supervisees can then apply to other relationships in the clinical setting.

Personal

Supervision of clinical practice can be carried out in a number of settings and styles. There are, however, common features: it should by definition centre on the clinical work of nursing, the main focus of which is the nurse–patient relationship; additionally, it will have an educational and quality control function.

Despite these common elements, it remains a personal experience and there will be differences in the personal styles of supervisors. The move to clinical supervision in nursing has been marked in many cases by a failure to understand not only the amount of skill required but also the personal nature of the supervisory relationship, which has only contributed to devaluing the process and reducing its effectiveness in improving practice.

The all-pervading notion that 'any nurse can nurse any patient' is transposed lock, stock and barrel to supervision and becomes: 'Any supervisor can supervise any supervisee'. This is patently not the case, and simply serves to perpetuate the celebration of the impersonal which runs throughout our development as a profession. It also reduces significantly the impact of individualised care for clients.

Practical

Nursing is a practically based profession, and clinical supervision must reflect that reality. Any supervision session in which the supervisee fails to focus on practice and its improvement has failed as far as the client's interests are concerned. In a profession which for decades has been plagued by the pragmatic approach concerned with the 'how' of practice with little regard for the 'what' and the 'why', we have recently, and somewhat self-consciously, reversed the coin in an attempt to understand theoretical and attitudinal issues in greater depth. The effective supervisor must guard against an over-intellectual, 'woolly' approach to essentially practical interventions; nor must the supervisor assume that the supervisee will automatically know 'how' to do 'what'. Given the current rush to describe what nurses 'do' and the 'outcomes' of their 'interventions' for the benefit of purchasers of services, it is all the more important for clinical supervision to focus on the supervisees' behaviour as opposed to their knowledge and attitudes.

Orientation

As Wolberg points out, important and often irreconcilable differences can and do appear in the theoretical background and orientation of supervisor and supervisee. Such differences may express themselves in any of the following ways:

- The relative weight placed on biological as opposed to psychological and social factors in the genesis of a patient's problems.
- The value of particular forms of intervention, particularly when such intervention may be seen as invasive and distressing for the client.
- The degree of stress placed on personality or character issues in determining individual behaviour.
- The prioritization of long-term and short-term nursing objectives.

The most effective supervision of nursing practice is the one that shows respect for the ideas and opinions of others. However, it is also the role of the supervisor to guide the supervisee to a position of recognising when extreme opinions are in conflict with the needs of the client and the delivery of appropriate nursing care.

Relationship

Nursing is delivered through the medium of the nurse–patient relationship and the supervisor's role is to assist the supervisee to apply theoretical knowledge, appropriate attitudes and the required level of skill to the care of clients. This is done through the supervisory relationship. The alliance between supervisee and supervisor is analogous to the therapeutic alliance defined as the bond of trust between nurse and client for the practice of high quality nursing. Quality supervision depends on the ability of both parties to exploit the potential of this relationship in promoting understanding and growth as professionals. Platt-Koch (1986) sums up the relationship of supervision thus: 'Despite occasional problems, supervision should feel like a safe place for the nurse. Concomitantly, the supervisor should feel pleasure in nurturing a younger or less experienced clinician.'

Trust

The establishment of trust also requires a high level of professionalism in the operation of supervisory boundaries. Supervision can place both parties in strong transference situations. The intimate discussion of clinical and personal issues can, and should, have the effect of producing closeness between the supervisor and supervisee. Some inexperienced nurses may misinterpret interest and concern on the part of the supervisor and may openly express feelings of love or sexual attraction. These represent very serious tests of trust for the supervisor who must handle this situation in a manner which leaves no room for doubt about the intention of retaining strictly professional boundaries, yet aims not to humiliate or hurt the supervisee.

The above model is suggested to represent a useful framework for an examination of the educational and training requirements a service should be planning to meet, prior to setting up a network of clinical supervision.

In another earlier attempt to categorise the roles of the clinical supervisor, Frankham (1987) offered the 'twelve role model of supervisor functions'. In an examination of this model, Simms (1993) has superimposed Proctor's 'three-function model' of supervision in order to draw out the primary aim of each role. For the purpose of this chapter, Frankham's model has been altered to address mental health nursing issues more directly:

- *Monitor*: to ensure the maintenance of professional standards (*normative*).
- *Manager*: to ensure the pursuit of agency practice and policy (*normative*).
- *Teacher*: to impart nursing theory and knowledge (*formative*).
- *Mentor*: to provide a supportive and sustaining relationship (*restorative*).
- *Therapist*: to provide counselling or therapy (*restorative*)
- *Analyst*: to provide insights into the process of nursing and the elements of the supervisory relationship (*formative*).
- *Mirror*: to facilitate the supervisee's explorations (*restorative/formative*).
- *Trainer*: to provide training in practical nursing skills (*formative*).
- *Evaluator*: to assess nursing competence and standards of individualised nursing care (*normative/formative*).
- *Reviewer*: to formulate and review nursing care plans, intervention and outcomes together with the supervisee (*normative/formative*).
- *Facilitator*: to assess the supervisee's levels of stress and establish support needs (*restorative*).
- *Professional representative*: to provide a role model of professional practice (*formative/normative*).

The group of models which have had perhaps the most significant impact on supervision and its practice in a number of disciplines are those coming under the broad umbrella of 'developmental models'. These models have their roots very firmly in the birth of clinical supervision in psychoanalysis and are currently practised widely by those who supervise psychotherapists and counsellors. However, I would contend that they have much to offer to mental health nursing practitioners who operate through relatively in-depth case work. As such, these models are easily adaptable to the community setting where nurses are frequently involved in such relationships with clients, and to the key worker/named nurse situations pertaining in many inpatient settings.

The two matrix model of supervision divides supervision into two main categories:

- supervision that focuses directly on the treatment/care matrix, in which supervisee and supervisor reflect together on observed practice, reports, written notes or recordings of the nurse client interaction; and

- supervision that focuses on the treatment/care matrix through its reflection in the 'here and now' experience of the supervision process.

These two main categories to supervision can be further subdivided into two approaches which will guide the supervision session.

Approach I

Mental health nursing practice is reported and reflected on in the supervision session: this is done in three stages, as follows.

Reflection on the content of nursing practice
Attention here is focused on the client, the client's life, what he/she has been able to share or explore with the mental health nurse, which area of his/her life, which health or other problem is currently in need of change or attention. This form of clinical supervision focuses on the relationship between client needs and the process of nursing.

Exploration of the strategies and interventions used by the mental health nurse to meet the client's needs
The focus here is on the choices used by the mental health nurse: not only what interventions were used but also when and why they were used. Alternative strategies and interventions might be developed and their consequences anticipated. The main goal of this form of supervision would be to increase the nurse's choices and skills in intervention.

Exploration of the nursing process and relationship
Here, the supervisor will pay particular attention to what was happening consciously or unconsciously in the process of delivery of mental health nursing care. Hawkins and Shohet (1989) refer to this as examining 'what happens around the edges': the metaphors and images, the worries and concerns of nurses about clients that may provide essential insights into vitally important issues for the maintenance of high standards of care.

Approach 2

Focus on the nursing process as it is reflected in the supervisory process: this is also done in three stages, as follows.

Focus on the mental health nurse's counter-transference
This is an extremely important aspect of mental health nursing practice, and supervision should improve awareness of the influence of such dynamic material on practice and relationships. Here, the supervisor concentrates on whatever is still being carried by the nurse from the process of nursing the client. The counter-transference may be of three different kinds:

- personal material from the nurse which has been re-stimulated by the process of nursing a particular client;
- the nurse's unconscious attempt to 'counter' the transference of the client; and
- projected material from the client that the nurse has 'taken in' somatically, physically or mentally (Casement, 1985; Hobson, 1985).

Focus on the here and now process as a mirror of the there and then process
Here, the supervisor focuses on the relationship in the supervision session in order to explore how it might be unconsciously playing out or paralleling the hidden dynamics of the relationship with the client. Difficulties in the relationship between therapist and patient are reflected in the relationship difficulties between therapist and supervisor. Ekstein and Wallenstein (1958) described what they termed the 'parallel process', which they observed more frequently in inexperienced therapists. This process frequently arises when the mental health nurse responds to those aspects of the patient's problems which highlight her own personal learning blocks as they are activated by the supervisory relationship.

Focus on the supervisor's counter-transference
Here, the supervisor primarily focuses on his/her own 'here and now' experience in supervision and on the feelings, thoughts and images which the shared material or discussion gives rise to. These insights can be used to provide reflective illumination for the nurse in supervision and assist the process of working on two levels because the material which has been unheard at a conscious level may emerge in the supervisor's thoughts, feelings and images of the supervisory process.

However, some of this material may need to be retained and remain unshared with the supervisee, and may be more properly dealt with in the supervisor's own supervision.

GROUP SUPERVISION

With a workforce of the size and complexity of mental health nursing, individual clinical supervision on a regular basis may be impossible. In some situations where there is a definite team nursing approach, it may also be inappropriate. On the other hand, the potential for group supervision in this and other branches of nursing remains enormous. However, the distinction must be made between group supervision, which is a formalised regular meeting in a setting covered by agreed ground rules on issues such as respect and confidentiality, and an informal peer group meeting which is simply a coming together of colleagues, usually for support at a particularly stressful time.

The selection and convening of groups for supervision needs time and consideration. Ideally, a group should be facilitated by a leader who is more experienced and skilled than the group members, and who has access to regular support and supervision. If set up properly and supported adequately, peer group supervision can be a useful means of improving practice in mental health nursing, particularly if a few ground rules are followed:

- The group should have shared values but contain within it experience of differing approaches and therapeutic skills, to avoid collusion and lowering of horizons.
- A group should ideally contain no more than seven people: supervision needs time and, if the group is to meet the needs of its members, it must be limited in size.
- The group should have a clear commitment from all its members. Resistance to supervision needs to be examined and used as a learning experience.
- The group should operate on the basis of a clearly established contract covering aspects of time, place, frequency, duration, confidentiality and boundaries.
- Groups must be clear about their focus. It is useful to attempt to ascertain members' expectations and agendas.
- There must be clearly defined roles within the group, in order to determine which member is going to be responsible for the organisation, who carries the main responsibility for facilitating and for managing time and interruptions.
- The group must plan regular review sessions and the regular input of external supervisors who can look at the work from different angles.

However, it must be remembered that groups may also present a number of pitfalls and, in the wrong hands, can be extremely destructive (Wright, 1989). Consequently, any service wishing to establish a network of peer group clinical supervision should invest first in training for group leadership, to ensure that nurses have some idea of the power of group dynamics.

Of similar importance in terms of investment is the development of senior clinical nurses who will act as the 'culture carriers' of mental health nursing. This key link individual in relation to both research and practice is in a pivotal position to ensure the right atmosphere for learning and research (Pembrey, 1980; Ogier, 1982). More recently, however, the role of the senior clinical nurse has been described increasingly as someone responsible for guiding the actions of others rather than providing direct patient care.

There is now a wealth of documentation on the central position occupied by senior clinical nurses or clinical nurse specialists in providing support to learners in the clinical environment, and on the subsequent benefits this has for improved practice (Booth, 1992; Sloan and Slevin, 1991; Clifford, 1992). However, many studies have demonstrated that senior nurses themselves, the very people expected to provide a positive supportive learning environment, have their own very real needs of support and will be unable to respond to requests for cooperation with educational and research initiatives without the provision of clinical supervision support for themselves (Mackay, 1989; Hingley and Harris, 1986). Many mental health nurses in a senior position, and therefore suitable candidates for the role of clinical supervisor to more junior staff, may feel threatened by change and simply develop a system which is unstructured and largely exists on paper. The responsibilities facing a professional supervisor are onerous: mental health nurses undertaking such work need to be sure that the advice and information they are giving is up to date, professional and research based. One can easily imagine how some senior nurses who have lost touch with practice will attempt to avoid this relationship. As Hawkins and Shohet (1989) have said:

> It is easier to use less structured types of supervision to avoid the rigours and concentrated focus of regular, formal sessions ... It is easy to create a climate where supervision is only requested when you have a recognisable problem and at other times you have to be seen to soldier on.

TRAINING AND PREPARATION OF CLINICAL SUPERVISORS

Mental health nurses who practise as clinical supervisors usually tend to supervise in the manner in which they themselves were supervised (Clarkson and Gilbert, 1991). Thus, training nurses to become more conscious of their roles as clinical supervisors may involve some 'un-learning': this is to ensure that they concentrate on mental health nursing and are not tempted to lead their supervisees only towards their own therapeutic approach.

Authors such as Robinson (1974) and Clarkson and Gilbert (1991) have suggested a structured approach to the preparation of supervisors by the use of models which propose a period of supervised practice. This implies that the trainee supervisor who is working with more senior trainers will also deliver supervision to less experienced nursing staff.

According to this approach, there should be three structured stages of training:

- *Awareness*: bringing the supervisor from unconscious incompetence to conscious incompetence.
- *Accommodation*: making the move from conscious incompetence to conscious competence.
- *Assimilation*: from conscious to unconscious competence.

In order to facilitate this process, the training of supervisors will need to address the extent of the senior nurse's knowledge base, as an expert command of the subject area is a prerequisite for quality supervision.

> Any trainer requires a firm grasp of the material, sufficient experience to provide a fertile source for examples, and an ongoing sensitivity to the vicissitudes of practice. Supervising clinicians who remain in the field, working with the ongoing challenges of their practice, are usually experienced as having greater authority and authenticity as trainers than supervisors who are no longer active in clinical practice. (Clarkson and Gilbert, 1991)

Working in Partnership, the review of mental health nursing (Department of Health, 1994) was obviously conscious of the role nurse educators could potentially play in clinical supervision and contains recommendations requiring them to continue to practise as do our medical and psychological colleagues in teaching positions.

Mental health nurses are subject to the common mental blocks to further learning affecting the general population. This, combined with the culture of nursing which has tended to view qualification as a certificate of continuing competence, produces a challenging climate for the introduction of clinical supervision.

My own experience as a practitioner and supervisor of nurses in primary health care has shown me how relevant the comparison made by Hawkins and Shohet (1991) is between clinical supervision and what the British coalminers used to call 'pit-head time', that is, the right to wash off the grime of the job in the bosses' time. Clinical supervision is 'pit-head time' for those who work at the coal face of emotional distress, disease, loss, death and confusion. There can be few groups of practitioners who would have a stronger claim on the time and support needed to develop clinical supervision than mental health nurses.

REFERENCES

Allanbach BC and Jennings BM (1990) Evaluating the effects of a nurse preceptorship programme. *Journal of Advanced Nursing*, **15**(1): 22–28.

Bion WR (1975) *Brazilian Lectures*, 1. Rio de Janeiro: Imago Editora.

Booth K (1992) Cited in: Butterworth CA and Faugier J (eds) *Clinical Supervision and Mentorship in Nursing*. London: Chapman and Hall.

Burnard P (1989) The role of the mentor. *Journal of District Nursing* **8**(3): 8–17.

Butterworth CA and Faugier J (eds) (1992) *Clinical Supervision and Mentorship in Nursing*. London: Chapman and Hall.

Casement P (1985) *On Learning from the Patient*. London: Tavistock

Clarkson P and Gilbert M (1991) The training of counsellor trainers and supervisors. In: Dryden W and Thorne B (eds) *Training and Supervision for Counselling in Action*. London: Sage.

Clifford C (1992) *The Clinical Role of the Nurse Teacher*. Paper presented to the Royal College of Nursing Research Advisory Group Annual Conference, University of Birmingham, April 1992.

Collins EGC and Scott P (1978) Everyone who makes it has a mentor. *Harvard Business Review,* July–Aug, 89–101.

Community Psychiatric Nurses Association (1989) *Clinical Practice Issues for CPNs*. London: CPNA Publications.

Critchley DL (1987) Clinical supervision as a learning tool for the therapist in milieu settings. *Journal of Psychosocial Nursing* **25**(8): 18–22.

Darling LA (1984) What do nurses want in a mentor? *Journal of Nursing Administration* **14**(10): 42–44.

Department of Health (1989) *The Children Act*. London: HMSO.

Department of Health (1990) *NHS and Community Care Act*. London: HMSO.

Department of Health (1993) *A Vision for the Future*. London: HMSO.

Department of Health (1994) *Working in Partnership. A Review of Mental Health Nursing*. London: HMSO.

Dryden W (1991) *Key Cases in Psychotherapy*. London: Croom Helm.

Eckstein R and Wallenstein RS (1958) *The Teachings and Learning of Psychotherapy*. New York: Basic Books.

Faugier J (1992) The Supervisory Relationship. In: Butterworth CA and Faugier J (eds) *Clinical Supervision and Mentorship in Nursing*. London: Chapman and Hall.

Ferguson K (1992) *Position paper on in-patient psychiatric nursing*. Unpublished paper, Department of Health, London.

Frankham H (1987) Aspects of supervision, counsellor satisfaction, utility and defensiveness, and tasks in supervision. Unpublished dissertation, University of Surrey, Roehampton.

Hawkins P and Shohet R (1989) *Supervision in the Helping Professions*. Milton Keynes: Open University Press.

Hill J (1989) Supervision in the caring professions: a literature review. *Community Psychiatric Nursing Journal* **9**(5): 9–15.

Hingley P and Harris P (1986) Burnout at senior level. *Nursing Times* **86**(31): 28–29.

Hobson R (1985) *Forms of Feeling: The Heart of Psychotherapy*. London: Tavistock.

Holloway EL (1984) Outcome evaluation in supervision research. *Counselling Psychologist (USA)* **12**(3): 167–74.

Houston G (1990) *Supervision and Counselling*. London: The Rochester Foundation.

Ivey A (1977) Foreword. In: Houston G *Supervision and Counselling*. London: The Rochester Foundation.

Kohner N (1994) *Clinical Supervision in Practice*. London: King's Fund Centre.

Laurent C (1993) Out in force. *Nursing Times* **89**(3): 29–30.

Mackay L (1989) *Nursing a Problem*. Milton Keynes: Open University Press.

Maslach C and Jackson SE (1982) The measurement of experienced burnout. *Journal of Occupational Behaviour* **2**: 99–113.

McFarlane J (1982) A charter for caring. *Journal of Advanced Nursing* **1**: 187–196.

Menzies IEP (1961) *The Functioning of Social Systems as a Defence against Anxiety: a report on a study of the nursing service of a general hospital*. London: Tavistock Publications.

Myrick F and Awrey J (1988) The effect of preceptorship on the clinical competency of baccalaureate student nurses: A pilot study. *Canadian Journal of Nursing Research* **20**(3): 29–43.

Ogier ME (1982) *An Ideal Sister?* London: Royal College of Nursing.

Pembrey S (1980) *The Ward Sister, Key to Nursing.* London: Royal College of Nursing.

Platt-Koch LM (1986) Clinical supervision for psychiatric nurses. *Journal of Psychological Nursing* **26**(1): 7–15.

Proctor B (1991) On being a trainer. In: Dryden W and Thorne B (eds) *Training and supervision for counselling in action.* London: Sage Publications.

Puetz BE (1985) Learn the ropes from a mentor. *Nursing Success Today* **2**(6): 11–13.

Robinson WL (1974) Conscious competency – The mark of a competent instructor. *Personnel Journal* **53**: 538–539.

Simms J (1993) Supervision. In: Wright H and Giddey M (eds) *Mental Health Nursing.* London: Chapman and Hall.

Sloan P and Slevin D (1991) *Teaching and supervision of student nurses during practice placements.* Discussion paper (OP/NB/2/91) for the National Board for Nursing, Midwifery and Health Visiting for Northern Ireland, Belfast.

Stoltenburg CD and Delworth U (1987) *Supervising Counsellors and Therapists.* San Francisco: Jossey Bass.

Stuart GW and Sundeen SJ (1983) *Principles and Practice of Psychiatric Nursing,* 2nd edn. St Louis: CV Mosby.

Watts G (1987) *Clinical Supervision in Community Psychiatric Nursing.* Unpublished report, Leeds University.

White E (1990) *The 3rd Quinquennial National Community Psychiatric Nursing Survey.* Manchester: University of Manchester.

Wright H (1989) *Groupwork: Perspectives and Practice.* London: Scutari Press.

Wolberg LR (1988) *The Teaching of Psychotherapy,* 4th edn, Part 2. New York: Grume and Stratton.

CHAPTER 5

Rolling Back the Years: Developing the Profession of Nursing After a Public Inquiry

PAUL TARBUCK

INTRODUCTION

There have been many dark days since 1987, first at Moss Side and Park Lane Hospitals and secondly since 1989 at Ashworth Hospital (after the amalgamation of the former two hospitals). There have been two periods of industrial action; one saw the patients unjustifiably confined to their rooms and saw nurses withdrawing their labour to the detriment of patients, and latterly a damning public inquiry. Throughout those sad and shameful days, a handful of nurses, qualified and unqualified and members of other disciplines (including clerical and ancillary staff) worked on – unsung heroes, vilified and sent to Coventry by their colleagues; occasionally intimidated and victimised – believing that keeping faith with the patient was more important than keeping faith with the majority and hoping that the truth would eventually be revealed and that some good would come out of the situation. Also, observers could not fail to notice that but for the goodwill and cooperation of the patients during the two industrial disputes (despite their being so blatantly treated in an unjust manner) calamity could not have been avoided.

November 1991 to January 1992 are months the like of which I hope never to see repeated again. Every member of staff at Ashworth Hospital, including the education and training team, was busily marshalling information in an attempt to justify her/his activities – I can assure all nurses and professional colleagues that being the subject of a public inquiry focuses the mind like nothing else. Those who had genuinely fulfilled their roles to the best of their abilities, doing all that had been asked of them and more, were ambivalent and desperately unhappy – they wanted to tell the world that they too were as shocked as everyone else about the daily revelations emerging from the Adelphi Hotel in Liverpool (the Committee of Inquiry into Complaints about Ashworth Hospital held some of its public hearings there), but they had to deal with feelings of loyalty towards and a wish to support colleagues and friends. I was also in a similar invidious position – wanting to demonstrate my own small efforts to introduce positive cultural change and yet feeling loyalty to the managers who had, according to the Committee of Inquiry, not correctly 'focused' my endeavours and those of my educational colleagues. In the final analysis, however, one's allegiances to the patient must come before all others and so there is no option but to be open and honest, to tell it like it is and let the facts speak for themselves.

This chapter is about the initiatives that have occurred within the Nursing Directorate at Ashworth Hospital in the first year after the public inquiry – initiatives designed to put the professional house in order and to start to conceptualise what the new future might look like – the public inquiry was in many respects the catalyst necessary to liberate thinking and start this process off. It concerns a professional group in search of the values that had been lost and striving to justify the steps it takes to arrive at the point where it is possible for it to once again feel legitimate self-respect. It is dedicated to the 'unsung heroes' of Ashworth Hospital, the patients and staff from whom I have learned the true nature of professionalism; which is that, in times of adversity when the mission seems to be unachievable, the vision becomes clearer and more inspiring.

INTO THE HISTORY BOOKS FOR THE WRONG REASONS

For the nurses of Ashworth Hospital, 1991/92 was a watershed period. The Committee of Inquiry into Complaints about Ashworth Hospital, whose findings later became known as the Blom-Cooper Report (Department of Health, 1992), was undertaking a systematic and rigorous analysis of the functioning of the hospital. It was uncovering malpractices in abundance regarding all aspects of the patients' life at Ashworth – of which the most worrying concerned managerial incompetence and unacceptable practices within the disciplines of medicine and nursing.

The catalogue of ills was reminiscent of Martin's (1984) conclusions concerning the many public inquiries into large psychiatric institutions over the years – multiple causative factors leading to a major failure of hospital systems designed to safeguard the patients' interests; the power of the working group being asserted as an irresistible force for compliance with the traditional norm; the distortion of the aims of the institution so that the original vision was lost; the isolation of the staff and working groups within the institution; the darker side of group loyalty within the staff complement allowing coercive, subversive and clandestine activities to go unchecked and the perpetrators to go unapprehended; the stunting of intellectual and professional enquiry; poor supervision of staff members and inadequate monitoring of strategy and policy within the institution by managers, officials and lay authorities alike.

The depressing picture being painted by the inquiry was further discoloured and compounded by a range of emotions, mainly unpalatable, that were experienced by members of staff at the time – bitterness, denial, doubt, fear, recrimination, shame and suspicion; it also rekindled the rivalries and internecine disputes that the hospital had sought to eradicate since the amalgamation of Moss Side and Park Lane Hospitals in 1989.

Some members of staff, enlightened mental health professionals ignored by the media and working largely behind the scenes, had for many years been trying to engender working practices within their spheres of activity that could be measured against the best in the country. Alas, these individuals could but hang their heads in bewilderment and dejection at the revelations unfolding before the public eye. Another group – those whose darker sides had been publicly and wretchedly exposed – sought to avoid direct personal criticism by hiding behind a smokescreen of legal wrangling and scapegoating 'the management', believing that the banner of official industrial action in some way negated personal professional accountability. A third group (perhaps the bulk of the nursing staff) were totally confused, their traditional icons and supportive organisations and mechanisms being discredited by the day. More seriously, a few of this latter group had totally lost their confidence and had started to withdraw from all but the most simple forms of patient contact – one member of staff had actually refused to speak to the patients in his place of work for 'fear of litigation'.

A year later, the nurse member of the Minister's Taskforce that was assembled to assist the hospital in its response to the Inquiry's recommendations published his own signing off plan for achieving change in culture and nursing practice called *Freedom to Care* (Rae, 1993). Phrased in characteristically upbeat and optimistic terms, this report none the less reiterated many of the difficulties in the organisation noted by the Inquiry, though Rae insightfully noted that members of staff as well as the patients were victims of the stagnant culture.

The Blom-Cooper Report (p. 226), commenting upon the education offered by the post-basic and staff development teams at Ashworth Hospital from 1987 to 1992, said that the educational staff had assisted many to 'achieve their full potential'. The Committee were less sure, however, that the efforts of the tutorial team had been 'focused' by the managers on the needs of the patients. Rae paints a similar picture, pointing out some of the deficits in the caring ethos and how training might be used to address them while acknowledging the value of some of the educational experiences on offer.

In fact, members of the education team were already aware of the deteriorating situation in the clinical areas and in 1989 had proposed a hospital-wide initiative to identify training requirements. Sadly, the plan was rejected in case it raised 'unnecessary expectations amongst staff that they might receive more training than could be afforded'. It was replaced by a series of meetings between educators, trainers and managers who decided upon the strategic focus of education and training for the next 2 years.

The Special Hospitals Service Authority (SHSA) had also been aware of some of the poorer aspects of practice within its three units – Ashworth, Broadmoor and Rampton, and had created a plan for modernising nursing. The plan was published in November 1991 and was called *Nursing in Special Hospitals*.

A CHARTER FOR PROFESSIONAL NURSING PRACTICE

Nursing in Special Hospitals (SHSA, 1991) contained eight key aims and associated objectives for achievement in the medium term and set down a blueprint for professional development around which the three special hospital units could build an individualised identity. The blueprint offered by the SHSA was made up of statements of intent concerning:

- individual care;
- meeting patients' needs;
- assuring the service;
- education and practice;
- nursing teamwork;
- clinical supervision;
- multidisciplinary teamwork;
- forging links;
- managing the service.

Despite this plan being available since the autumn of 1991, none of the units had really contemplated the potential benefits of the blueprint for clinical nursing practice. At Ashworth it was decided that this plan, when taken with the Strategy for Nursing Revisited (National Health Service Management Executive, 1992) would be a suitable bedrock on which to base professional developments. The Director of Nursing Services, who joined the hospital in April 1992, realised the importance of these documents and entrusted the strategic development to a small team of senior nurses who began to meet together informally to consider the ramifications of the aims of *Nursing in Special Hospitals* for Ashworth.

During this period, the hospital was forecasting a large budgetary overspend incurred by nursing overtime which meant that resource management issues dominated the thoughts of all the Clinical Area Nurse Managers. Because of this, developments on the professional front were somewhat protracted and infuriatingly slow. However, by November of 1992 a draft Charter for Professional Nursing Practice at Ashworth Hospital was ready for consultation and an operational version was made available to all service and ward managers by April 1993.

The Charter received mixed responses at the draft stage – 'breathtaking in its vision and scope'; 'very welcome'; 'too over-inclusive'; 'totally unrealistic'; 'not achievable without staff who share the same values'. Although the Charter could be viewed from many different perspectives and undeniably it would take a great deal of sustained effort to attain its full implementation, that did not mean that its tenets would be unattainable. With this in mind, the educational programme and the senior nurse managers' performance-related pay were modified to reflect the achievement of the Charter attainment targets.

The Charter represents a detailed strategic plan for professional developments based upon the needs of patients and focusing resources on the clinical areas. It is composed of the following:

- Core principles concerning nursing practice in the essential areas of nursing theory (Fawcett, 1989) and statements about other professional activities.
- Core professional nursing practice standards.
- Audit tools for each standard.
- Attainment plans (who should do what by when) for each standard.
- Budgetary forecasts for each standard.

Overall the Charter would take some 3 years to deliver at a cost of £4.2 million above base budget! However, £3.6 million of that related to the cost of introducing 24-hour therapeutic care to all the wards in the hospital. Areas of core principles outlined by the Charter are shown in Table 5.1. It was intended that the statements should be discussed by the ward team and suitably tailored and amended and be incorporated into the ward philosophies. Core practice standards were also proposed for adoption by the nurses in the clinical areas (Table 5.2).

Core practice standard statement 4.04 concerned education and practice and stated that:

> **Knowledge and skills will be enhanced via the development of educational programmes with direct relevance to practice and the creation of excellence.**

The outcome criteria for this standard required an analysis of patients' nursing needs and the utilisation of an *Investors in People* (Department of Employment,

Table 5.1   Core principles of professional nursing from the Charter for
Professional Nursing Practice.

Core principle statements	
The hospital	Corporate identity
The individual	Human being
	The nature of human being
	Human rights
	Limitation of rights
	Entitlement to free choice
	Equal opportunities
Human society	Human societies
	The nature of human societies
	Ashworth Hospital
	The nature of Ashworth Hospital
Health/illness	Health and illness
	The nature of mental health
	Entitlement to health care
Nursing	Nursing
	The nature of psychiatric nursing
	Nursing at Ashworth Hospital
	Professionalism within nursing
Quality assurance	Quality assurance of nursing
	Standards of care
Nursing practice	Advanced nursing practice
	Primary nursing and clinical supervision
Staff support	Staff support
Nursing management	Professional leadership
	Nursing management
	Multidisciplinary collaboration
Nursing education	Nursing education
	The nature of the curriculum
	Multidisciplinary education
	Responsibility for learning
Nursing research	Research
	The nature of nursing research
	The focus of nursing research

Table 5.2   Standards for professional nursing practice from the Charter for Professional Nursing Practice.

Core standard statements	
Individualised Patient care	Patient's rights
	Partnership of care
	The named, primary nurse
	Patient's advocacy
	Access to treatment/services
Meeting patients' needs	Individualised patient care
	Advanced nursing practice
	Nurses' role
	Multidisciplinary treatment
	Allocation of resources
Assuring the service	Standards setting
	Clinical nursing audit
	Individual performance review
	Clinical audit action plans
Education and practice	Education and practice
	Nurses' continuing education
	Good practice
	Patients' needs-related education
	Collaborative education
Nursing teamwork	Professional/clinical supervision
	Staff support services
	Personal accountability
	Participation in change
Multidisciplinary teamwork	Multidisciplinary working
	Collaborative working
	The nurse and team building
Forging links	Communication networks
	Mutually beneficial links
	Sharing good practice
Managing the service	Professional management skills
	Devolved authority
	Nurses' strategic contribution

1991) staff development model. It was envisaged that, via the Charter, the strategic agenda for nurse education and training would henceforth become more intimately related to nursing practice developments focused upon the patients' requirements.

LETTING GO OF THE PAST

Up to the time of the Inquiry, the nurse education and training deparments within the hospital had enjoyed a good reputation within the profession (Topping-Morris, 1992) and had an outstanding record of achievement, including:

- Preregistration courses for both Registered Mental Nursing (RMN) and Registered Mental Handicap Nursing (RMHN) qualifications in association with NHS training partners.
- Enrolled nursing courses in both mental handicap and psychiatric nursing as well as conversion courses in both specialities.
- The first RMN course in the country to be offered conjointly with the independent sector in the country.
- The first English National Board (ENB) 955 Care of the Violent or Potentially Violent Individual, ENB 960 Principles of Psychiatric Nursing within Secure Environments and ENB 770 Nursing in Controlled Environments courses in the country.
- The first ENB 811 Community Psychiatric Nursing course in Mersey Region.
- The first ENB 870 An Introduction to the Understanding and Application of Research course in the North-West.
- The first ENB 934 Care and Management of Persons with Human Immuno-Virus and Acquired Immune Deficiency Syndrome (HIV/AIDS) Related Conditions course in the North-West, and the first nationally to be focused upon mental health requirements of individuals with HIV/AIDS.

However, by March 1992 it had become obvious that these substantial achievements had been at the cost of allowing practice standards (in the absence of adequate monitoring) to find their own minimal and unacceptable levels and that, to elaborate on a metaphor, the education and training staff had been in the audience while the managers fiddled with Rome burning all around! The education team had demonstrated to the public inquiry that every member of staff had received some form of training every 3 years (in 1 year more than one-third of the qualified nurses had attended an educational event of one sort or another) but it was not possible, for the most part, to demonstrate practice or cultural changes as a result of the teaching received. It had become obvious that the requests for training courses from managers in 1989, while valid in some respects, failed to predict some of the more fundamental training requirements of the nursing staff.

All this merely confirmed the informal advice given by the two nursing experts appointed by the Committee of Inquiry to review the profession of nursing on its behalf – David Sines, Professor of Community Health Studies at the University of Ulster and Tony Thompson, Senior Lecturer at the Mid-Trent College of Nursing and Midwifery. They had suggested that the education and training staff in the hospital needed to be more assertive in ensuring that the programme of events on offer not only fulfilled those of the nursing staff members' training and updating requirements but could clearly be associated with the patients' health care needs.

This challenge offered a startling new possibility for the future of the education team – for at that particular point their colleagues throughout the country were busy integrating schools of nursing with universities and polytechnics and the underlying assumption was that the educationalists at Ashworth might similarly follow suit. Yet here was an independent view stating that an internal educational team empowered to be clinically assertive might be of more value to the hospital than a group of external academics whose primary loyalties would rest elsewhere.

Thinking about the impossible was beginning to emerge; the traditional notions of accountability and line responsibility were beginning to be challenged and alternative models were being considered. These were heady days indeed!

Two initiatives were already under way that prepared the ground for this strategic shift in thinking. One move in this direction had been taken in January 1992 when, despite the immense personal pressures brought about by the public inquiry, the Director of Nursing Services had the foresight to create the Department of Advanced Nursing Studies (DANS). Its mission was to provide a flexible response to the training and education requirements of the Nursing Directorate and to support the hospital with its corporate training requirements. The DANS effectively amalgamated all the previously disparate functions associated with nurse education and training under one banner and thus gave an opportunity for a hospital-wide response to initiate the necessary strategic and tactical responses to the educational and training agendas for nurses.

A second factor was that the registered nurse tutors on the staff had concluded that they should adopt a clinical role. They had been shaken by the public inquiry and had lost confidence in those whose responsibility it was to ensure that what was being taught was being integrated into practice. They felt it important to be in a position to see for themselves how much integration of new knowledge and skills into practice was occurring and wished to be in a better position to influence the culture.

By October 1992 the new thinking was reaching a concluding phase and it was decided that the new role of the lecturer/practitioner could best be consolidated by the adoption of a new identity for the department – a Mental Health Nursing Forensic Practice Development Centre, the first of its kind in the country. It incorporated the activities of the DANS team, the quality assurance team, the advanced nursing practice team and care and responsibility training staff. The tutorial staff had successfully redefined their roles. Clinical teaching and role modelling within therapeutic groups were to be considered preferable to class-room teaching and members of the teaching staff began to work on various projects of clinical relevance with their clinical colleagues and to rediscover the value of action learning. The scene was now set and the time was right to under-take a fundamental review of the curriculum and to address the imperative of core practice standard 4.04.

INVESTORS IN PEOPLE

Investors in People (Department of Employment, 1991), an initiative by the Depart-ment of Employment, had indicated a model approach for employers to develop their staff, which consisted of four stages:

- commitment (to the corporate vision);
- planning (training and development to prepare staff to meet the com-mitment);
- action (acquisition of new skills as part of the corporate and individual provision); and
- evaluation (new skills should be measured for their effects upon the achievement of the business plan).

In 1992 the hospital was introducing Ward Management with the first appoint-ments being made in the spring and an Individual Performance Review (IPR) system was also being brought on line. It appeared that the adoption of an *Investors in People* approach by the DANS team and the introduction of ward man-agers might complement the emerging view of education and training.

The Charter for Professional Nursing Practice had outlined the 'Commitment' and it was now necessary to 'Plan' the content of the education programme in order to comply with the spirit of *Investors in People*. It was decided to attempt to identify the patients' requirements by the creation of a dedicated tool to be used by those closest to the patients – the primary nurses – and that a corporate agenda might emerge from a composite of the primary nurses' perceptions con-cerning the patients in their care. This composite agenda would then be used to re-engineer the education and training programme to anticipate the requests for training being made by the ward managers over the medium term as a result of the IPR of their nurses.

It seemed that new ground might be broken here, for using this approach it would be possible to:

- Identify the fundamental aspects of the nurse's role – what it is that a nurse needs to do to meet the patients' requirements.
- Focus the education and training programme on those areas – what should be provided to assist the nurses to meet the patients' requirements.
- Check requests for training emanating from ward managers and other managers to ensure a strategic orientation and value for money.
- Provide an arbitrary point against which to measure the education and training provision for its effectiveness in improving the quality of care and/or increased efficiency in the delivery of care.
- Relate the strategic national professional nursing agenda more concretely to the patients' requirements.
- Address some of the Charter standards.

The aim was to ensure that any future educational experiences offered by the hospital to its nursing staff could be related immediately to an application within the clinical environment (while always accepting that there will be a limited but enduring requirement for research and development activities not immediately applicable clinically but of strategic significance).

PERCEPTIONS OF PRIMARY NURSES ABOUT PATIENTS' NURSING NEEDS

The next stage of the project was concerned with the identification of a mental health nursing assessment tool that could be used to complement the *Investors in People* approach. Most nursing theoreticians over the latter part of the twentieth century have suggested frameworks for assessment based upon their own ideological perspectives, usually arising from a developmental, interactional, stress adaption or systems model perspective (George, 1989). This has led to a proliferation of approaches to the assessment of patients/clients and the adoption of an eclectic view of nursing assessment (outside a few 'dedicated' centres in the United States). In other words, the nurse adopts the model approach that best fits the patient's circumstances. This has the effect of putting nurses at a disadvantage when compared to the unidimensional theoretical position of other professions, for clinical nurses and nurse educators (sometimes within the same hospital, and even occasionally within the same ward) use different assessment approaches and also different associated vocabularies to describe the therapeutic objectives that they are seeking to achieve.

The absence of any substantive academic knowledge base, including the lack of

Table 5.3   The structure of the primary nurses' perceptions of patients' needs tool.

Professional Standard 1: Nursing

> The nurse applies appropriate theory that is scientifically sound as a basis for decisions regarding nursing practice
>
> 1.0   Professional issues

Professional Standard 2: Assessment

> The nurse continuously collects data that are comprehensive, systematic and accurate
>
> 2.0   Classification data
> 3.0   Criminological data
> 4.0   Physical conditions
> 5.0   Sleep patterns
> 6.0   Patients' early experiences
> 7.0   Developmental issues
> 8.0   Sociocultural issues
> 9.0   Community assessment
> 10.0   Drug/alcohol/tobacco intake
> 11.0   Patients' self-perception
> 12.0   Patients' appearance
> 13.0   Psychological profile
> 14.0   Sexual assessment
> 15.0   Spiritual assessment
> 16.0   Educational/occupational/recreational
> 17.0   Patient support

Professional Standard 3: Diagnosis

> The nurse utilises nursing diagnoses and standard classification of mental disorders to express conclusions supported by recorded assessment data and current scientific premises
>
> 18.0   Nursing diagnoses

Professional Standard 4: Planning

> The nurse develops a nursing care plan with specific goals and interventions delineating nursing actions unique to each patient's needs
>
> 19.0   Mental health care planning

Table 5.3   The structure of the primary nurses' perceptions of patients' needs tool (continued).

Professional Standard 5: Implementation

The nurse intervenes as guided by the nursing care plan to implement nursing actions that promote, maintain, or restore physical and mental health, prevent illness and effect rehabilitation

20.0   Clinical interventions/specialism

Professional Standard 6: Evaluation

The nurse evaluates patients' responses to nursing actions in order to revise the data base, nursing diagnoses and nursing care plan

21.0   Evaluation of care planning

22.0   Generic training requests

---

theoretical thinking and critiques of the application of existing nursing theoretical approaches within forensic nursing, had been noted by the Reed Report (DoH and Home Office, 1992) which commented upon services for mentally disordered offenders (though in fact a dedicated forensic nursing model has now been proposed (Tarbuck, 1994)). Some work undertaken by MacKinnon and Yudofsky (1986) stimulated thought on the issue, and indicated the possible content of some assessment tools for psychiatric care and Kovel's *A Complete Guide to Therapy* (1987) similarly informed thinking.

Eventually a tool was generated which was felt to be reasonably comprehensive – indeed some later critics felt that it was too inclusive, being likened to a pot-pourri in parts while others felt that it resembled more of an audit tool than a needs assessment document. The tool actually consisted of 22 fields of enquiry containing 280 items associated with the primary nurses' perceptions of patients' nursing needs. The fields were structured around internationally accepted standards of nursing (RCN, 1986) and were formatted to emulate the nursing process (see Table 5.3).

A number of items in the tool were of a professional nature and others were of direct clinical relevance – prompts were included at the appropriate points to assist the surveyors and responders. The tool was piloted by the DANS team prior to its usage in the field and several grammatical errors and misleading items were amended at this stage. It was realised that a number of issues concerning reliability and validity needed to be addressed if the tool was to be accepted as a suitable means to generate useful data. In particular, because there were so many people involved in administering the tool and in responding to it, it was difficult to predict and control inter-rater reliability.

Unfortunately, during 1992/93 the Nursing Directorate was on a predicted over-spend of some £800 000 and because of this staff release from wards for training purposes was prohibited. It was also necessary to have some information available by September in order to meet deadlines associated with bids for new development money being presented to the SHSA. Much debate occurred over whether or not it would be wise to see if more money appeared on the table (as had been the case after other public inquiries) and bid for some of that to pay for the training associated with a research project, or to start the activity now in the knowledge that it would not be methodologically exact but would none the less yield some information that was not previously available on which to base management decisions about strategy.

If one cares to examine the recent history of the special hospitals there has been no shortage of committees, internal inquiries and reports that have recommended very positive ways forward, but the necessary action to bring about change has often been absent. It seemed that to procrastinate and wait for new money (if any might appear in the future) was just another form of inertia and therefore it was decided to go ahead. This was not an ideal situation but with hindsight necessary: the feeling of pressure, both from the public inquiry and the corporate agenda to somehow kickstart the profession of nursing via a stimulating educational and training programme was irresistible. Incidentally, no new money ever appeared on the table as a consequence of the public inquiry.

A centralised system of carrying out the project was developed, relying heavily on a common understanding among members of the DANS team who, after briefing, used semi-structured interviews with primary nurses (who were selected for their abilities to meet minimal specified educational parameters). Except for a small number of items in the first section related to the profession of nursing, the requirement of primary nurses was that they should hold a diploma level qualification or have evidence of recent study which would have exposed them to nursing theory and the use of the process of nursing at diploma or first degree level. This requirement was imposed in an attempt to set a baseline for understanding, although there was evidence (items not responded to, margin comments and verbal reports by DANS staff) that several items were not totally comprehended by the primary nurses responding to the survey.

Ten members of the DANS staff made contact with all the wards in the hospital, the intention being to survey the primary nurses responsible for the entire patient population of the hospital (621 patients) who were accommodated within the 28 wards. A number of wards appeared unable, or unwilling, to assist with the survey. Reasons for non-participation included:

- lack of substantive ward manager (others were unwilling to assume responsibility);
- pressure of work;

- bitterness of senior nurses on some wards concerning their lack of success at ward manager interviews;
- shock, dismay and anger concerning the public inquiry;
- anger concerning the lack of previous training opportunities offered to staff which was being blamed for some of the inadequacies becoming apparent from the public inquiry (daily transcripts were being made available to all staff);
- uncertainty among nurses about their future in the post-public inquiry period; and
- staff members being demoralised, leading to managerial and motivational problems at operational level.

Eventually 19 ward managers and/or charge nurses and 38 primary nurses participated in the project. The semi-structured interviews took, on average, some 3 hours to complete over at least three sessions and on some wards the DANS staff left sections of the tool with the primary nurses to complete; the data was checked by the DANS staff later. The information obtained reflected the views and professional opinions of 10 nurse educators, 19 ward managers and charge nurses and 38 primary nurses about their perceptions of the nursing needs of 389 patients within their care. The participating nurses were responsible for providing care for the patients on:

- 4 female wards,
- 1 gender integrated ward and
- 14 male wards,

which made it possible to ascertain nurses' perceptions about:

- 61 female patients (83.6 per cent of the female population)
- 309 male patients (56.4 per cent of the male population) and
- 389 patients in total (62.2 per cent of the patient population), including 19 patients on the gender integrated ward.

PROFESSIONAL NURSING ISSUES

Section 1.0 of the survey concerned the conceptual base of the profession of nursing and of the primary nurses' notions of mental health nursing practice. While the majority of nurses could offer reasonable definitions of nursing paradigms, there was a significant level of ignorance concerning nursing theoretical constructs, models of nursing and other models. Ignorance of some elements of statute, the Code of Conduct (UKCC, 1992) and Code of Practice (MHAC, 1991) was a grave cause of concern – it was obvious that the nurses would benefit from a rolling programme of training concerning the Codes of Conduct and Practice. The nurses' desire to provide care was obvious few of them could express a cogent rationale for their activities, or appeared to have been involved in the construction of a ward philosophy, mission statement or model approach to caring. More than half the wards surveyed did not relate care plans to any theoretical construct for nursing or contemporary research findings and a small proportion of nurses could not defensibly explain their care plans or relate simple principles for evaluation. Just under one-fifth of nurses could not define their roles as primary nurses. These findings were affirmed by data arising from the clinical nursing auditing system within the hospital which confirmed the DANS team thinking that the nurses should be introduced to systematic care planning and be made aware of research methods and the extant literature on nursing care planning.

Nursing diagnoses was the subject of Section 18.0 and it was discovered that no nurses were familiar with any NANDA diagnoses (Gettrust and Brabec, 1992), although a number of common diagnoses made by nurses could be related to the NANDA taxonomy. Others in use were borrowed from the medical model and others still were simple descriptions of mood; 57.1 per cent of patients were perceived as dangerous by staff (only 6.9 per cent of patients were said to describe themselves as dangerous), yet nurses' understanding of what constituted dangerousness was fragmented. No single nurse gave a cogent exposition on clinical indicators of dangerousness. As both these areas, nursing diagnoses and the prediction of dangerousness are somewhat problematic the DANS team felt it appropriate to recommend that nurses should undertake higher degree studies within these areas who might then create a debate within the hospital and who would participate in educating others.

With regard to clinical specialisms, nurses generally felt that the people most skilled and experienced (regardless of discipline) should engage in the more advanced forms of therapy with patients. The information obtained (see Table 5.4) was used to formulate a development bid to the SHSA for the introduction of clinical nursing specialisms and to indicate the possible focus of diploma level courses offered internally.

A list of training requests made by the primary nurses was identified for planning purposes and it was obvious that in some instances staff members tended to identify courses that would lead to qualifications that were perceived as desirable but would not directly benefit the client group, although a minority of requests clearly identified competency and knowledge-deficient areas of direct clinical relevance. Global requests for training included items about cardiopulmonary resuscitation, care and responsibility training, competency based courses for health care assistants, human relationships skills training, information technology skills and issues around leadership and resource management. Various other departments in the hospital were alerted to the findings as appropriate, although in a hospital facing a crippling overspend it was extremely frustrating to have an insight into what was required but to be

Table 5.4   Indicators for the development of clinical nursing specialisms

Of the patients the Primary nurses said:

% (n=389)	Could benefit from
34.2	Counselling
21.9	Group psychotherapy
21.1	Social skills training
15.1	Anger management training
14.9	Behaviour therapy
13.9	Psychodynamic counselling
13.6	Reality therapy
11.8	Cognitive behaviour therapy
11.6	Relaxation therapies
8.7	Drama therapy

largely impotent to change matters. However, sufficient resources were liberated to respond to some of the information technology and health care assistant training requirements and a variety of information technology courses and a pilot competency based course (National Vocational Qualification) for health care assistants, in association with South Sefton Health Trust, commenced.

THE PATIENT POPULATION

The primary nurses noted that 48.1 per cent of patients were classified as mentally disordered; 32.4 per cent were personality disordered (it was thought by the primary nurses that more than half the female patients were personality disordered (64 per cent)). The comparatively small number of mentally impaired (10.3 per cent) and severely mentally impaired (2.6 per cent) patients required nursing by appropriately qualified staff (RNMH, EN(MH)) and the Director of Nursing Services was reminded that this group, small but significant, should continue to have their special training needs addressed. Some recent manpower deployment analyses had given cause for concern with regard to appropriate skills mix; in particular, how well RNMHs at Ashworth had been prepared to care for mentally disordered individuals and non-RNMHs to care for people with a learning disability. Whatever the outcome of this particular conundrum another fundamental question emerged – how well are both RMNs and RMNHs prepared to care for individuals with a personality disorder? The SHSA encouraged the debate around personality disorder to unfold and formed a working group to examine the issues, including nursing aspects.

Table 5.5   Criminological data.

	%Female (n=61)	%Male (n=309)	%Total (n=389)
Admitted from courts	14.8	28.8	29.6
Admitted from prisons	50.8	19.1	23.4
Committed arson	57.4	14.9	22.3
Committed non-fatal assault	86.9	64.1	66.8
Committed fatal assaults	8.1	28.8	24.6
Assaults upon children	0	9.4	7.7
Lacking insight into the crime	62.3	47.9	48.6
Fantasise about criminal acts	27.9	12.6	14.6
Offence committed while disinhibited by alcohol/drugs	34.4	17.5	19.8
Consider self addicted to alcohol/drugs	60.7	58.3	59.6

More than one-quarter of patients were admitted from the courts, with slightly less than this being admitted from the prisons (see Table 5.5). The greatest number of offences that had been committed by the patients were of an assaultive nature and the majority of those were non-fatal for the victims. More females had committed arson than males; more males had taken the life of another than females; more females had been convicted of using assaultive behaviours. The female patients were perceived to be different to males in some areas of offence behaviour. For example, no females had committed crimes against children; they lacked insight to a greater extent than the male patients into the effects of their crimes; and their levels of criminal act fantasy were thought to be higher than those of males. It would appear that from the information contained in this section, both in terms of quantity and type of offences and of the internal experiences of female offenders, that their needs are sufficiently different to males to warrant special care and management considerations.

More than one-third of females and one-sixth of males committed offences while under the influence of alcohol/drugs and more than half believed themselves to be addicted to alcohol/drugs. Since acquiring this information, nurses at Ashworth applying for assistance with funding for higher degrees have been encouraged to consider issues related to offence behaviour and women's studies. The internal educational programme was considered for its content in regard to criminological and penal aspects of mental health nursing, and for its provision regarding women's studies. One lecturer/practitioner, with a colleague from the Patients' Education Department, commenced 'Awareness Groups for Women',

Table 5.6   Developmental issues.

	%Female (n=61)	%Male (n=309)	%Total (n=389)
Parent(s) with mental disorder	19.7	10.4	11.8
Criminal behaviour as a child	34.4	17.2	19.5
Temper tantrums in childhood	24.6	18.8	18.8
Exposed to child abuse	50.8	9.7	15.9

the outcomes of which in terms of females' self-perceptions were encouraging. Funding for two nurses, one to undertake diploma level studies in alcohol abuse and the other to continue studies in health education, was provided.

ETHNIC ISSUES

Of male patients, 9.5 per cent had originated from different cultural and ethnic groups – this represented approximately 60 patients. Their differing cultural and religious requirements should not be ignored and, indeed, the SHSA has suggested heightened vigilance by members of the nursing staff in this regard (SHSA, 1993).

DEVELOPMENTAL ISSUES

The primary nurses reported that members of both sexes in their care appeared to have had difficulties in their early lives and stages of development, including birth and postnatal difficulties and separation from family at birth or being orphaned (Table 5.6). Females seem to have been exposed to a higher incidence of factors potentially injurious to their later psychological health. For example, just under one-fifth of females had been reared by parents with a mental disorder, more females had exhibited criminal behaviours in childhood and had a higher incidence of temper tantrums. In the primary nurses' experience significantly higher proportions of females had been exposed to child abuse than males. With regard to the latter point, it was decided to seek an opinion from the Gracewell Institute which later led to a multidisciplinary workshop being provided for a target audience, who might then take the information that they had acquired about victims of child abuse back to their clinical areas for dissemination.

More than one-quarter of patients did not experience refreshing sleep without

Table 5.7   Psychosocial aspects of care.

	% Female (n = 61)	% Male (n = 309)	% Total (n = 389)
Unable to maintain socially acceptable attire	45.9	17.5	21.9
Unable to offer socially useful greetings	16.4	11.0	11.3
Believed to be institutionalised	78.7	57.3	58.9
Unrealistic expectations about discharge	62.3	33.7	37.3
Do not attend work	47.5	13.0	17.7
Gain no satisfaction from work	32.8	27.9	27.2
Not orientated towards work	55.7	33.0	35.2
Not motivated to achieve educationally	54.1	38.8	40.4
No wish to socialise with others	18.0	13.0	13.2
Disinterested in recreation	34.4	23.3	23.9
Wish to sit alone	16.4	18.5	17.2
Receive no visitors	34.4	24.9	26.5
Believe that no one cares	26.2	10.4	12.3
Exploit others to fulfil needs	55.7	26.9	30.6

the aid of medication and a higher proportion of females had more difficulty in getting to sleep and awoke unusually early. A minority of the overall sample group had enduring physical ailments, although no pattern was observed. It was felt that nurses might not be sufficiently aware of non-pharmacological approaches to assisting patients to relax and have a sound night's rest, and that pharmacological updates and stress management sessions should form part of the rolling staff training programme to rectify this situation.

PSYCHOSOCIAL ASPECTS OF CARE

One-fifth of patients were said to have an inability to maintain socially acceptable attire and for a similar number grooming was of concern (Table 5.7). One-fifth of patients were said to have inappropriate facial expressions and one-fifth used inappropriate eye contact. More than one in ten were perceived to be unable to offer socially useful greetings and three-quarters of females and more than half of the males were believed to be institutionalised (these figures were treated with caution as other indicative factors of institutionalisation, for example apathy, were not attributed such high values). More than one-third of all the patients harboured unrealistic expectations concerning their future discharges. Just less than half of females and more than one-tenth of males did not attend work and approximately one-third of females and more than one-quarter of males did not enjoy their work. Significant numbers of patients did not feel

Table 5.8   Patients' self-perceptions/psychological issues.

	% Female (n=61)	% Male (n=309)	% Total (n=389)
View self in a negative way	52.5	24.0	28.8
View own body as unacceptable	41.0	5.5	11.8
Not motivated to change	66.6	44.0	45.8
Describe self as dangerous	9.8	6.6	6.9
Feel unable to control urges	57.4	30.7	33.4
Inappropriate affect	27.9	24.9	24.4
Unable to maintain concentration	41.0	21.4	23.6
Perceptual problems	63.9	21.4	27.2
Lacking clarity of thought	32.8	17.2	19.3
Illogical/irrelevant thoughts	29.5	11.3	13.9
Thought content problems	54.1	32.0	35.2

orientated towards working or motivated to achieve educationally, nor saw the relevance of education. More than one in ten patients lacked a desire to socialise and more than one-third of females and more than one-fifth of males were disinterested in recreational activities. One in seven females and one in six males wished to be left to sit alone for the majority of the day. This information was related to colleagues within the rehabilitation team in the hospital for their consideration. More than one-quarter of patients received no visitors at all and a minority of patients were perceived not to trust their families, with one in four patients believed not to trust the staff. One in four females and one in ten males believed that no one cared for them. However, the primary nurses perceived that more than half of the females and one-quarter of the males exploited others to fulfil their agendas.

ASSESSMENT OF PATIENTS' SELF-PERCEPTIONS AND PSYCHOLOGICAL ISSUES

More than half of the females and just less than one quarter of the males were believed to view themselves in a negative way and 41 per cent of females viewed their bodies as being unacceptable (more than one third were said to have an eating disorder) (Table 5.8). Nearly half the patients were not motivated to change. Few patients thought that they were dangerous; however more than one third thought that they would be unable to control their urges if discharged from the hospital. Primary nurses perceived that significant numbers of patients displayed some elements of inappropriate affect and that with nearly one in four

Table 5.9   Unpleasant emotions experienced by patients

Emotion	% Total (n=389)	Emotion	%Total (n=389)
Abandonment	2.6	Hostility	15.9
Ambivalence	4.1	Insecurity	4.4
Anger	16.5	Jealousy	7.5
Apathy	0.8	Loneliness	6.4
Boredom	14.9	Loss	4.9
Compound	9.3	Powerlessness	4.4
Fear	0.3	Remorse	16.1
Frustration	18.8	Resentment	12.9
Grief	1.3	Revenge	5.9
Guilt	8.5	Sadness	7.5
Hopelessness	1.3	Unworthiness	1.5

patients it was difficult to create a therapeutic relationship. However, more than 10 per cent of patients experienced a variety of difficulties with speech that might impede their ability to communicate and socialise. Nearly one-quarter of all patients found it difficult to maintain concentration and one in ten had memory recall problems. It was thought that more than 14 per cent of patients might benefit from a reality orientation programme. Patients experienced the following to varying degrees: perceptual difficulties; lack of clarity of thought; illogical/irrelevant thoughts; 24.9 per cent had difficulties with the flow of their thoughts and one-third had thought content disorders. One in ten patients had ritualistic thoughts and behaviours, one in four patients were deluded and 12.9 per cent regularly experienced hallucinations. This picture stimulated debate about the difficulty of creating and maintaining a collaborative therapeutic partnership with patients whose enduring perceptions of reality differ substantially from the experiences of the majority of people and of the need for nurses to avoid unrealistic short-term health gain expectations for the patients at Ashworth Hospital. It also confirmed beliefs about the requirement for a modified Thorn Initiative to commence at Ashworth.

More than one in five patients had moderate levels of anxiety; more than 13 per cent of females experienced panic attacks and 18 per cent severe anxiety problems. Patients were said to express, or display, a variety of unpleasant emotions (Table 5.9).

Some of this data did not agree with that to be found in some other areas of the survey. This internal inconsistency may have been due to compartmentalised thinking by the respondees and the somewhat extensive nature and protracted

Table 5.10   Perceived antisocial behaviours.

	%Total (*n*=389)
Poorly judge the reaction of others	33.7
View negative reaction as a gain	15.1
Fantasise about self-harm	11.3
Swallow foreign bodies	4.4
Self strangulation	4.9
Seek seclusion	7.7
Other forms of self-harm	13.6
Suicidal behaviour	10.8
Fantasise about harming others	18.0
Assaultive behaviours	30.9
Weapon making/secreting	4.4
Hostage taking	2.8
Splitting/manipulation	24.4

length of the survey. This information was used to confirm the thematic components of a certificated counselling course. Further, each course was ascribed a specific therapeutic focus in addition to the core knowledge and skills components.

Primary nurses described a variety of antisocial behaviours arising from the patient group (Table 5.10). Almost one in ten patients were said to be afraid of their own angry thoughts and one in five were believed to have difficulties in controlling their impulses. This information was used in association with the Mental Illness *Health of the Nation* (Department of Health, 1993) targets to plan specialist higher education modules to be provided in the education programme second and third years post-inquiry.

SOME SEXUAL AND SPIRITUAL ASSESSMENT ISSUES

It was believed that more than one in ten patients engaged in sexual activities enforced by confinement and that one in five required basic sex education (more than one third of the females), including structure and function of sexual organs (Table 5.11). A minority of the patient population practised a religion, while many could not articulate a reason for living. Some patients harboured feelings of spiritual isolation/hopelessness/alienation; of being unforgivable and unlovable. Females appeared to be more orientated towards suicidal thoughts and

Table 5.11   Some sexual and spiritual issues.

	% Female (n=61)	% Male (n=309)	% Total (n=389)
Engaged in sexual activities enforced by confinement	16.4	13.0	12.9
Require basic sex education	34.4	16.5	20.6
Practising a religion	9.8	16.5	14.6
Unable to articulate a reason for living	6.6	7.1	7.7
Describe self as unforgivable	11.5	2.9	4.9
Describe self as unlovable	6.6	4.5	5.4
Not motivated to change	66.6	44.0	45.8
Express suicidal thoughts	16.4	5.2	7.5
Made recent, genuine effort to end own life	8.1	0	1.3

behaviours than were their male counterparts. Despite the above data only 3.3 per cent of females and 7.8 per cent of males were said to require regular spiritual reassurance, figures lower than those concerning patients experiencing spiritual distress – causing some doubt as to the ability of some nurses to pick up 'spiritual' cues from the patients. Skills training courses related to nurses providing reassurance, support, assessment and interventions for spiritual distress were considered for incorporation into the training programme in the medium term, and the Special Hospitals Chaplains' Conference was made aware of the information obtained.

MANAGING THE RESOURCE TO CREATE OPPORTUNITIES

In the latter half of 1992 and early 1993 the Director of Nursing Services and the two Assistant Directors of Nursing Services responsible for operational services and professional development respectively, had been in consultation with the staff and in negotiation with their staff representative bodies about a proposed change to the structure of the working week. A period of time surrounding the lunchtime overlap of shifts was noted to be under-utilised and it was suggested that this time (approximately half an hour per day over 3 days per working week) could be accumulated and the time be reinvested into educational activities – the scheme later became known as the 'Reinvestment of the Working Week'. The scheme was accepted by the staff and their representatives and became operational on 1 April 1993.

This initiative was an outstanding example of the cooperation between the management and staff representative bodies that had become possible at Ashworth. It would not have been possible prior to the public inquiry. Effectively, 10 days of working time per annum had been liberated for every nurse, qualified and unqualified, to receive education and training. It was decided that 5 days should be given over to annual updates on key health and safety issues:

- Cardiopulmonary resuscitation;
- Care and responsibility training;
- Fire prevention;
- Food hygiene;
- Infection control;
- Pharmacy updates; and
- Security updates.

A further 5 days would be devoted to professional development issues in anticipation of the recommendations of the UKCC Post-Registration Educational Preparation Project (subsequently known as PREP). From 1 April 1993, the nurses of Ashworth Hospital began to receive 15 PREP days every 3 years, compared to the 5 days in 3 years proposed by the UKCC, and this was achieved from within the base budget. With the advent of this exciting prospect a Personal Professional Profile (PPP) was piloted in the Spring of 1993 and issued to every member of the Nursing Directorate in May; all members of staff were encouraged to record the educational activities that had been completed in their PPPs with career achievements and aspirations and reflective practice and clinical supervision notes.

Bearing in mind the requirements of the Charter for Professional Nursing Practice, the primary nurses' perceptions of patients' needs and the PPP endorsements of reflective practice and clinical supervision, the PREP programme for 1993/94 was prescribed in order to pump-prime the strategic thrusts. On offer to Ashworth nurses for 1993/94 were the following educational events:

- Code of Conduct/MHAC Code of Practice appreciation;
- Patient advocacy/human rights;
- Care planning;
- Research awareness; and
- Clinical supervision awareness.

Because of limited resources in terms of manpower and classroom accommodation, each study day had an associated Open Learning Pack requiring 3.5 hours of private study. The packs enabled students to study flexibly and reduced the pressure of time on the lecturer/practitioner and classroom space. Health care assistants were not required to undertake a care planning or research awareness course but instead were to receive 2 days of human relationships skills training.

The menu for PREP days was to become more varied and sophisticated with time, and it was anticipated that attendances at conferences, workshops and staff exchange experiences would also be credited towards PREP time.

A decision had been taken in mid-1992 by the new Director of Nursing Services, with the Director of Advanced Nursing Studies, to withdraw from the commitment to preregistration preparation of nurses – the hospital was funding around 12 P2000 students per annum and paying associated on-costs. The manpower forecast for the Nursing Directorate indicated that qualified nurses would not need to be recruited in any significant numbers for at least 5 years. The staff turnover rate of less than 1.5 per cent per annum was below the NHS average.

It would appear that the special hospital financial lead (over £2000 in addition to base salary) continued to act as a strong incentive for staff to stay with the hospital (this may be a perverse incentive from the corporate perspective as the organisation requires a regular injection of new personnel with fresh ideas and diversity of experiences to invigorate the culture). If the labour market continues to be labile and a surplus of qualified nurses exists, which seems to be the emerging medium term picture, serious thought will have to be given about the necessity for the continuation of the special hospital lead. Perhaps this money could be better invested in other areas of patient care; or the lead be paid in educational credits which the individual employee might exchange for appropriate educational/training experiences; or simply be accrued and paid as a lump sum when the employee leaves the special hospital. This latter proposal might encourage a regular throughput of staff as leavers claim their 'nest-eggs', which would become more attractive to take as each year passed.

It was also felt that preregistration training might not be preparing nurses to care adequately for patients within secure environments and that new recruits to Ashworth Hospital should be able to 'hit the ground running', so to speak. In light of the public inquiry serious questions had also started to emerge about the ability of newly qualified nurses (who might not be sufficiently experienced and professionally robust) to withstand some of the negative and coercive aspects of the culture. The money liberated from the withdrawal from preregistration preparation was to be reinvested in the postregistration development of the existing Ashworth nurses.

When recruiting additional members of the workforce, the special hospitals would look first to hire mature and experienced individuals. They, along with other employers of mental health nurses, would undoubtedly find registered nurses with diplomas in behavioural therapy, counselling or psychodynamic therapy a far more attractive proposition than newly registered nurses with a diploma in generic health studies (the current status of P2000 finishers). Nurse human resource managers and educators must become more adept at anticipating the vagaries of the market-place, as skills requirements within the workforce will force fundamental structural changes within foundational nursing courses by the turn of the century. Nurse education planners beware!

HIGHER EDUCATION CONSIDERATIONS

In the spring of 1992, the Director of Advanced Nursing Studies had undertaken an option appraisal of higher education links (actual and potential) enjoyed by the Nursing Directorate, and in the summer of that year had produced a strategy paper suggesting that the Directorate should create an enduring link with one institution for the accreditation of its education provision and thereafter engage a number of higher education institutions on a variety of projects. This strategy was accepted by the Hospital Management Group and negotiations commenced with Sheffield Hallam University (SHU). SHU had had many years of experience in assisting with educational programmes at Ashworth's sister hospital at Rampton and the opportunities afforded by possible tripartite developments between Ashworth, Rampton and SHU were very attractive. Rampton Hospital achieved SHU Associate College status in October 1992, the first Associate College to be approved, and Ashworth Hospital became the second SHU Associate College in March 1993.

The higher education link is viewed as being professionally desirable and necessary to fulfil some of the Charter for Professional Nursing Practice requirements, but also the overwhelming majority of nurses in the hospital have not had the opportunity to study at higher education level (while today's nurses are being prepared to level two (diploma) standard). The link established with SHU would be of value in assisting Ashworth nurses to undertake diploma level studies, thus ensuring parity with their P2000 colleagues.

The strategic imperatives of the Charter for Professional Nursing Practice and the primary nurses' perceptions work were used to inform the content of three diploma level courses in Counselling, Forensic Care and Management and Research – all of which were validated via SHU and carried the appropriate English National Board for Nursing, Midwifery and Health Visiting (ENB) awards. Both SHU and the ENB were extremely supportive and helpful in facilitating the adoption by Ashworth nurses of the professional standards related to education in the Charter for Professional Nursing Practice and, in particular, their willingness to speed up the usual academic processes was greatly appreciated. More clinically focused modules of study were planned for subsequent years and these would have more of a multidisciplinary flavour to them.

The Patients' Council, created in early 1993, now forms an integral part of the process of curriculum planning and is consulted about all new proposed developments. It is a sign of the growing confidence within nursing that nurses feel able to suggest agendas to other disciplines and to expose their strategic thinking to user-representative groups.

MANAGEMENT PREPARATION

Because of the large budgetary overspend within the hospital, a training programme envisaged for the newly recruited ward managers (which should have commenced in the summer of 1992) did not take place. This was a serious strategic error as the ward managers were said to be pivotal in the process of culture change in the post-public inquiry period and had to acquire many new skills very quickly. They would have benefited from a detailed training programme. The training they did receive (except for a 4-week induction period) was delivered in an unsystematic manner. If these managers were to be 'hero innovators' and 'culture change agents' appointed to signal the dawn of a new era of enlightenment (many took up post at the time that the Committee of Inquiry was deliberating) they were being sent into the fray without a full armoury of managerial skills at their disposal. The Director of Personnel, alert to this very unfortunate situation, had bid for management training monies to be specifically devoted to multidisciplinary management preparation and had been successful in obtaining some non-recurring funds for the year commencing 1993/94. By September 1993 a multidisciplinary competency based (Business and Technical Education Council) Management Certificate and Diploma programme had commenced in association with Touchbase Associates of Southport (Newton and Wilkinson, 1993) for 100 members of staff, and further courses with specific resource management focuses were planned and made available as part of the corporate development programme.

With these four new ways forward – the reinvestment of the working week, the savings from the withdrawal from preregistration training, Associate College status of SHU and the management training initiative – the potential to 'kickstart' the profession via an educational programme acquired some sense of reality. It was possible that movement could start to occur on a number of fronts.

CONCLUSION – TURNING OPPORTUNITIES INTO STRENGTHS

By April 1993 the revelations of the Blom-Cooper Report, the Charter for Professional Nursing Practice, the results of the primary nurses' perceptions of patients' needs survey, the information being generated by nursing clinical audit and the insights supplied by the nurse member of the Minister's Taskforce were starting to come together in a meaningful way. However, the air of optimism was tinged with an awesome sense of reality, for the total picture of need was daunting. It was acknowledged that any substantial professional culture change could only be achieved by a sustained educational and training effort over a long period of time, probably 3–5 years. The introduction of designated culture change agents from outside the existing culture would undoubtedly facilitate the process; indeed, the introduction of a more fluid staff complement should become more of a possibility once the hospital became a Trust. A purchaser-provider environment would stimulate the hospital to focus its resources ever more carefully and effectively upon patient-centred activities, which would act as a strong incentive to employ nurses whose skills were more demonstrably related to the patients' requirements.

Perhaps the entry of Ashworth Hospital into the health care market-place may be the best guarantee that nurses retain an enduring orientation towards practice and professional issues, and that the dark days of a public inquiry will never again dawn upon Ashworth Hospital.

REFERENCES

Department of Employment (DOE) (1991) *Investors in People*. London: Department of Employment.

Department of Health (DOH) (1992) *Report of the Committee of Inquiry into Complaints about Ashworth Hospital*. London: HMSO.

Department of Health (DOH) (1993) *Health of the Nation: Mental Illness Key Area Handbook*. London: Department of Health.

Department of Health and Home Office (1992) *Review of Health and Social Services for Mentally Disturbed Offenders and Others requiring Similar Services*. London: HMSO.

Fawcett J (1989) *Analysis and Evaluation of Conceptual Models of Nursing*, 2nd edn. Philadelphia: A Davis and Co.

George J (1989) *Nursing Theories: The base for professional nursing practice*, 3rd edn. USA: Prentice Hall International.

Gettrust K and Brabec P (1992) *Nursing Diagnosis in Clinical Practice: Guides for care planning*. USA: Delmare Publications.

Kovel J (1987) *A Complete Guide to Therapy: from psychoanalysis to behaviour modification*. London: Pelican Penguin.

Mackinnon R and Yudoksky S (1986) *The Psychiatric Evaluation in Clinical Practice*. Philadelphia: JB Lippincott.

Martin JP (1984) *Hospitals in Trouble*. Oxford: Blackwell.

Mental Health Act Commission (MHAC) (1991) *Code of Practice MHA 1983*. London: HMSO.

Newton R and Wilkinson M (1993) Securing change through management development. *Directions*. NHSTD Newsletter, October 1993.

National Health Service Management Executive (NHSME) (1992) *Strategy for Nursing Re-visited*. London: NHSME.

Rae M (1993) *Freedom to Care*. Merseyside: Graphics Dept, Ashworth Hospital.

Royal College of Nursing (RCN) (1986) *Standards of Care in Psychiatric Nursing Practice*. London: Royal College of Nursing.

Special Hospitals Service Authority (SHSA) (1991) *Nursing in Special Hospitals*. London: SHSA.

Special Hospitals Service Authority (SHSA) (1993) *Report to the Committee of Inquiry into the Death in Broadmoor Hospital of Orville Blackwood and a Review of the Deaths of Two Other Afro-Caribbean Patients: 'Big, Black and Dangerous?'* London: SHSA.

Tarbuck P (1994) The therapeutic use of security – a model for forensic nursing. In: Thompson A and Mathias P (eds) *Mental Health and Disorder*. London: Churchill Livingstone.

Topping-Morris B (1992) Historical review of forensic nursing. In: Burnard P and Morrison P (eds) *Aspects of Forensic Psychiatric Nursing*. London: Avebury Press.

United Kingdom Central Council for Nursing, Midwifery and Health Visiting (UKCC) (1992) *Code of Professional Conduct*, 2nd edn. London: UKCC.

CHAPTER 6

Women and Mental Health Nursing

Sally-Ann Newton

> ...there is at present no consensus about women's needs which informs practice in the mental health field. It certainly feels like an uphill struggle to put such issues firmly on the agenda when reviewing services and making recommendations for appropriate practice in institutions which are male dominated and gender blind. (Potier, 1992, p. 17)

Women are overrepresented in their contact with mental health professionals compared with men. This is not a new development but a facet of women's life which is well documented and has remained constant with the growth of psychiatry. Showalter (1987) cites evidence from the seventeenth century which demonstrates that there were twice as many women diagnosed as having mental disorder as there were men. By the 1850s women were occupying the majority of beds in lunatic asylums, a trend which continues to the present day. Women are still more likely to be admitted to psychiatric hospitals than men. In 1986, 113 386 women compared to 83 865 men were admitted to mental illness hospitals and units. Women are also more likely to be diagnosed as depressed than men. In 1986 23 469 against 11 740 men were diagnosed as clinically depressed, 10 537 women compared to 4978 men were diagnosed as neurotic and 7667 women but only 6531 men were diagnosed with personality and behaviour disorders (Table 6.1). It is not surprising, then, that of the 46 million prescriptions for psychotropic medication issued in 1987, two-thirds were for women (Ashton, 1989).

It is evident that society has certain expectations of female behaviour. This is apparent in a number of areas. For example, women who deviate from the accepted standards of 'normal' monogamous, heterosexual relationships with children are overrepresented among women in prison because the courts are excessively punitive to them (Heidensohn, 1989). Women in custody are also more likely to receive medical disposals. Women constitute only 4 per cent of the total prison population yet a survey of Risley remand centre showed that 20 per cent of women compared to 9 per cent of men received a medical disposal (Nacro, 1991). The majority of men diagnosed with psychopathy receive a

Table 6.1   Mental illness hospitals and units – England: all admissions by diagnostic group 1986.

Diagnostic Group	Males	Females
All diagnoses	83 865	113 386
Schizophrenia, paranoia	15 271	14 148
Affective psychoses	8107	16 526
Senile and presenile dementia	7624	13 234
Alcoholic psychoses	509	266
Other psychoses (including drug psychoses)	7455	10 537
Neurotic disorders	4978	10 291
Alcohol dependence syndrome	8301	3508
Non-dependent abuse of alcohol	2095	1204
Drug dependency	1382	806
Non-dependent abuse of drugs	614	278
Personality and behaviour disorders	6531	7667
Mental retardation	305	284
Depressive disorders not elsewhere classified	11 740	23 469
Other psychiatric conditions	287	346
Mental illness – diagnosis not stated	65	48
Other conditions and undiagnosed cases	8601	10 774

Source: Department of Health & Social Services (1986).

custodial sentence, whereas women with the same diagnosis are dealt with by psychiatry.

The reasons for this overrepresentation can be explained in a variety of ways. There are obvious inequalities defined by gender and by gender role. Women have a distinct position in society which is defined in social, political and economic terms, often placing them in a disadvantaged position in comparison to men. The woman's stereotypical role within the family is predicated upon assumptions of maternal, wifely and home-making instincts. A woman is still expected to be responsible for the unpaid domestic labour within the home. If she works outside the home she is expected to accept employment opportunities that are less skilled and therefore rewarded with low pay. These serve to make her dependent on either a male breadwinner in a traditional heterosexual family setting, or on the state for income supplements. The views of normal acceptable behaviour are male-centred with variations being seen as abnormal. Man has declared himself to be the 'Self' and woman as 'Other'. The concept of woman as Other, as described by De Beauvoir (1988), suggests that women are defined by their difference from men and not as individuals with a unique function that is not dependent on the understanding or approval of man. Woman is described as

Other because she is not man. Man is the self, he determines the world, structures and boundaries within which woman has to live. In this patriarchal system there is no mechanism for woman to reverse this thinking and she is expected to function within this dominant order. Thus this male perspective on behaviour is viewed by society as the prototype of human behaviour.

Society uses the courts and psychiatry in an attempt to control woman's behaviour when she deviates from limits which are defined and set from this male perspective. The need to control women's behaviour can be traced at least to the mediaeval period when they were accused of witchcraft and sentenced to violent deaths following trials which offered little opportunity of defence.

This management, or perhaps more correctly, mismanagement of witches can be linked to the oppressive treatment of women that developed in the name of madness and psychiatry. Szasz (1977) notes how 'In the past, men created witches; now they create mental patients' (p. 20).

An early example of the use of psychiatry to control women by men was described by Wollstonecraft (1987, first published 1797) in her unfinished novel *Maria; or, The Wrongs of Women*. Although a fictional piece, it was illustrative of the fate of many women of that period. It discussed 'the misery and oppression, peculiar to women, that arise out of the partial laws and customs of society'. The character:

> ...Maria has been forced into a madhouse by her abusive husband, who wants control of her fortune and liberty to pursue his sexual adventures. To Maria, the 'mansion of despair' in which she is incarcerated becomes a symbol of all the manmade institutions, from marriage to the law, that confine women and drive them mad. (Showalter, 1987, p.1)

In understanding women's mental health issues it is therefore important to consider the historical oppressive treatment of women as patients by a medical and male-dominated psychiatric profession. The stereotypical role of woman which has and still does dominate western culture is that of the obedient wife and the nurturer of children, husband and society. It is when woman attempts to remove herself from this stereotypical role that society labels her mad or, in more professionally and legally acceptable terms, mentally ill. Traditionally women who attempted to distance themselves from the prescribed role of monogamous heterosexuality and the accepted 'norm' of perceived feminine behaviour of the day were considered rebellious and even, by some, mentally disturbed. This included those pioneering women who attempted to avail themselves of the educational and professional opportunities afforded to men. Showalter (1987) describes the case of Edith Lanchester, who in 1895 was kidnapped by her father and three brothers and admitted to a private asylum with a diagnosis of 'over-education'. She was the daughter of a wealthy family, had been educated at

London University and became involved in Socialist and Suffragette politics. When she started living with her working-class lover, outside marriage, Dr G Fielding Blandford justified her compulsory admission. In his defence for signing the 'urgency order' he used the fact that he believed her opposition to conventional marriage made her unfit to take care of herself. It would appear that she was 'guilty' in several areas. The first was that her opposition to conventional matrimony was considered as evidence of her inability to take care of herself. However, there is a contradiction in that conventional matrimony, at that time, involved the woman giving up her independence and autonomy to the husband. Secondly she used her education to campaign for improving the lives of women and the working class. Finally she broke the conventions of traditional marriage and the class structure.

This case is just one of many examples of how psychiatry has been used in an attempt to enforce patriarchal limits and control the behaviour of women. It was difficult for women to fight against these constraints because psychiatry, which was based on traditional white middle-class male values, was used as a powerful method of control legitimised by the state. This is illustrated by considering the position in relation to hysteria. The diagnosis of hysteria was one that was frequently applied to women who were judged as behaving outside the limits set by patriarchal values. The described features of hysteria are numerous and involve various anatomical systems and disorders of function. They mimic physical disorder but are inconsistent with pathology.

Patients so diagnosed were predominantly women within the age range of 15–40 years. The origin of the term 'hysteria', from the Greek *hysterikos*, meaning womb, relates to the theory that the disorder was due to 'the wandering womb' which could only be present in women. Thus hysteria was associated with sexuality and the essential and unique nature of being a woman.

At the time of the Great War men who displayed all the symptoms of hysteria could obviously not be given this feminine diagnosis, so the term 'shell-shocked' was coined. In this way these symptoms were legitimised as indicative of illness for men in the special circumstances of the battle field (in which women did not take part).

Popular psychiatric belief supposed that a relationship with an emotional trauma precipitated an attack in women. This focused upon women as psychologically vulnerable and prone to the disorder, whereas men were deemed to be stronger and more capable of controlling their emotions. Examples of emotional traumas were given as the expectations of marriage and pregnancy, critical life events which were often out of the woman's control. There was some validity in this; an illustration of the lack of control and power over life events for women is that it was as late as 1882 that the Married Women's Property Act was passed. This gave women legal control over their own earned income. Prior to that time, upon her marriage, as well as enslaving a woman to her husband, she and her belongings became his property!

A feminist analysis of hysteria as described by Smith-Rosenberg (1984) accepts that the disease did exist, but places it within a social framework. This view suggests that the woman is retreating into her own private space to demonstrate her rejection of the role she is forced into by society and her immediate family. Woman is rejecting the stereotypical female nurturing role by becoming sick and dependent, thereby forcing the male as either father, husband or physician to adapt to her needs and nurture her. This behaviour results in males feeling threatened, professionally rejected as therapist as the patient does not respond, while fathers and husbands are denied attention and nurturing.

In an attempt by professionals to regain power treatments were devised which were humiliating, aggressive and ineffective. These included wet towels, showering with ice water and suffocation during a fit. There was no medical evidence to support such 'treatments' and it can only be concluded that such behaviour was an attempt to 'punish the naughty child' and to reverse her behaviour, which was seen to be under conscious control and attention-seeking in its intentions.

No attempt was made to analyse the problem within a social context; the presentation was viewed singularly as within the woman herself. This lack of understanding, or of any comprehensive analysis by professionals, is described by Greer (1987).

> Psychiatry is an extraordinary confidence trick: the unsuspecting creature seeks aid because she feels unhappy, anxious and confused, and psychology persuades her to seek the cause in herself. (p.82)

Bruch (1974) and other commentators suggest that one way in which women have attempted to communicate their anger to society about their powerlessness, about the damage done to them by treating them as objects of adornment and pleasure and about their rejection of stereotypical roles, is in the disorder labelled anorexia nervosa.

There are numerous and conflicting explanations why a woman chooses this method of starvation. This potentially fatal behaviour has been evident throughout history, but it is only within the last 100 years that the diagnosis of anorexia nervosa has been universally accepted. It is also now generally accepted that there exists a collection of eating disorders (of which anorexia nervosa is the most common) that affect one woman in ten.

Bruch (1974) suggests that it is women's struggle against feeling enslaved, exploited and not being permitted to lead a life of their own that lies behind the condition. Bruch's theory is increasingly congruent with the views of people so diagnosed.

> Eating distress is a part of a struggle against socio-political gender oppression. A painful but sane response, particularly in Western culture. When we get together and change how we view ourselves and fight against injustice, then liberation is ours. (Pembroke, 1992, p.13)

Contemporary treatment of anorexia nervosa includes a compulsory high calorie diet. If refused, some institutions will physically restrain the patient and institute force feeding. It is somewhat ironic and disconcerting that this aggressive behaviour should be conducted in hospitals in the name of 'treatment' in the late twentieth century, when in many respects the situation is little different from the equally barbaric prison force feeding of the Suffragettes during their campaign for equal rights at the turn of the century.

The position becomes worse. In the name of behaviour therapy psychiatry treats the adult woman as a naughty child. As part of a treatment plan so-called incentives are withheld until target weights are reached. These incentives can be such basic rights as access to private bathroom facilities, relatives, media communication, etc. Patients are faced with very large portions of food and drinks with high calorie substitutes and observed until all is consumed. Very frequently there appears to be no recognition that the process of dieting to such an excess as seen in anorexia nervosa will result in a physiological shrinking of the stomach, thus reducing the quantity that can comfortably be consumed. These treatment plans rarely involve a negotiated dialogue on the reasons for the behaviour, or alternative methods of improving eating habits. Patients are often discharged upon reaching their target weight and returned to the same circumstances with the same pressures that led to them developing an eating disorder. This behaviour, contrived in the name of treatment, demonstrates the ability of a dominant group such as psychiatrists to categorise individuals legally within a medical diagnosis which is based on limiting and oppressive representations of women.

In a patriarchal society, a network of systems exists to reinforce this. The World Health Organisation, for example, classifies 'anorexia' as a mental disorder, thereby legitimising diagnosis and treatment within a medical framework. Misunderstanding of the problem is perpetuated and a disorder that is predominantly female in origin (women accounting for currently 90 per cent of all diagnoses) is denied a more therapeutic response, which acknowledges that the problem has many components, including the problem of the pressure on women to conform to societal norms within a male perspective.

A fundamental change in the therapeutic approach to caring for women would enable problems to be addressed from within a feminist framework, to include psychological, familial, biological, sociocultural, political perspectives and issues of abuse.

Spender (1988) observes how:

> Most of the knowledge produced in our society has been produced by men; they have usually generated their explanations and the schemata and then have checked with each other and vouched for the accuracy and adequacy of their view of the world. (p.l)

Perhaps one of the most influential men who has generated knowledge and understanding, or more accurately misunderstanding, of women is Sigmund Freud. Freud's psychoanalytic theory relating to the development of the female personality has received mixed views from feminists, which can clearly be divided into two groups. The first group would consider his work to be derogatory to women. Walsh (1987) suggests that it should be dismissed as 'misogynist and based on biological determinism' (p. 1). Weisstein (1987) is somewhat stronger in her criticism of psychology as a whole.

> Psychology has nothing to say about what women are really like, what they need and what they want, essentially, because psychology does not know. (p.268)

The alternative view is that Freud's '...theories actually form a useful basis from which to start answering questions about the implications of sex differences for women's position' (Whitelegg et al, 1982, p.253). For most feminists, however, it is somewhat difficult to attribute Freud's theories with any credibility when the basis of his work describes woman as inferior and Other. He describes and analyses her behaviour, normal and abnormal, within the boundaries of his accepted 'norm' of masculine behaviour.

If his work has contributed anything to the understanding of woman it is probably only in a negative sense and is responsible in part for society viewing women as inferior. This perception as inferior derives from Freud's castration complex. In this the female child, on exploring her genitals, discovers she has no penis. His theory suggests that because of this she accepts the male child as superior and therefore it follows that she must be inferior to him:

> ...She acknowledges the fact of her castration, and with it, too, the superiority of the male and her own inferiority. (Freud, 1982, p.288)

It may be argued that this precis of Freud's contribution to the understanding of the psychology of women is minimalistic and therefore devalues his theories. The opinion which is being offered, however, is that his work is derived from some unacceptable and erroneous concepts, and that his contribution is flawed because it only serves to misrepresent women in a manner which is unhelpful and destructive.

Psychoanalysis, based on Freudian theory, has been described as a means of social control and as such is dangerous to the mental health of women. This view is based on the premise that the 'Assumptions about the inherent inferiority of women are embedded in the very core of psychoanalytic theory' (Lerman, 1987, p.44). This view of women as inferior dominated his work and his response to criticisms of this area of his theories is dismissive of:

> ...the feminists, who are anxious to force us to regard the two sexes as completely equal in position and worth. (Freud 1987, first published 1925).

This unrelenting view of woman as inferior as late as 1925 was increasingly out of step with contemporary thinking at the time. Members of the Women's Social and Political Union (the Suffragettes) had in 1918 secured the vote for women householders over the age of 30 years. They were also only 3 years away from establishing parliamentary equality by securing votes for all women over the age of 21 years in 1928. Women were therefore instigating changes in their political position in society while Freud and his colleagues were still diagnosing 'nonconforming' women as hysterical. The power and equality which some women were achieving in Parliament was overshadowed by the ability of male psychoanalysts to use their power as a means of social control of behaviour.

Is it, perhaps, the legacy of Freud's sentiments that still lingers in some aspects of women's lives and society in general and which forces them to seek solace at their general practitioners, the first step to becoming a mental health statistic? Furthermore, does the expected role of women, with the pressures to conform to impossible and conflicting demands, result in them experiencing a greater degree of distress and unhappiness?

It can be argued that perhaps it is women rejecting this role and demonstrating behaviour outside societal expectations that results in a lack of understanding and the potential for misdiagnosis with increased contact with mental health professionals. Do women internalise their oppression, absorb feelings of inferiority and dependence and turn their violence inwards on themselves?

It is generally at this early stage of presenting with distress that the societal causes of women's problems are not addressed, so leading them to be treated and encouraged to adjust their behaviour and emotions to living in a world which is dominated by male values and therefore sexist in practice.

A lack of understanding and acceptance of lesbianism can be seen as an example of society's dominant male values. It was only in the early 1970s that mental health professionals stopped describing lesbianism as a developmental problem and prescribing heterosexuality as the cure! Sayce (1993) describes how lesbians have been discriminated against by current attitudes of mental health workers with the suggestion that their lesbianism is a direct product of their sexual abuse. This creates a barrier to effective therapy. The real issue of the abuse may not be aired and the possibility that the woman has chosen her sexual preference can be missed by the therapist, thereby leaving clear communication and therapeutic problems for the therapist and the woman.

Chernin (1989) makes the point that it is:

> ...our right to be women in this culture, with our right to grow and develop ourselves and to be accepted by our culture in a way that ceases to do damage to what we are, in our own most fundamental nature, as women. (p. 3)

It is essential that mental health care is provided in an environment 'that ceases to do damage', just as one of Florence Nightingale's central tenets was that hospitals should do the sick no harm. Mental health care should facilitate the growth and empowerment of women to enable them to redress the imbalance of power within relationships and society.

There is growing evidence to support the view that a disproportionate number of women who come into contact with mental health professionals have at some time suffered physical and sexual abuse. Copperman and Burrowes (1992) state 'it is estimated that 40 per cent of women who become in-patients in hospital have already experienced sexual violence...' (p. 4). Palmer et al (1992) found that up to 50 per cent of women who had seen a psychiatrist had been abused as children. It is generally accepted that sexual abuse is nationally one of the most underre-ported crimes. It would therefore follow that these figures are an understatement of the true extent of the problem. Gravett, in his oral evidence to the Ashworth Hospital Committee of Inquiry (1992), stated '...the vast percen-tage of female patients have been seriously sexually abused and been subject to violence by men in their past' (p. 229). This 'vast percentage' has been estimated to be at least 80 per cent of the women in Ashworth Hospital.

There is empirical evidence to suggest that the effect of child sexual abuse has an impact on the mental health of the individual adult woman. Specific studies are starting to demonstrate the relationship between self-harm and suicide attempts in women who have been abused (see Beck and Van der Kolk, 1987; Bryer et al, 1987; Carmen et al, 1984; Herman et al, 1989; Watson and Williams, 1992). It should be noted that this is not a new discovery for women with mental health pro-blems. What has changed is that awareness of child sexual abuse has become more evident in society, thus facilitating adult women speaking out about their childhood abuse. Reflecting this recognition, it is essential that mental health services are planned and resourced to meet the growing needs of this patient population. It is inappropriate to continue to diagnose women as mentally ill and provide traditional treatments such as psychotropic medication and ECT and not address the real issues within the context of their life and the distress caused.

The process of facilitating growth for these women as sufferers of abuse must begin with acceptance and believing in the abuse, and providing an environment which is safe both physically and emotionally. The well documented case of Miss D in the Ashworth Committee Inquiry Report (1992) is a shocking yet typical example of how institutional care can be unnecessarily imposed or prolonged by society's failure to offer appropriate help at various stages:

> At the age of fourteen she had begun to drink cider and lager. Later she increased her consumption to two bottles of sherry per day...Miss D described frequent binges and accepted that much of her difficulty with the police occurred in the context of her heavy drinking. (Ashworth Committee Inquiry Report, 1992, p. 75)

Would her 'problem' with alcohol have been dealt with differently had she been a male juvenile? Heidensohn (1989) discusses the 'double standard' that is operated by the courts in relation to male and female juveniles. Male misbehaviour is more likely to be accepted as normal developmental activity, whereas female behaviour is seen as linked to sexual promiscuity and the adolescent girl therefore needs protection and control, which is provided by society's institutions of prison, hospitals, etc. The differentation between the sexes is scaled to protect girls from themselves, but it allows boys to be boys (Casburn, 1989, p. 47).

These cameos serve to illustrate how there is a lack of appropriate facilities and inability on the part of staff to understand and address the underlying cause of the disruptive behaviour exhibited by women such as Miss D. It could be suggested that had her attempt to disclose her previous abuse been addressed in a more supportive and therapeutic environment, then her progress through the system might have been altered and her distress minimalised.

Before one can address the question of how mental health nurses can provide a therapeutic milieu which affords physical safety and facilitates growth and empowerment for women, it is necessary to scrutinise and understand the organisational developmental of current service provision.

The philosophy of the 1960 in psychiatric establishments was to develop mixed-sex environments in place of the sterile segregated wards which had characterised the asylum movement. Rehabilitation wards were the first to be integrated, followed by acute admission wards. The integration involved mixing of both staff and patients. This was seen as a progressive process of 'normalisation', justified by the belief that it was abnormal for men and women to live apart from each other. Segregation also mirrored prison environments, which were viewed as non-therapeutic.

The philosophy gathered so much momentum that it became regarded by some as the most appropriate method of providing a therapeutic milieu not only in mental health settings, but also in general hospitals. There has also been an expressed belief that mixed-sex environments produce less disturbed behaviour in male patients, and that male patients are more likely to take an interest in their appearance when women are around. Another described advantage (for men!) is of the effect on improving the standard of living:

> When male psychiatric patients are kept together you do not get a high standard of hygiene and there are none of the homely touches which women naturally bring. (Pitt, 1992, p. 23)

There are, however, questions that need to be asked about the effect on women. What are the costs of accepting the negative experiences of sharing intimate living space with men who are strangers? If mixed-sex wards are supposed to be part of the process of 'normalisation' it begs the question about how many people would voluntarily share their intimate living space with strangers of the opposite gender. If (as previously discussed) a disproportionate number of women in mental health settings have been physically and sexually abused, does mixing them with men, at a point when they are trying to reconcile them-selves to the impact of these issues, only serve as reminders of their previous abusive relationships and therefore hinder their recovery?

It is important to state at this point that the intention is not to infer that all men are abusers of women. It is, however, accepted practice in some psychiatric hospitals to mix male patients who have abused, with women (either staff or patients) as part of a therapeutic plan to assess their behaviour and attitudes to women. What is clearly unacceptable, both morally and professionally, is that there appears to be little if any consideration given to the effect on the women as either patient or staff.

Weddle (1992) conducted a survey of psychiatric patients in the Glasgow area. His study found that both men and women had experienced sexual violence and that about three-fifths of women felt vulnerable in mixed-sex wards during the acute stage of their illness. Most women agreed that mixing was appropriate only during rehabilitation.

If patients are mixed during the acute stage of their illness, what is the image that is portrayed of man, and the potential for damage to his character? Admission to an acute ward can by definition suggest that an individual's behaviour has been changed by his illness with the potential for disinhibited or violent behaviour.

Does this in fact not reinforce the image of the violent man to a woman who is in acute distress herself? Disinhibited and violent behaviour can lead to physical and sexual assaults on women and there is substantial evidence to suggest that this frequently happens in psychiatric hospitals. This produces the potential for a criminal record and an extended stay either in hospital or custody for the man, quite apart from the untold damage to women, who find themselves violated in what they supposed was a place of safety and therapy.

Numerous incidents have been reported ranging from harassment to rape. Bennetto (1993) in the *Independent* describes seven cases of alleged rapes at one London hospital. Hughes (1992) asks the question 'Therapeutic for whom?' and describes the disturbing case of a young woman admitted to a secure unit. She had a history of severe sexual abuse by her father and brothers from an early age and was admitted to a mixed ward. She was the only female patient with 11 men, five of whom had committed sexual offences. During her stay she faced daily harassment, including attempts to touch or kiss her. The article raises many other areas of concern, including the basic lack of privacy in mixed wards, where sleeping and bathroom facilities are often divided only by flimsy curtains. It also describes the suggestion of a relative that her daughter was raped while heavily sedated. This unacceptable incident was made even more distressing when the mother was informed by the police that because her daughter was mentally ill 'it would be virtually impossible to make the case stand up in court'. In reporting similar issues Tonks (1992) notes that 'underfunding and overcrowding may be putting women at risk of sexual assault in psychiatric units in London's hospitals' (p. 1331). Cohen (1992) and Copperman and Burrowes (1992) have made similar observations.

What has to be acknowledged by mental health nurses is that their establishments mirror the culture of the society they serve. In this context, women and vulnerable people are just as likely to be assaulted, abused and harassed inside hospital as well as in the grounds, on the streets and in their own homes.

As with abuse within society, nurses must recognise that the abuser may be someone they know, a patient, a member of staff, a legitimate visitor or the opportunist stranger. Nurses need to become more vigilant in relation to the safety and security of patients and themselves.

Recent UKCC (1993) figures indicate that a disconcertingly high number of professional misconduct cases relate to the abuse of women by male nurses. While the causes of this scenario are undoubtedly complex, it is important that mental health nurses are aware of such issues. If we are to fulfil our duty to ensure the safety of all patients in our care, not only the vulnerable, but also the potential abuser, we have to address much more fully aspects of our own practice and of the environment in which we work. This will involve identifying both the surreptitious and overt ways in which we reinforce the existing status quo. For example, in the literature there has been scant attention given to the concerns regarding male staff caring for women patients. It is often accepted practice that male staff are used for control purposes in relation to disturbed behaviour, self-harm, etc. In environments where seclusion is used, women may still be forcibly placed in seclusion and items of clothing removed by male staff. Where strong suits are used, it may still be policy to use male staff to undress women. This reinforces the stereotypical view of man as the all-powerful controller and aggressor. This is not therapeutic or empowering for the woman and is equally damaging to the image of male staff. There can also be issues raised concerning attitudes and inappropriate (for example, sexist or macho) language of male staff when nursing women. At the least this is uncomfortable and distressing for women patients and at the worst can develop into explicit sexual harassment.

It has not been the intention to alienate male (nurses) staff in any way. Males have a part to play in caring for women, but they need to understand what their gender and its associations may represent to some women. They need to learn not to become defensive or hostile but accept that their gender can be a problem. They can assist in improving services for women by cooperating and adding their support to women-only programmes and services. Nurses have not perhaps listened sufficiently to users of their services and encouraged and facilitated their ability to become proactive in influencing service provision. Growing evidence is emerging from women users of mental health services that if offered a choice they would prefer to be cared for on single-sex wards.

MIND's Langbaurgh Campaign Group (1993) conducted a survey as part of MIND's National Stress on Women Campaign. The survey found that of 127 women asked, 48 per cent wanted a women-only ward, and only 3 per cent wanted mixed-sex wards.

Thomas et al (1992) conducted a survey of 150 patients comprising 79 men (53 per cent) and 71 women (47 per cent). Their results showed that 28 (19 per cent) of the total surveyed would have preferred a single-sex ward. Of the women in this survey who said they would have preferred a single-sex ward 19 (27 per cent) said 'they would have felt safer within a woman-only unit because there would be less violence and more privacy'. While this apparently represents a minority in favour of single-sex wards, it is none the less a sizeable minority, whose needs should not be lightly dismissed.

There has been a growing emphasis in government statements on the principle that mentally ill people should not be slotted into existing patterns of service. The reforms of the National Health Service (Parliament, National Health Service and Community Care Act, 1990) are based on greater choice for users. It is a right that the growing concern among patients, relatives and carers, expressed by Cole (1993), Hadden et al (1992), de Rochas (1993) and others about the limitations of mixed-sex wards be listened to and acted upon. It is an area in which nurses have a very significant role to play.

The main concern from all these contributions relates to the lack or potential lack of privacy afforded in such settings. It is suggested 'that their present popularity has more to do with money than therapy' (Cole 1993, p. 16). The nurse's role is crucial in creating health care environments where women and others can expect to be cared for in conditions which afford physical and emotional safety.

In their interventions they need to accept that this is not an imaginary part of a woman's mental illness but that harassment and sexual assaults are really happening. They must ensure that they do not collude with the abuse by denying that it is real. Women need to be believed and supported in making complaints to the hospital management and the police if a crime is suspected. Health authorities should have clear policies which are not ambiguous. The decision to involve the police or not should not be left to the staff's individual discretion. The Special Health Authority Draft Policy (1993) provides a useful model.

An area that has been raised by Mind's Stress on Women campaign is the need for women to choose the gender of their key worker. It is government policy to allow women the right to choose a female GP but it is not practice for women to be given the choice of their key worker or psychiatrist.

The issue which is being raised is the degree to which many people feel comfortable sharing their distress, often of a very personal nature, with staff of the opposite gender. In a small study, Mathieson (1991) found that 88 per cent (22 of 25) of female psychiatric patients would prefer to be cared for by female nurses. Women reported feeling uncomfortable discussing sexual problems with male staff. The study also reported women objecting to physical interventions and discussing physical problems with male staff. Of male patients, 37 per cent (10 of 27) stated that they would be unwilling to discuss sexual problems with a female nurse.

The issue of choice of key worker is therefore not limited only to women patients. The rationale for allowing patients the choice of their key worker can also be extended to other groups with specific needs, the central issue being that of the user being offered maximum appropriateness and informed choice of a nurse who is most suited to understanding and responding to their individual needs.

THE WAY FORWARD

The particular problems facing women in mental health settings arise from sources embedded in society itself. Women are more prone to the diagnosis of mental disorder because of the way their problems and responses are viewed and judged. Once diagnosed their treatment, be it in hospital or community, is similarly discriminatory, because of preconceptions and prejudices on the part of lay and professional people. There is now ample evidence to support these assertions.

Nurses have not been particularly successful in preventing the occurrence of these problems nor in countering their effects. This is not because of an absence of female nurses. The live UKCC register shows that some 55 per cent of RMNs are female. Since women are less likely to attain senior posts than men, it is reasonable to assume an even higher preponderance of women in direct care roles. If this is so, why then are women not being adequately cared for? The answer lies in the way women are bound up in the same systems, whether they are patients or nurses. Women, as nurses, are subjected to the same judgemental value systems and expectations of female subservience as their patients. An area where this is often evident is in the nurse–doctor professional relationship. Nurses and nursing practice traditionally have been undervalued by members of the medical profession and others. This has often led to their voices not being heard in relation to day to day patient management and service provision. However, it is nurses that collectively are responsible for the cycle of 24-hour patient care, and as such should be proactive in developing facilities and treatment programmes that are based on the real needs of the users. Nurses need to empower themselves to be more influential in the development of service provision, and in their own employment, for facilities and working practices that do not discriminate against them as women. An area that needs to be developed to remove discriminatory practice is in the provision of child-care facilities for both the woman as a patient and as an employee.

The good news is that there is now a developing awareness of the societal pressures and professional influences that have created this situation and an increasingly robust call for change. In this context, mental health nurses are in a prime position to influence service provision. It is of paramount importance that they listen to the voice of the user and provide safe services. It is especially relevant that single-sex accommodation is offered, and that people have a choice of the gender of their named nurse. Actively antidiscriminatory policies and more appropriate therapy and support must follow. These are the essential first steps in ensuring service provision that is not blind to either gender or culture. The aim is complementary to the empowerment of all service users, be they male or female, and supports the rise in consumerism in the 1990 which is being underpinned by the named nurse initiative, the Patient's Charter, individualised care and the user movement. The goal will be safe health care provision that is an interactive and negotiable process, with the user and providers entering into a more egalitarian partnership.

Developing appropriate therapy and support for women is a particular challenge. The study of the psychology of women has interdisciplinary representation from anthropology, psychology, sociology, psychoanalysis, psychiatry and medicine. If there is to be a change in how this body of 'experts' study women's mental health there has to be a strong representation from within feminist theory.

A fundamental change in the therapeutic approach to caring for women is required to enable the problem to be addressed from outside a medical framework that is fundamentally based on male assumptions. Therapy should include exploration of the issues from a feminist perspective, approaches that female mental health nurses are well placed to adopt given the appropriate education. They should challenge the existing systems, knowledge base, discourses and attitudes to offer alternative models of care, or develop new ones in areas where they are not yet present.

EDUCATION

Gender issues need to be in evidence in the education and training programmes of all nurses and health care workers. However, the root of the problem starts much earlier than nurse education! Nurses, and the general public, are educated in what is mainly a sexist education system which reinforces stereotypical views on gender roles. Education reproduces inequality through the reinforcing of these stereotypical gender roles. Traditional learning reinforces gender hierarchy with males more highly valued, a view which is perpetuated by women teachers as well as men. Girls in school need to be able to discuss inequality and sexual harassment in a safe environment and develop ways of effectively coping and of challenging such practices. Boys need to be helped to understand their behaviour based on stereotypical gender roles and the effect this has on girls and women.

Teachers need to practise (teach) in a manner which is not blind to gender or culture. Gender and cultural studies have to be a major part of the national curriculum for both boys and girls to develop personalities and behaviour free from prejudice and ideas of women as inferior. Education of children should aim to remove sexual divisions to prevent them developing in a gender-stereotypical mould that is not beneficial to the child or society.

Nurse education, both pre- and postregistration, should build upon and maintain a curriculum that is based on gender and cultural equality. This should include representation from feminist practice in both education and clinical practice.

PRACTICE AND SERVICE PROVISION

Nurse education and practice needs to develop a knowledge base and attitudes which reflect an awareness of women as patients with specific needs related to their gender and position in society. There is a need to develop assessment tools specific to women which address the 'real' issues and which do not marginalise their problems or cloud them by traditional medical assessment, treatment and diagnosis.

Nurses are in a unique position to develop their skills to facilitate management of specific issues in therapeutic group work. Women who have experiences unique to them should be supported in closed groups, for example: women who self-harm, women with eating disorders, women who have been abused, women who are dependent on medication, etc. Therapy should be delivered in a environment which affords emotional and physical safety and does not reinforce the medical model by using medication as a first response. Therapy must deal with issues related to their experiences and needs as women in a society which is often unsupportive. As well as therapy groups, they should be offered individual counselling, support groups and complementary therapies such as aromatherapy, therapeutic massage, etc. Nurses need clinical supervision and support when nursing these patients as issues covered may be distressing and relevant to their own personal circumstances. Nurses need to ensure they do not contribute to discriminatory practice and that they work against such practice in others and the system as a whole.

In ensuring that women as users are able to influence and monitor service provision, nurses have to encourage women to speak out for facilities that are necessary for them as women. This includes the provision of or access to child-care facilities. In developing services for women, consideration should be given to developing a charter of rights which is specifically written for women. A useful start would be the inclusion of the four main issues highlighted in the MIND Stress on Women Campaign:

- an end to sexual harassment and sexual abuse in mental health settings;
- the right for women to choose a woman care manager or key worker;
- child-care for people who use mental health services; and
- service provision monitored by gender and action to end unfair treatment (MIND, 1992).

When planning a comprehensive care package attention should be given to ensuring that discharge and community care plans reflect issues that are central to building on the growth and independence of the woman. Avenues should be found which maintain and support (emotional and practical) and address social and relationship issues which may in part contribute to her problems.

The explicit aim is to influence the development of comprehensive services in which women can be physically safe, to think, feel, explore and be themselves as women with their own language and discourse.

> If we continue to speak this sameness, if we speak to each other as men have spoken for centuries, as they have taught us to speak, we will fail each other. Again...words will pass through our bodies, above our heads, disappear, make us disappear. (Irigaray, 1992, p. 69)

The psychiatrisation of women's mental health lies within the parameters that society defines for women. Nurses, in their wider public health role, have a key part to play in reassessing these boundaries to ensure that the 'fault' does not continue to be seen within the woman herself, but rather within society and its structures.

References

Ashton H (1989) Cited in: Neustatter A. *Head Counting*. Cited in: *Guardian* 26 October 1989. Cited in: *Women and Mental Health* (1991). London: MIND Information, MIND Publications.

Ashworth Committee Inquiry Report (1992) *Report of the Committee of Inquiry into Complaints about Ashworth Hospital*, Volume II: The Case Studies. London: HMSO.

Beck JC and van der Kolk B (1987) Reports of childhood incest and current behaviour of chronically hospitalised psychotic women. *American Journal of Psychiatry* **144**(11): 1474–1476.

Bennetto J (1993) Patients raped at mental hospital. *The Independent* April.

Bruch H (1974) *Eating Disorders Obesity, Anorexia Nervosa and the Person within*. London: Routledge and Kegan Paul.

Bryer JB, Nelson BA, Miller JB and Krol PA (1987) Childhood sexual and physical abuse as factors in adult psychiatric illness. *American Journal of Psychiatry* **144**(11): 1426–1431.

Carmen EH, Rieker PP and Mills T (1984) Victims of violence and psychiatric illness. *American Journal of Psychiatry* **141**(3): 378–383.

Casburn M (1989). Women and Justice. In: Heidensohn F (ed) *Women and Crime*. Basingstoke: Macmillan.

Chernin K (1989) *Womansize: The Tyranny of Slenderness*. London: The Woman's Press.

Cohen P (1992) High risk mix. *Social Work Today* **23**(31): 4–6.

Cole A (1993) All mixed up. *Nursing Times* **89**(41): 16.

Copperman J and Burrowes F (1992) Reducing the risk of assault. *Nursing Times* **88**(26): 64–65.

De Beauvoir S (1988) *The Second Sex*. London: Picador Classics.

Department of Health and Social Services (1986) *Mental Health Statistics for England 1986*. Booklet 1, Mental Illness Tables A2.2 and A2.3, Government Statistical Service. London: HMSO.

De Rochas J (1993) Mixed sex feelings ignored by NHS. *Nursing Standard* **8**(12): 10–11.

Freud S (1982) Female sexuality. In: Whitelegg E, Arnot M, Bartels E, Beechey V, Birke L, Himmelweit S, Leonard D, Ruehl S and Speakman M A (eds) *The Changing Experience of Women*. Oxford: Basil Blackwell in association with The Open University.

Freud S (1987) Cited in: Walsh M R (ed) *The Psychology of Women: Ongoing Debates*. New Haven/London: Yale University Press.

Gravett P (1992) *Report of the Committee of Inquiry into Complaints about Ashworth Hospital*, Volume 1. London: HMSO.

Greer G (1987) Cited in: Walsh M R (ed) *The Psychology of Women. Ongoing Debates*. New Haven/London: Yale University Press.

Hadden DSM, Dearden CH and Ross G (1992) Mixed sex wards. *British Medical Journal* **6847**(305): 251.

Heidensohn F (1989) *Women and Crime*. Basingstoke: Macmillan.

Herman JL, Perry JC and van der Kolk BA (1989) Childhood trauma in borderline personality disorder. *American Journal of Psychiatry* **146**: 4.

Hughes P (1992) Therapeutic for whom? *The Guardian* 2 July.

Irigaray L (1992) What is Feminist Theory? In: Crowley H and Himmelweit S (eds) *Knowing Women, Feminism and Knowledge*. Cambridge: Polity Press in association with The Open University.

Langbaurgh Campaign Group (1993) *Langbaurgh Campaign Group*. Redcar: MIND Press Release.

Lerman H (1987) From Freud to Feminist Personality Theory: Getting There from Here. In: Walsh M R (ed) *The Psychology of Women, Ongoing Debates*: New Haven/London: Yale University Press.

Mathieson E (1991) A question of gender. *Nursing Times* **87**(7): 31–32.

MIND (1992) *Stress on Women Pack*. London: MIND Publications.

Nacro (1991) *A Fresh Start for Women Prisoners: The Implications for the Woolf Report for Women*. London: Nacro.

Palmer RL, Chaloner DA and Oppenheimer R (1992) Childhood sexual experiences with adults reported by female psychiatric patients. *British Journal of Psychiatry* **160**: 261–265.

Parliament (1990) National Health Service and Community Care Act 1990, Chapter 19. London: HMSO.

Pembroke L (1992) Eating distress. *Openmind* **54**: 12–13.

Pitt B (1992) Cited in Sullivan J. How unisex wards are providing an ideal mix. *Medical Forum*, 28 May, p. 23.

Potier M (1992) Clinical psychology. *Openmind* **58**: 16–17.

Sayce E (1993) Given a voice. *Nursing Times* **89**(36): 48–50.

Showalter E (1987) *The Female Malady: Women, Madness and English Culture 1830–1980*. London: Virago Press.

Smith-Rosenberg C (1984) The hysterical woman: sex roles and role conflict in 19th century America. In: Black N, Boswell D, Gray A, Murphy S and Popay J (eds) *Health and Disease: A Reader*. Milton Keynes: Open University Press.

Special Health Authority (1993) *Draft Policies for Dealing with Allegations of Sexual Assault, Sexual Abuse and Rape Involving Patients of the SHA*. Unpublished.

Spender D (1988) Cited in: Gelsthorpe G and Morris A (eds) Feminism and criminology in Britain. *British Journal of Criminology* **28**(2): 93–110.

Szasz TS (1977) *The Manufacture of Madness*, 2nd edn. London: Paladin Granada Publishing.

Thomas B, Liness S, Vernals S and Griffin H (1992) Involuntary cohabitees. *NursingTimes* **88**(49): 58–60.

Tonks A (1992) Women patients vulnerable in mixed psychiatric wards. *British Medical Journal* **6838**(304): 1331.

UKCC (1993) Gender trouble. *NursingTimes* **89**(46): 3, 5, 18.

Walsh MR (ed) (1987) *The Psychology of Women, Ongoing Debates*. New Haven/London: Yale University Press.

Watson G and Williams J (1992) Feminist Practice in Therapy. In: Ussher J and Nicolson P (eds) *Gender Issues in Clinical Psychology*. London: Routledge.

Weddle I (1992) Cited in: Tonks A. Women patients vulnerable in mixed psychiatric wards. *British Medical Journal* **6838**(304): 1331.

Weisstein N (1987) Cited in: Walsh MR (ed) *The Psychology of Women, Ongoing Debates*. New Haven/London: Yale University Press.

Whitelegg E et al. (1982) *The Changing Experience of Women*. Oxford: Blackwell.

Wollstonecraft M (1987) Cited in: Showalter E (ed) *The Female Malady: Women, Madness and English Culture, 1830–1980*. London: Virago Press.

CHAPTER 7

Alternatives to Seclusion

Dᴀᴠɪᴅ Sᴀʟʟᴀʜ

INTRODUCTION

In attempting to find alternatives to seclusion, what must be done first must be to answer the perennial question once and for all: is seclusion a skill for the management of disturbed behaviour, and as such to be included in the skills repertoire of the psychiatric nurse? This debate has now been given greater prominence due to the conclusions of the Ashworth Inquiry Team (Department of Health, 1992) in respect of seclusion. The Department of Health in conjunction with the Special Hospitals Service Authority have rejected the recommendation that the practice of seclusion should be phased out of the hospital within 2 years. The reasons for the rejection are not at all clear, but one could not help but speculate that it may be due to financial constraints. It is hoped, therefore, that the decision to defer the full implementation of the recommendation is only temporary. The implementation of the recommendation has a wider implication for the rest of psychiatric nursing. That is why the recommendation must be revisited. More and more psychiatric hospitals and units will have to change their methods of delivering quality and appropriate care which best meets the needs of patients, which will become paramount as purchasing authorities and commissioning agents become more involved in all stages of the process of care and not just the end results.

DEFINITION

The current Code of Practice for the Mental Health Act 1983 published by the Department of Health and Welsh Office (1990) defines seclusion as 'the supervised confinement of a patient alone in a room which may be locked for the protection of others from significant harm'. This definition implies that the individual who is secluded has no voluntary means of access from the room in which the confinement is taking place. It does not mention the fact that this room ought to be so designated. Consequently, a patient who is in his or her bedroom with the door unlocked, but with a nurse sitting on the other side of the door, who cannot move in and out of the room voluntarily is being secluded. However, as Mason (1992) concludes, the literature on the definition of seclusion lacks consistency. The definition advanced by the Code of Practice and quoted above is one which is widely used in psychiatry today as a working definition. It is worth noting further that the revised Code of Practice (Department of Health and Welsh Office, 1993) states that the 'sole aim of seclusion is to contain severely disturbed behaviour which is likely to cause harm to others'.

HISTORICAL PERSPECTIVES

In this century the practice of seclusion in mental institutions was originally regulated by the Mental Deficiency Acts of 1913 and 1927. Long before that, however, the Commissioners in Lunacy expressed their disapproval of the use of seclusion in Broadmoor Maximum Security Hospital, 5 years after the opening of the hospital in 1830 (Commissioners in Lunacy, 1868). This concern continued to be expressed throughout the nineteenth century. Often this concern is heightened by the inappropriate use of and practices occurring in the seclusion room and the eventual effect on the patient. Some of these incidents have resulted in the death of patients (Prins, 1993). The statutory regulations governing seclusion were repealed when the Mental Health Act 1959 came into being but the misuse of seclusion continued.

LEGAL PERSPECTIVES

The Department of Health (1992) notes that a person is:

> deemed to be kept in seclusion if at any time between the period commencing at 8 a.m. and ending at 7 p.m. he is isolated in a room, the door of which is fastened or held so that he is unable to leave the room at will, but not if he is isolated in a room in which the lower half of the door is so fastened or held but the upper half left open. (Regulation 34(2), Mental Deficiency Regulations 1948; Rule 57(2), Mental Treatment Rules 1948)

There are, however, legal constraints relating to the use of seclusion. These in the main address the issues of procedure and responsibilities of staff, including the treatment plan, attire for the patient, limited articles for the patient's use, observation intervals and record keeping. These constraints have been emphasised as a result of the case of *A* v. *United Kingdom* which was considered by the European Commission on Human Rights (Harding, 1990). The case was brought to the Commission by a patient in Broadmoor Hospital who was secluded for 5 weeks in 1974. The Commission found that the conditions in which he had been held amounted to a breach of Article 3 of the European Convention on

Human Rights which prohibits 'torture or inhuman or degrading treatment and punishment'.

The legal aspects of seclusion have been outlined by Gostin (1986) and more recently by Hoggett (1990) who pointed out that the justification for secluding the mentally disordered patients without their consent:

> 'can probably be summed up by the proposition that there is a right to restrain a patient who is doing, or is about to do, physical harm to himself, to another person or to property'

The legal justification for seclusion can be found in common law. This implies that the nurse who is responsible for the seclusion of a patient merely needs to demonstrate that the action taken is for the good of the individual or others. The responsibility to act reasonably is therefore essential and has constituted an area of debate within the profession, focusing principally on the reason for the seclusion, as previously discussed. Despite the law and the general trend of the focus for guidelines which has remained consistent throughout time, the European Commission's ruling, occasional deaths and vigilance to prevent improper use of seclusion, the practice still lingers on. Why then is seclusion still deemed necessary?

JUSTIFICATION FOR SECLUSION

One of the main reasons for the seclusion of patients has been the perceived shortage of staff to deal with the problem behaviour that the patient is displaying. This, seen as a backdrop to the argument that anything that will benefit the majority is a good thing, raises many ethical questions. For example, who derives the greatest benefit when the patient who refuses food is secluded? It is easy, therefore, to form the opinion that the way in which this patient was treated was to simply remove a 'nuisance' from the ward environment. Others postulate that there are some patients who may need seclusion and indeed benefit from the experience. There is very little evidence to show that the patient who has been in seclusion attributes the change in behaviour totally to the use of seclusion. The question of who is benefiting from the experience needs to be asked. However, the answer cannot always be that it is the patient. Why do we think the experience is good for the patient? Or is this a case of professional pride or perhaps even arrogance which leads us to think that we know best?

The intention here is not to deride those who still use seclusion. It must be said that there is still a widespread belief that seclusion may be helpful. There is certainly considerable difficulty in agreeing on who benefits most from the experience. Plutchic et al. (1978) are among many reasearchers who express the view that there are variances in the opinions of clinical staff as to who benefited most from the experience. There is a view in this particular research that the most common feeling expressed by all clinical staff was 'satisfaction with helping the ward run more smoothly, satisfaction with helping the patients, as well as regret that the crisis was not resolved differently'.

PATIENT PERSPECTIVE – EMOTIONAL EFFECTS

Apart from the potential and sometimes apparent physical harm to both the patient and/or staff emotional and psychological harm is difficult to assess. This is because different patients may experience seclusion in various ways and these beliefs and perceptions will be dependent on their mental state and the type of disorder that they suffer. Reviews of clinical aspects of seclusion have been compiled by many researchers, notably Begin (1991) and Brown and Tooke (1992), who supported the view that seclusion is harmful. For example, seclusion may reinforce the delusion of persecution in the psychotic patient, while feelings of mistrust and hostility may be exacerbated in the personality disordered patient and yet again distress may be caused in the neurotic patient.

Hammill et al (1989) note that some patients tend to play down the contribution that their own behaviour may have made to their being secluded. They added, however, that recollections of psychotic experiences in seclusion are generally factually accurate. Many patients who have been secluded view the experience negatively. Hammill et al (1989) expressed the opinion that seclusion is a:

> painful one associated with feelings of helplessness, fear, sadness and anger.

While they do not find any evidence to support the view that patients feel safe and protected in seclusion, other studies find mixed reactions. Plutchic et al (1978) reported that some of the patients found the experience had a calming effect, while others in their sample population reported boredom, anger, confusion and disgust. In an article in the *Nursing Times* (1993) an anonymous writer described the experience of seclusion as follows:

> I felt completely alone. The corridor went silent...In a way I felt that I deserved to be punished – although I felt that if I had been treated in a different manner it would not have occurred.

This statement added greater substance to the view held by many patients who have been secluded that the experience is degrading and humiliating. While it may be argued that the use of seclusion ought to be included in the portfolio of management options for the mentally ill, its frequent use is undeniably an indicator of poor quality service.

CHALLENGING BEHAVIOUR – A DEFINITION

In psychiatry challenging behaviour can be described as any psychiatric condition necessitating the increased use of staff resources and expertise. This definition is deliberately broad to demonstrate the fact that it is not only the patient who is throwing property about or assaulting others who requires this specialist and highly focused individual care. A depressed patient who is inactive, feeling despondent and who experiences low self-esteem also presents behaviour which makes increased demands on the staff. A severely mentally ill person whose physical condition is deteriorating fast due to refusal to accept sustenance also requires this type of increase in staff resources. It is true, however, that the the majority of patients who may be categorised as having challenging behaviour are those who are aggressive, disruptive and sometimes violent towards others, but it must not be overlooked that some patients present a challenging behaviour as manifest by their propensity to self-harm. The case study below demonstrates an example of what might be described as a challenge.

CASE STUDY

Charles, a 30-year-old man of Afro-Caribbean origin was referred to the forensic psychiatric service (RSU) because of the management problems that staff from a catchment area hospital were experiencing. He was admitted 2 days previously to that hospital, having been refusing medication in the community.

Obviously there had been a deterioration of his mental condition. He again refused medication while in his local hospital and all attempts to persuade him failed. The decision to administer the medication by injection was therefore taken. During the process of restraint, the patient and some of the staff were injured; the patient managed to escape and took refuge in a corner of the ward. He had a table that he was threatening to use on anyone who came any closer to him. The staff decided to call in the riot police, who managed to bring the situation under control after a considerable time. However, this took a total of eight nurses and six policemen.

This patient had previously spent 8 years in a special hospital. He had originally committed manslaughter while experiencing paranoid delusions and was conditionally discharged under Section 37/41 of the

Mental Health Act 1983. His assessment took place in the ward's seclusion room, where he was placed following the incident. High doses of major tranquillising medication were adminstered with very little effect. The decision to admit him to the forensic service was made as relationships had broken down.

The immediate difficulty, however, was the question of how to transport this unwilling individual, who was also antagonistic and apparently willing to fight for what he perceived as justice denied. After appraising all the options available to us, including that of involving the police, we decided to take him with us in the hospital car.

The first step on this uncertain journey was to form some degree of trust by clarifying our purpose and how we proposed to care for him while with us. He finally agreed to come with us but with great reluctance. The journey back with the nurses from the forensic unit was not an easy one. While there were no aggressive incidents en route, the silence felt like walking on eggshells – just waiting for something to happen.

During a review of the circumstances leading to his admission to the forensic service, he informed us that 'I felt cornered, I had to fight'. His behaviour had changed, apparently because we were able to communicate what we wanted to do with options. He felt, therefore, that he had a choice and that his opinions were being taken into account.

This case study shows how effective the use of communication could be at the time of difficulty. The patient felt he was being listened to and therefore responded in a positive manner, even though he did not agree with the suggested final outcomes; at least he knew what the options were and could make a choice on informed basis. The use of the nurse's negotiating skills can be very effective, but of course they do not work all the time. Making a stand during the earlier stages of the discussion leaves very little leeway for compromise. The patient must feel he or she is being consulted.

One of the key factors that precipitates aggressive behaviour is the alienation of the patient throughout the care process. Other factors, perhaps to a lesser degree, are lack of or excessive environmental stimulation, unsuitable mix of patients and lack of satisfying an expressed need and irritation. Although it is recognised that the mentally disordered individual may exhibit disturbed behaviour as a result of the disorder from which they suffer, the environmental factors contributing to the onset of this behaviour cannot be overlooked. Indeed, the patient in the case study felt he had been excluded throughout the care process. This point is stressed further by Topping-Morris (1993), who stated that 'professionals should be aware that disturbed behaviour which may seem odd or irrational at a given time needs to be seen in the context of events over a longer period. Behaviour should therefore not be categorised as disturbed without taking account of the circumstances surrounding it'.

SECLUSION AS A MEANS OF MANAGEMENT

Seclusion has emerged through the ages as a means of managing the person who presents a challenging behaviour. Its intention and, in most cases, its purpose is to derive the most satisfaction of tranquillity for the other users of that particular environment. There is evidence that some of the decisions to seclude are based on the evidence of staff shortages. Similarly, it can be argued that the decision to seclude takes into account the best available care option for the individual. If this assertion were to be sustained then it is equally legitimate to ask why the whole process leading to the eventual seclusion decision was left to degenerate to such a level to justify the final action. Many advocates for the use of seclusion argue that it is only for a short term and used as a last resort. Topping-Morris (1992) observed that despite the many assurances that it is used as a necessary skill to deal with an otherwise unmanageable situation, 'it can easily become an inhumane and commonplace method of control'. How else can the practice be changed? Replacing it without defining the boundaries will, of course, only raise the anxiety levels of staff who work closely with the patient. Nurses must strive to find alternatives to seclusion. So – what are the alternatives?

SOME ALTERNATIVES

Prolonged physical restraint and high doses of medication have been cited as an alternative to seclusion. Kinsella et al (1993) described the functions and purpose of the Intensive Care Area (ICA), which is a 'lockable, self-contained and closely supervised living space, which provides a place where one or two disturbed and potential violent patients may be cared for away from the open clinical area'. It is also a controlled environment in which most aggressive outbursts can be managed safely. The advantage of this approach, they claimed, is the ability to preserve the peace and quiet of the main clinical area, ensuring optimum care to the individual or individuals, closer contact from the allocated nurses and the opportunity for the nurses to focus on identifying the trigger factors. Duration of the placement can range from several hours to several weeks; return to the main clinical area is staged to ensure effective reorientation. They claimed that the placement of patients in the ICA is not seen as a punitive intervention, but it may be viewed negatively by the patients. The authors assert that other patients like the increased attention and find it difficult 'to give up such a high level of input and individualised care'. Norris and Kennedy (1992), following a study of the views of patients on the process of seclusion, concluded that 'whatever nurses can do before or during the seclusion process that results in more positive perceptions by patients should be helpful in promoting more comfortable feelings and appropriate behaviour'.

The process for the no-seclusion policy, however, is a long and difficult one that needs to be carefully managed. It also requires total commitment of the multi-professional staff to see the decision through.

THE REASIDE CLINIC EXPERIENCE – A NON-SECLUSION ENVIRONMENT

The Reaside Clinic is the largest medium secure facility (Regional Secure Unit (RSU)) in England. It was designed principally to admit the mentally disordered offender, though other groups of patients who present challenging behaviour but have not offended are also admitted. The patient population at the end of 1993 was 77. The clinic is based in Birmingham and provides care to patients resident within the West Midlands Health Authority region, amounting to a population size in excess of 5 million multicultural people.

The clinic is divided into seven areas known as residential units, each specialising in an approach of care provision in terms of patient need. The purpose of the specialisation by need is to provide an environment that is responsive to the assessed needs of the patient. The nursing staff in these residential areas are regarded as specialist nurses as development of skills which best meet the needs of the patients is encouraged. The staff are able to gain experience in skills for intensive care nursing, admissions and assessment, specialised assessment (post-treatment of acute phase), cognitive behavioural therapy, therapeutic community and living skills development. There is only one seclusion room, which is on the intensive care unit (ICU) and is being used as a storage facility. The management of the disturbed patient is not centralised on the ICU. All the residential units are expected to deal with most challenging behaviours without recourse to transferring the patient to the intensive care unit, even though the unit provides a crisis management facility. The reason for this policy decision is to ensure that if possible, the patient receives care from staff who are familiar to them and understand their needs best. This also ensures that the staff build up the relevant skills necessary for the management of the disturbed and aggressive patient.

THE ENVIRONMENT

One of these residential units is the intensive care unit (ICU). It is a seven-bedded unit, comprising a kitchen, toilets and lounges. In the original design it had a seclusion room, which is now used as a storage space. All the patients have unlimited access to their individual rooms and keys are available for the use of any of the patients who are able to take responsibility for their safety. Seating arrangements within the unit and indeed throughout the clinic itself comprise armchairs and settees. None of the doors to communal areas is locked and patients use normal crockery and cutlery. Patients in this unit are encouraged to mix with all other patients within the clinic. The use of the main dining area of the clinic, which is centrally situated and accessible to all the patients, is encouraged unless the patient's mental condition prevents this. In this case food can be brought to the unit for the patient. Like most purpose built RSUs, the Reaside Clinic has a large activities area, a gymnasium, a five-a-side football pitch and a large full-sized football pitch. These facilities are used by all the patients, particularly those from the ICU. The security of the clinic depends mainly on the vigilance of staff and the quality of assessment of the degree of dangerousness. Security, therefore, is concentrated on the individual patient with the reason for the precaution well identified and communicated to all clinical staff, the patient and relevant others. The sources of referrals and the throughput of patients is as detailed in Table 7.1.

Table 7.1   Sources of admission and discharges.

Year	Beds	Admissions				Discharges			
		SH	NHS	Comm	CJS	SH	NHS	Comm	CJS
1987	46	3	31	–	12	1	22	7	1
1988	46	9	16	3	20	4	14	25	2
1989	55	9	9	7	25	4	12	20	3
1990	77	13	15	21	50	10	21	48	7
1991	77	8	29	28	50	6	40	50	9
1992	77	8	19	32	61	5	32	60	16
Totals		50	119	91	218	30	141	210	38

SH = special hospital; NHS = ordinary NHS hospital; Comm = community; CJS = criminal justice system.

Table 7.1 shows that 46 per cent of patients admitted to the Reaside Clinic over the period covered by this review (October 1987 to December 1992) are from the Criminal Justice System (CJS). This is followed by those admitted from National Health Service (NHS) psychiatric facilities (25 per cent), 19 per cent admitted from the community (COMM) and 11 per cent from the Maximum Security Hospitals (SH: Special Hospitals). It is possible that the figures are slightly exaggerated in the case of the community category because of readmissions during the period. For example, 48 patients have been readmitted once, 18 patients readmitted twice, four patients were readmitted on three other occasions. The records also show that one patient was readmitted on five occasions and another patient on seven occasions. Nearly all these readmissions should not normally have occurred, as most of the patients concerned would have benefited from a short stay on a general psychiatry hospital ward. The difficulty stems from the lack of readily available beds in local hospitals and the reluctance of some provider units within the patients' catchment area to admit patients who might be too disruptive. Another dimension is the legal status of the patient with respect to the Mental Health Act at the time of discharge.

There is also a debate within the service that the Reaside Clinic may have been discharging their most difficult patients to special hospitals. Statistical information reveals that from the opening of the clinic on 1 October 1987 to 31 May 1993, a total of 30 patients were transferred to the Special Hospitals; the actual number of patients involved is 27 (one female accounts for three transfers and two transfers are attributable to a male patient). Of these, 15 patients were returned after a period of trial leave from the Special Hospitals, leaving a total of 14 new patients transferred from the Reaside Clinic. This, if weighed against the size of the clinic – 77 beds – and the population within its catchment area – 5.5 million (the West Midlands Health Region being the largest in the country) – does not seem excessive, relative to other RSUs.

The majority of patients admitted to Reaside are severely mentally ill and have committed offences ranging from murder to possession of illicit substances. A smaller proportion is diagnosed as suffering psychopathic disorder and a further few have learning disabilities. About 10 per cent of the patient population is female. People of Afro-Caribbean origin account for about 27 per cent of the total patient group and about 5 per cent are Asians. The average age of patients is about 26 years and most of them are on Sections of the Mental Health Act 1983 with restrictions on discharge.

PHILOSOPHY OF CARE

Our core values are embedded in our philosophy which, in assuming the principles of normality, states that:

> Within the constraints of the law, potential for dangerousness towards others, and the need for his/her protection, a recipient of the services should have the same liberty, rights, autonomy and choice as any other member of the community.

It concluded by saying that any infringement of these rights should be justified.

This statement of our values and philosophy for care shapes everything that involves staff and people who use the service. Use of sanctions is discouraged as it is felt that this fails to encourage nurses to find alternative solutions to difficulties presented by patients. In the case of seclusion, it is accepted that this is a sanction and therefore an unacceptable skill for the psychiatric nurse to possess. This philosophy, with its resultant values, underpins recruitment policy. The first step on the appointment ladder therefore is the acceptance and commitment to the philosophical framework for providing care by all staff employed in the service. Great emphasis is placed on the attitudes of all staff, as it is believed that technical competencies alone can never be sufficient criteria on which to base staff selection. All staff are encouraged to work towards finding alternatives to difficulties and therefore are flexible in their approach in the way they deal with service users.

This non-confrontational approach to care enables the patients to learn from their own mistakes, which in turn helps them to develop the necessary coping strategies required to deal with any difficulties they may have. One of the key effects of this philosophy is that patients who are assessed as requiring similar care have the same rights, liberties and freedoms. Whenever it is necessary to withdraw any of these, then this is communicated to the patient and the reasons for the withdrawal explained. The gist of the philosophy, therefore, dictates that the patient is not always expected to earn these rights, liberties and freedoms but they are withdrawn and reinstituted when the desired behaviour (which the patient is aware of) is achieved.

RESOURCE COMMITMENT

Many may argue that the answer to working towards a no-seclusion policy is increased staffing. This may be the case in some instances, for as consistently seen in the Reaside Clinic increase in staffing during crisis time alone seems to have been sufficient. The evidence seems to point to the fact that when staffing levels are increased to deal with any psychiatric emergency, the need to return to a lower but effective level of staffing as soon as possible is very important. This is because when there are more staff in the immediate environment of the patient, it can also act as catalyst in aggravating or precipitating difficult behaviours in patients. The ICU is a six-bedded facility serving a total patient population of 77. The staff/patient ratio of the clinic varies depending on the assessed needs of patients. There are no minimum staffing levels in the clinic. The overall staff/patient ratio is 0.89 staff to one patient although the ICU usually operates on a ratio of 1:1. These figures are often reduced at night. The flexibility of the staff in agreeing not to work to minimum staffing levels also ensures that the numbers of staff on duty reflects the level of activity. This may seem a far-fetched situation to some, but in practice this system of workload determination does reflect the ownership of the clinic's values and the responsibility of the nurse to practise as a professional. The fact that most of the disturbed behaviours are dealt with on the base units also reduces the demand on the ICU. The staff of the unit therefore concentrate on dealing with emergencies that are without doubt a long-term problem.

CRISIS MANAGEMENT

The management of the patient during the period preceding the actual disturbed behaviour is very important. The allocation of staff to patients on a one to one basis and on the degree and quality of the rapport between the allocated nurse and the patient is also important. There is an expectation that the 'sickest' patient receives the best qualified and experienced staff to coordinate their care. Another aspect worth mentioning is the way in which the care process is managed within the clinic. The clinical teams have senior nursing staff as members as well as the named nurse for the patient. The senior staff, therefore, are expected to support the junior staff, especially during crisis periods. This has its benefits in that introduction of the senior staff in care provides the patient with distraction from focusing for too long on what they may perceive as the source of their displeasure. In addition most of the decisions can be made on the spot by the senior nurse without resorting to consultation with all the clinical team members. The accent, therefore, is on the effective management of the problem at hand. Most of the patients who use the crisis management facility do so after all attempts to calm the situation safely have failed.

MEDICATION-FREE ASSESSMENT

Patients are admitted to the unit that best meets their needs and do not need to progress through a series of stages. Where discharge is indicated the patient can be discharged from any one of the six residential units within the clinic, including the ICU. The majority of patients who are admitted to the clinic undergo a period of assessment which does not involve the use of any neuroleptic medication.

The value of this is obvious and importantly the care team is able to review various options which could be of potential benefit to the patient. In the case of patients who are admitted from prison environments they may have presented as seriously mentally ill when assessed in the prison setting. In some cases the patient may have found it difficult to cope with the pressures and demands of life in prison and felt anguish and frustration to such a degree that the equilibrium of mental well-being was disturbed. A period of medication-free assessment may provide a useful insight into the behaviour of the patient outside the prison environment. In some cases this approach means that the patient never has the need to receive any medication.

LEVELS OF AGGRESSION – A 4-YEAR PERIOD AT THE REASIDE CLINIC

While we would like to say that the measures outlined above have led to the Reaside Clinic being 'aggression free', this is unfortunately not so. However, we feel we can argue that the level of aggression in the clinic is less than in similar facilities in the country. In a 4-year retrospective study (yet to be published) 981 violent incidences were recorded, a rate of 13.5 incidents per 1000 occupied bed days involving 127 patients (36 per cent of the patient population). A total of 63 incidents are attributable to one patient only and 27 patients were responsible for a minimum of 10 incidents each. The latter group are responsible for 705 incidents, i.e. 72 per cent of the clinic total. These incidents took place mainly on the three acute units. The study also reveals that 30 per cent of the incidents (293) were directed against property, 688 directed at people (366 against staff, 292 against patients and 30 against patient and staff).

The classification of the incidents is also worth noting. While many studies of aggression, notably Fottrell et al (1978), concentrated on injuries sustained our study concentrated on the actual strike or blow and whether or not they touched the intended target. The authors of the study will assert that such a novel way of classifying physical aggression will exclude the tendency to underrepresent the seriousness of assaults as it does not take into account the intention of the aggressor. The consequence of this method of classification is that the level of aggression as far as frequency is concerned will be high, as even a punch which did not hit anyone is recorded as an incident. The conclusion of this study highlights the fact that physical restraint (contact between staff and the patient) in order to deal with the situation was used on 357 incidents (36 per cent of incidents) and medication was used during 130 (13 per cent) of the incidents. The rest of the incidents were managed by the removal of the patient from the scene without physical contact and by a process involving persuasion, counselling and maintenance of supervision alone.

There is further evidence that 50 per cent of the incidents resulted in no injuries to victims, 41 per cent sustained minor injuries, bruises, swellings and superficial cuts and 9 per cent of the incidents involved the use of weapons, such as cups, chairs, hot tea or ashtrays. The classification of the injuries is as follows:

> *Group A* (single blow to non-vital area).
> *Group B* (multiple blows or single blows to vital area, e.g. head, genitals).
> *Group C* (use of weapon, cups, hot liquids, furniture).

Between October 1989 and September 1993 there was a total of 981 incidents within the clinic. Of these 41 per cent were incidents relating to group A, 45 per cent to group B and 14 per cent to group C. There were no injuries sustained in 50 per cent of all incidents and 46 per cent involved cuts and bruises. However, 4 per cent of all those involved in aggressive incidents sustained injuries that were serious. The direction of the aggression is also significant in that 75 per cent of all incidents were against the person – patients and staff – and 30 per cent against property.

Operating a service of this nature on a policy of not secluding may lead to the accusation that patients and staff are being excessively exposed to too much and unnecessary aggression. On the contrary, we feel that the level of injury sustained by patients and staff is low and the resultant absence from work due to injuries sustained by the staff is a very small proportion of the general sickness rate.

SICKNESS RATE

In a survey of sickness patterns from between 1990 and 1993, 2900 days were lost to the service in terms of absence; 772 days (3.36 per cent) were for long-term medical reasons and 2068 days (9.04 per cent) were for short-term reasons. The actual number of days lost to the service through absence attributable to all injuries sustained at work amounted to 6 days (0.26 per cent), including all those injuries which did not involve patient assaults, e.g. sporting injuries sustained during recreational activities with patients. Within the same period 50 per cent of those involved in these incidents sustained no injuries, 46 per cent sustained minor bruises and cuts and 4 per cent of the victims sustained injuries which were thought to be serious or potentially serious, for example a blow to a vital area.

The numbers injured in aggressive incidents are equally spread among the qualified and unqualified staff group and between female and male groups (the male/female nursing staff ratio is 50:50). As discussed above the total number of incidents over the 4-year period amounted to 981. Of these 137 resulted in the staff sustaining minor injuries and on 48 occasions there was some form of serious injury. Most of the serious injuries required hospital intervention, for example for X-ray or for suturing, and there was admission to hospital on two occasions only. The system for reporting incidents also ensures that the staff who are involved in an aggressive incident and sustain any form of injury attend casualty as a precaution. This is the case even in situations where there is no obvious injury.

You may think by now that the staff of the Reaside Clinic are saints! To achieve this quality of staff requires a great deal of planning. For example, the policy we adopt for the selection of our workforce is to ensure maximum exposure for all advertisements for any vacancy. Equal opportunities in recruitment provide a common foundation from which to start. The Reaside Clinic selects only the best of the applicants available for selection and places great importance on the attitudes of our staff, as it is our belief that technical competencies alone can never be sufficient criteria on which to base staff selection.

STAFF ATTITUDE TO SECLUSION

A survey of nurses' attitudes to seclusion in 1992 reveals that the majority of the nurses of the service view seclusion as ineffective, untherapeutic and punitive. The respondents emphasised the view that it does not solve the problem presented but rather masks the real issues to be resolved. They cited effective training, high staffing ratios and effective leadership from senior nurses as some of the many factors minimising the use of seclusion. There is also the view that secluding the patient is against the clinic's philosophy, highlighting the prerequisites of flexible attitudes and a level of expertise that will enable delivery of an effective nursing care in forensic psychiatry. There are now opportunities for nurses to change this outdated practice but first there must be a major change of attitude by many care providers regarding the effectiveness of seclusion and a radical change in response to the way patients express their frustration and, in some cases, aggression. The use of seclusion is a practice issue and not an academic or theoretical one. The people who are best placed to make changes are those who are involved directly in the use of this procedure – nurses.

THE USE OF DISCRETION

One of the ways in which nurses may impact on the process of change is how they exercise discretion during their contact with the patient. Nurses in psychiatry and particularly forensic psychiatry are given a very high degree of freedom to exercise discretion in the way they allocate resources and the quality of that resource. It can be argued that most of the incidents that may result in injuries to individuals are usually due to the way the nurse exercises this discretion. It may be that the patient is given little information, left out of the decision-making process and thus alienated further. The result of this may be displayed in various ways, one of which is, of course, aggression. The Reaside Clinic's key philosophy is that the involvement of the patient is central to effective nursing practice. Consistency and fairness of approach is another aspect of this process.

CONTROL AND RESTRAINT

The use of control and restraint techniques in the management of aggressive and violent behaviour is as contentious as is seclusion in psychiatry today. While some nurses agree to its use as a form of effectively controlling dangerous behaviour others argue that it is also a form of intervention which uses the infliction of pain to control asocial behaviour. They concluded therefore that, if possible, nurses should not use this form of intervention. In a year-long study (1991–92) involving a study population of 77 patients, there was a total of 585 incidents; 140 incidents where the skill was used were examined. The factors considered were the duration of the interventions, time of day and injuries to staff.

In the majority of cases when a patient is disturbed there is restraint followed by removal to a seclusion room. The approach adopted in the Reaside Clinic is only changed in terms of destination and what happens when they reach there. The patient is restrained as in all cases and where removal is indicated the patient is removed to their own bedroom. The social withdrawal which would have resulted from seclusion is therefore maintained.

In conclusion, the non-seclusion environment does not only have to define the strategy necessary to spell out clearly the service's intention; more importantly, the bold and imaginative plans must be carried through. At this stage the culture or the spirit of the service to enable the strategy to be implemented effectively must be seen to be willing. In developing the culture for not secluding the patient, all the staff of the service must be consistent in their approach in the way they respond to the patient's challenging behaviour. They must also be properly trained to rethink and adjust to the new way of thinking – they must be flexible. Equally important is the need to ensure that the new message is shared by all and is communicated effectively to patients. It is true to state that the delay in providing a patient with information can result in frustration on the part of the patient, which might increase the possibility of aggression. It is too easy to say that aggression should be prevented while the effort to carry out the intent is not there. As discussed earlier nurses do exercise a great deal of discretion in their practice, particularly in the decision to seclude the patient. In ensuring that this discretion or autonomy is not abused, everyone in the organisation must exercise it in a way which is consistent with the service's philosophy, values and aims. These values must be shared by all staff of all disciplines. These shared values are important in ensuring that the behaviours of the staff are not corrupted by the few but very influential staff who may be against its implementation at the point of service delivery.

Setting up the non-seclusion service, or changing to one, requires very bold decisions coupled with a strong sense of purpose and commitment to see the vision through. A little more time will have to be spent during the recruitment process in paying attention to explaining what the objectives of the service are.

The induction programme for staff must also communicate this purpose clearly. Managing the culture, having decided on the goals to be attained, requires strong leadership with emphasis on training and evaluation of effectiveness of care.

REFERENCES

Begin S (1991) Isolation and restraint – literature review and focus on their impact and associated normative components. *Canadian Journal of Psychiatry* **36**(7): 485–491.

Brown JS and Tooke SK (1992) On the seclusion of psychiatric patients. *Social Science and Medicine* **35**(5): 711–722.

Commissioners in Lunacy (1868) *Report on Broadmoor Criminal Lunatic Asylum*. London: House of Commons 1869.

Department of Health (1992) *The Report of the Committee of Inquiry at Ashworth Hospital*. London: HMSO.

Department of Health and Welsh Office (1990) *Code of Practice*: *Mental Health Act 1983*. London: HMSO.

Department of Health and Welsh Office (1993) *Code of Practice*: *Mental Health Act, 1983*. Published August 1993 pursuant to section 118 of the Act. London: HMSO.

Gostin L (1986) *Mental Health Services*: *Law and Practice*. London: Shaw and Sons.

Fottrell E, Bewley T and Sepeizzoni M (1978) A study of aggressive and violent behaviour among a group of psychiatric inpatients. *Medicine, Science and Law* **18**: 66–69.

Hammill MSN, McEvoy JP, Koral H and Schneider N (1989) Hospitalised schizophrenic patient views about seclusion. *Journal of Clinical Psychiatry* **50**: 174–177.

Harding TW (1990) The application of the European Convention of Human Rights to the field of psychiatry. *Medicine and Law* **9**(4): 1078–1098.

Hoggett B (1990) *Mental Health Law*, 3rd edn. London: Sweet and Maxwell.

Kinsella C, Chaloner C and Brosnan C (1993) An alternative to seclusion. *NursingTimes* **88**(17): 50–52.

Mason T (1992) Seclusion – definitional interpretations. *Journal of Forensic Psychiatry* **3**(2): 260–270.

Norris MK and Kennedy CW (1992) The view from within: How patient perceive the seclusion process. *Journal of Psychosocial Nursing and Mental Health Services*. **30**(3): 7–13.

NursingTimes (1993) Mental health, seclusion – making a fresh start. *NursingTimes* **89**(18): 65.

Plutchic R, Karasu TB and Conte HR (1978) Toward a rationale for the seclusion process. *Journal of Nervous and Mental Disease* **166**(8): 571–579.

Prins H (1993) *Big, Black and Dangerous. Report of the Committee of Inquiry into the Death in Broadmoor Hospital of Orville Blackwood and a Review of two other Afro-Caribbean patients*. London: SHSA.

Topping-Morris B (1992) Prisoners of the system. *NursingTimes* **88**(24): 39.

Topping-Morris B (1993) *Guidelines on Seclusion*. London: Royal College of Nursing.

CHAPTER 8

Exploring the Myths and Stereotypes of Mental Health in Old Age

STUART J. DARBY

INTRODUCTION

Old age is a part of human development and lifestyle about which there are many myths and stereotypical views. Assumptions about the process of ageing influences society's attitudes and behaviour towards older people. These beliefs and values impact upon the older person's perception of themselves and their position within society. Ageist attitudes therefore can lead to prejudicial and discriminatory practices that affect the provision of health and social care services.

This chapter aims to explore the ways in which mental health nurses can address the stereotypes of old age. It will provide an overview of these myths and give examples of the ways in which ageism is formed and displayed. Finally the chapter sets out to consider the approaches that nurses can take to address attitudes and behaviour that are detrimental to the well-being of all older people.

AGEISM

The term 'ageism' was first used by Butler (1974), who linked the same bias and prejudice displayed in sexism and racism to the behaviour shown towards older people. Ageism has been defined as a set of widely shared generalisations about the characteristics of older people, which may contain an element of truth but are generally simplistic assumptions that become one-sided, exaggerated and normally prejudicial to a group of people (Abercrombie et al, 1988). Ageism can therefore lead to inequitable treatment and discrimination towards older people. As a consequence of prejudice, older people may be denied the same rights as younger people or be denied access to appropriate forms of health and social care simply because of their age and regardless of their physical and mental abilities.

Unlike sexism and racism, ageism can be generally more covert and subtle in its manifestation, with the attitudes of society shaping the social policies that govern it. Stevenson (1989) suggests that ageist attitudes are also considered to be a contributory factor to abuse and inadequate care in old age. Older people are therefore marginalised both by society and by individuals and can find themselves in a position where they are looked upon with contempt that leads to discrimination, violation of rights and abuse and inadequate care.

SOCIAL AND DEMOGRAPHIC FOUNDATION

Social policy is often based upon demographic information in relation to age and not on epidemiological needs and trends. The provision of health and social care services may therefore be planned on the basis of, for example, the number of children under school age and the number of people over retirement age. Demographic trends over time have shown that the proportion of older people has increased over the last century, due in part to the decrease in adult mortality, infant mortality and fertility rates. In addition these numbers are set to rise. In 1990 there were 10.5 million people over pensionable age – a rise of over 1 million since 1971. These numbers are expected to reach 14.5 million by the year 2031 – a rise of nearly 40 per cent on the 1990 figures (Social Trends, 1992).

The problem with using raw data to provide a simple analysis of need is that the experience of ageing is often viewed as being the same for everyone. All people over retirement age are therefore characterised as one single homogeneous group irrespective of the diversity of their circumstances before the onset of old age. They are often portrayed as dependent, lacking in social autonomy, unloved, neglected by their immediate family and as a burden on society that consumes without producing. In addition, older people also run the risk of being labelled 'mentally ill' where they are unable or unwilling to keep pace with present-day thinking.

Population figures can also be used to organise older people into a second negative method of division, by ranking people into 'young elderly' and 'old elderly' subgroups. This brings its own myths, with the former being considered to belong to a twilight group of grandparents who are white-haired and loving individuals, while the latter are perceived as suffering from incontinence, immobility and mental instability. Both stereotypes can, however, set out to paint the older person as a ridiculed figure, worthless, slow and unproductive.

MENTAL HEALTH IN OLD AGE

To a large extent the view of mental health in old age is based upon stereotypical views about the process of mental health changes. These myths include assumptions that old age brings about mental health decline that is irreversible and largely associated with 'senility', that little can be done about it, and that there is no point in early detection since there is no treatment.

As with any other age group, older people suffer from various forms of illness. The stigma of mental health, however, is a powerful deterrent to seeking out and accepting help with mental health problems, particularly where fears of being labelled 'mad' or committed to institutional care are also present. Two major categories are used to define 'medical' mental ill health in old age. These include organic mental illness, in which definite changes in cerebral function take place, albeit for a temporary period, and functional mental disorders where no specific physical cause can be found.

Current estimates suggest that between 6 and 10 per cent of all older people have some degree of identifiable organic brain disturbance, namely dementia. Even in the very oldest groups, however, only one third of all older people experience some degree of organic brain deterioration and then usually not to such an extent that it impairs their ability to function normally in the community.

Functional illness, including disturbances of mood such as depression, affects about one-quarter of the elderly population. It is fairly rare, however, for a clinical affective disorder to manifest itself for the first time in old age. The majority of disorders are found in older people who have a history of this type of problem in earlier life. Where the onset of affective disorder takes place in later life, attributes such as the death of a significant person, removal from home or some other exogenous cause are indicated (Gearing and Slater 1988).

In addition to this, a large proportion of mental health problems in old age can be related to temporary or permanent sensory losses, ill health and the physical effects of medicines (Stokes, 1987). A significant relationship between lifestyle events and mental health in old age can also be seen. These prominent milestone events of retirement include altered lifestyle, altered relationships and altered personal image.

Altered lifestyle arises from the exchange of employment and paid activity for retirement and increased 'leisure time'. Although some theories promote this as a fair exchange (Dowd, 1984), the impact of reduced income, possible changes to housing and a general disturbance of 'normal' lifestyle are all factors that could influence an individual to such an extent that mental health problems might ensue.

Altered relationships occur where partners are required to spend more time together in the home and include a number of factors such as the movement of families away from parents, the loss of work colleagues and interests and the loss of peers and relatives through death. These are all considered to impact upon the loss and bereavement process associated with the phase of retirement.

Finally, older people in retirement can develop an altered image of themselves. In addition to physical biological changes their worth, value and status combined with society's expectations about how they should behave or act serves to change the way in which they perceive themselves and their role and function in the community (Palmore, 1985)

Self-concept and ideal self-concept, in which an individual tries to match up to the expectations of others or what they ought to be, has been said to create problems where individual expectations cannot be met. This leads to loss of self-esteem and loss of control which perpetuates myths, stereotypes and expectations by others.

Mental ill health in old age is therefore made up of a complex set of biological, psychological and social interactions. One of the enduring stereotypes about old age is that physical and mental illnesses are attributed to the process of ageing and therefore appropriate assessment, treatment and diagnosis is not sought. The old adage 'it's your age my dear' has been used in the past to attribute illness to ageing and could possibly be used where there are limited resources and there is a need to prioritise health and social care to those deemed to be more 'needy'. While statistics show that the fraction of old people consulting their own GP increases with age, there is some evidence that they also under-consult for their level of morbidity in comparison to younger age groups (Ford, 1985).

Given the range of factors that can contribute to mental health and well-being in old age it can be seen that mental illness is not inevitable. Many of these factors will generally respond well to improved attitudes towards ageing and to nursing, medical, psychological and social care and intervention.

SOCIOLOGICAL PERSPECTIVES

Images of ageing exist at two levels; the personal image held by an individual themselves and the images held by the wider society. It is important therefore to understand the way in which relative status is applied by society and the impact this has upon the self-image of the older person.

SOCIETAL IMAGES AND STATUS

While ageing is a biological process, growing older is a social process determined by attitudes, expectations, culture and traditions of society. The theories of Modernisation and Idealism can be considered as examples of the socialisation process applied to ageing.

Modernisation theory considers that social structure can affect the altered status of older people, while Idealism considers that society demands more equality between the younger population and the older population.

Modernisation theory

Modernisation theory focuses on the lowered status of older people and shifts in social structures in modern industrial society. Negative stereotyping is said to be a result of transformations from traditional agricultural society to industrial society. This perspective provides a 'moving picture' of how society's attitudes towards older people have been shaped over a period of time.

Before modernisation the bulk of the population was located in rural areas. The levels of education and literacy were generally low and links were closely tied between extended families where tradition was the basis of culture. After modernisation it is purported that urban environments, public education and nuclear families became the norm. Coupled with this came the evolution of the welfare state and its associated services. Innovation rather than tradition formed a new central cultural component of everyday life.

Shifts in social structures are therefore seen to be the central causal factors in Modernisation theory. Beliefs and values are seen as being of little importance in themselves, and behaviour is seen to reflect the dominant structure of society. The effect has been to reduce the status of older people.

Examples provided by Cowgill and Holmes (1972) include:

1. Older people once derived a high status because of their rarity, since fewer people lived into old age before improvements in health and social care.
2. Retirement (an institution in its own right) decreases the status of older people in terms of society's most valued medium of status, namely money. Modern economic technology has created new occupations and forced out old trades, so that experience is a less valued position.
3. Greater geographical mobility and urbanisation have been said to have destroyed extended family networks and destroyed the status of older people who were often a necessary source of financial and social support systems.
4. Finally, public mass education has led to widespread literacy and has

challenged the position of older people as transmitters of cultural knowledge and wisdom.

Idealist theory

Idealism offers an alternative to Modernisation theory. Fischer (1978) considers that political and social revolutions have changed the order of respect, deference and reverence afforded to older people. As a result of these conflicts, society demands more equality between the younger population and the older population.

In this sense Idealism emphasises a shift from social structural arrangements (Modernisation) causing a breakdown in relationships between young and old, to factors relating to the experience of ageing. Individual knowledge and experience of the external world therefore influences the way in which we interpret and define it (Gross, 1987). Examples of the way in which shifts in relationships between younger people and older people can affect status include:

1. Past admiration for the wisdom and experience of older people has disappeared, for example where skills and trades needed to be taught and passed down between generations, because of a demand for equality by younger people (Palmore, 1985)
2. Older people have been eased out of key positions where there has been a growth in technology, political advancement and a 'cult of youth'.
3. A breakdown in social institutions such as close family networks and reliance upon support from older relatives has led to a decreased value in the importance of the role of older people (O'Donnell, 1981).

Status within industrial societies therefore changes with retirement. Legislation dictates that an older person becomes old as a consequence of retiring and not on the basis of their physical or mental abilities. In pre-industrial society older people often have greater status since their knowledge, wisdom and contribution to everyday living is based upon their life experience and not their ability to earn money or work productively.

Preparation for old age and expectations for the future have been said to be derived therefore from long-term social changes. Lasch (1981) considers that these changes occur through attitude, which has in its roots an irrational fear, panic and terror of old age and death, and that these attitudes are associated with narcissistic personalities as the dominant type of personality structure in contemporary society. Individuals look to others to compare and validate their sense of themselves. The inability of the older person to be admired for beauty, charm or power leads to their inability to achieve through work or love. Self-destruction takes place, as older people are unable to live vicariously through their children and eventually this leads to further 'fraying' of links between generations.

PSYCHOLOGICAL PERSPECTIVES

Individual attitudes, values and beliefs about the process of ageing are influenced therefore by what a person believes objectively, what a person feels subjectively and the behaviour or way in which a person responds to these feelings and values. While growing up is normally taken to be something desirable and almost an end in itself, growing old has traditionally had very negative connotations.

SELF-IMAGE AND STATUS

Contrasting psychological theories provide illustrations of the way in which self-images of ageing can affect the individual older person. Examples of these psychological theories include the Decrement model, Social Exchange theory and the Disengagement theory.

The Decrement model is a term used to describe a negative image of ageing (Gross, 1987). The fundamental characteristics include decay or decline in physical and mental health and a reduction in intellect and social relationships. In contrast, the Social Exchange theory stresses the potential and advantages of increased leisure time and a reduction in day to day responsibilities. Dowd (1984) suggests that older people give up paid employment to receive honourable discharge and increased leisure time. This is seen as a 'contract for older people'; although individuals may want to refuse to undertake this contract, societal expectations and social pressure can often force the individual to withdraw from society. This image is clearly a conflict of interest affecting individuals over which they have little or no control.

Finally, the Disengagement theory concentrates on the way in which older people withdraw from society. Cumming and Henry (1984) consider that work and social life are inextricably linked. When retirement takes place this link is broken, resulting in disengagement from the society and world that older people once knew. Disengagement theory attempts to explain why people play a less important role in old age than they do in middle age. The theory holds that retiring from important social roles performs important functions both for society as a whole and for the individual older members of society. Freedom from the burden and responsibility of work and the conservation of energy to perform tasks found to be meaningful are proposed benefits. The theory itself, however, has been attacked as promoting negative images although most people do express a wish to give up paid employment and to retire from full time occupation (Havinghurst, 1984).

This perspective therefore views society as being composed of competing and conflicting groups, rich versus poor and young versus old (Morris and

147

Williamson, 1982). Retirement from paid occupation has clear disadvantages in loss of status, decreased income and reduced societal value in the eyes of society. The amount of control that a person feels that they have over their lifestyle and future is clearly linked to them succumbing to ageist policies that impact upon their feelings of self-worth and value.

RESEARCH

Although there is some agreement on the biological changes in ageing there is little research-based agreement on the psychological dimensions. As with physical status the popular image of psychological health in old age is one of gradual but inevitable decline.

Research attempts to provide a scientific and true picture of 'normal' mental health changes in old age. Of the three types of methodology commonly used to investigate these changes, namely cross-sectional studies, longitudinal studies and sequential studies, each has problems in avoiding the bias associated with stereotyping (Ford, 1985). Many of the studies upon which pessimistic conclusions are reached are based upon research that reflects the inferences attributed to ageing.

Cross-sectional studies compare age differences between age groups. They do not therefore reveal individual age changes. This can lead to over-generalisations about groups of people that are consequently applied to all older people.

Longitudinal studies compare people over a given period of time. Inevitably people may die during this period, leaving perhaps the fittest and intellectually most able at the end of the study. This serves to present a skewed picture that is not truly representative of the total number of people under investigation.

Sequential studies have problems in removing all the variables that have been mentioned earlier. These variables may include environment, culture and ageist attitudes. Studies have shown that variables such as lifestyle development and differences between people born as little as 10 years apart, living in rural or industrial areas, having differing education, nutrition, medical care and employment opportunities can all contribute to intellectual and mental health development (Gearing and Slater, 1988).

The difficulty with research studies is that while attempting to provide a snapshot of the reality of mental health in old age that can be generalised to a larger group of people, they cannot always reflect or provide answers to meeting individual needs. Building upon personal abilities, using the past history and background of an older person can be crucial to planning care services and meeting individual care needs.

The major areas of psychological investigation and research include the decline of learning abilities, memory, personality changes and intelligence. All are considered to be prominent features of mental health changes in old age.

LEARNING AND MEMORY

Learning is related to the ability to perform a task and commit this performance to memory in order for the same task to be carried out in the same or a similar way. Data relating to memory and learning in work situations shows that, given a longer training period, many older people do manage to learn but that the degree of success is likely to depend upon the nature of the task, the type of relationship to previous experience and the method of training (Chown, 1972). Expectations by the rest of society therefore pose a major problem in the learning ability of older people. Anxiety in new learning situations and time taken to complete tasks completely and competently, for example payment at supermarket counters, leads to a societal expectation of incompetence. The problem therefore lies not in the ability to continue to function intellectually, but in the lack of opportunity and time to process information in the learning period.

Memory problems may be a feature of old age, particularly where a diagnosis of dementia has been made. It is unlikely, however, for a younger person to be considered to have a mental health problem if they inadvertently leave a tap running or forget to lock the front door.

PERSONALITY TRAITS

Personality traits of older people often arouse negative views and can be seen in the language used to describe their personality. 'Withdrawn', 'isolated' and 'emotionally unstable' are descriptive words found in common usage. Personality surveys conducted by Age Concern (1974) showed that older people do not feel that they change as they age, and that they still possess the same traits, attributes and characteristics.

However, if the opportunities for social activities are reduced then an individual may deal with this by becoming more introvert and withdrawn. The response of the older person could therefore be seen as an internal reaction rather than as a process of ageing. What is 'normal' and what is desirable are clearly key factors in differentiating between personality change as a result of old age and personality change as a way of dealing with the situation in which older people find themselves.

A large number of studies on intelligence testing in older people and the identification of age differences in intellectual function is based upon cross-sectional studies. Decreased intellectual performance with age therefore may well simply reflect differences in the educational levels of cohorts. It could also be argued that intelligence itself does not change with age but that skills and information held by older people become obsolete. Changes in technology, new equipment and advanced methods of working, for example, with the computerisation and automation of equipment tend to be anathema to people who are unfamiliar with these systems.

In psychological tests older people seem to sacrifice speed for accuracy, perhaps reflecting their general feelings of inadequacy. When time limits are removed from psychological experiments, age differences in performance are much less marked and older people achieve and perform tasks equal to younger subjects (Chown, 1972).

Current research-based evidence shows that ageing does not bring about inevitable and profound decline in mental ability (Gearing and Slater, 1988). Older people can learn and improve their intellectual functioning given the right sort of educational programmes and the right setting. The increasing popularity of the University of the Third Age in a variety of countries testifies to the general high level of intellectual functioning and desire for education amongst older people (University of the Third Age, 1984). Older people learn best in non-threatening environments in which they regain confidence in their own abilities. The scope for re-teaching skills where physical or mental illness has reduced the individual's functional ability clearly needs to be taken into account. However, as with physiological changes it is difficult to distinguish between what is ageing alone and what influence cultural and environmental factors play.

EXAMPLES OF AGEISM

Chronological ageing

Chronological ageing myths relate to the way in which all older people are considered to belong to one homogeneous group, sharing the same values, the same lifestyle and therefore acting and behaving within a given range of functions. The physical 'look' and mental abilities of a person are simply related, therefore, to the number of years that they have lived. Although it is true that older people are more likely to experience ill health and disability in later years it is not necessarily an inevitable consequence of the ageing process.

This view can be easily reinforced since health professionals usually come into contact with a disproportionate number of older people and this serves to augment their views and attitudes. The consequent danger is that health and social care providers will either under-treat or over-provide. On one hand is a tendency to deny older people access to the most up to date or more expensive treatments, while on the other hand there is over-provision of care that reduces independence and freedom of rights. In this way chronological age definitions serve to reinforce views of increasing dependence upon others.

Rejection and isolation

Loneliness is a trait often attributed to older people. In reality only about 20 per cent of people over 65 years of age live entirely alone and assumptions must be made that some actually do this out of choice. It may be that those people who live in residential or nursing home accommodation are more likely to be childless, be the poorest in financial and social situations and to be without siblings.

It is frequently said that children find their ageing parents sickly and boring and edge them out of the family. While it is clear that changes in the size of the family and the participation of women in the labour market over the past century will have a marked effect on the number and availability of family members to provide care for older dependants in their own homes, there is little data to support the view that the family neglects the care of the old and dependent when services are provided by the state. Older people are also able to contribute to the life of the family by taking responsibilities within the home as well as contributing to finances through independent income and pensions. The flow of help and assistance is not, therefore, unidirectional and demonstrates that reciprocal care arrangements within families does take place.

The unquestioning acceptance of rejection may serve to reinforce government policy of putting pressure upon carers, relatives and neighbours to provide care in the community instead of looking at strategies for meeting health and social care needs based upon the number of people over a certain age, their individual abilities, housing stock and financial income.

Self-fulfilling prophecies

Individual images of ageing and self-concept are based upon attributes that each person ascribes to themselves and these can also be linked to societal and cultural expectations. Self-concept, beliefs and behaviour of older people have been shown to arise as a result of ageist attitudes. Older people are more inclined to behave in a way that society expects them to and therefore to collude with a social construction of reality and set themselves as a group apart (French, 1990).

The impact of this may delay people from seeking medical and social help, since they attribute problems to ageing and do not wish to present themselves as a burden to health and social care providers, or indeed to family and friends (Haug, 1986). Clearly this can then exacerbate problems and contribute further to negativistic attitudes.

Older people fail to seek financial benefits and opportunities as this serves to reinforce their feelings of inadequacy, unworthiness and as having charitable status that takes without giving in return. The resulting behaviour of older people therefore has been said to be in alignment with the societal expectations and not the expectation of the older person themselves (Midwinter, 1986).

It is not the young alone who have negative expectations of old age (Gearing and Slater, 1988). Gerontophobia (the fear of ageing) is present in many people until they become 'old' themselves. Recognising that life is not so terrible for them, they then consider themselves to be exceptions to the rule and thus add to the stereotypes and myths of old age. Problems that affect some older people – often a minority – are then presented in an 'over-drawn' picture of inevitable decline seen as a necessary accompaniment of old age and entrenching an 'inevitable myth' (Saul, 1974). In the long term, images that are often intended to generate concern about the real and serious problems of some old people can actually perpetuate a negative affect.

GENDER AND SEXUALITY

Discussions about old age are often largely concentrated on women. There are twice as many women aged 65 years as men and four times as many at 75 years. Older women experience both ageism and sexism, discriminated against because they are both old and female. Retirement at 60 years of age indicates that old age starts much earlier for them and because of their longevity, old age lasts much longer. Thomas (1988) considers that this double disadvantage is socially defined and socially constructed.

The attributes of male masculinity are associated with qualities such as competence, autonomy, self-control and are combined with stereotypes such as 'grey hair in males is distinguishing' and 'older men make better lovers'. This serves to denigrate even further the qualities for which women are commonly desired; beauty, physical attractiveness and child-bearing. The feminist movement has been criticised for contributing to this gender issue through concentrating on the issues raised by young women, such as abortion, contraception and premenstrual syndromes and ignoring the needs of older women (Macdonald, 1984).

Older women are also handicapped because they can no longer fulfil a reproductive function and are considered to be less sexually attractive. It is commonplace to consider that sexuality is not a prerequisite in old age and that older people have little exploitable value for both the contraceptive and pornography industries (Andrews, 1989). An example of this surrounds beliefs about the risk factors associated with HIV and AIDS infection. Surveys have shown that universal precautions are rarely taken with older people. It is considered that people over 65 years were, generally speaking, raised in an era where sexual morality was much more conservative and therefore are not likely to be sexually active in old age (Sadler, 1993). Recent reports have indicated the danger of assuming that HIV and AIDS is a younger person's problem. 'A crisis of silence' (Age Concern, 1993) considers that the number of older people with HIV is likely to be underestimated and this is simply because of ageist attitudes about older people and their sexual lifestyles.

This difference in outlook provides further evidence to support the views that older people are repressed and unexciting. Society is therefore much more permissive about ageing in men, giving older single men greater status than unmarried women, sanctioning men marrying women many years their junior and yet considering it to be humorous when older women have younger male partners. There is also evidence to suggest that males who are disabled at home or are providing care to a female dependant are more likely to receive support at home, such as meals on wheels and home help than women in the same situation (Finch, 1989). Phillipson (1982) suggests that because the majority of older people in institutional care are women, the standards may be lower and that women were far more likely than men to be depersonalised on admission to a geriatric ward (Evers, 1981).

In this context, D'A Slevin (1991) conducted a study of the attitudes of student and newly qualified nurses. The results demonstrated not only a rise in negative attitudes in nurses during their period of training, but also that males demonstrated more negative attitudes than their female counterparts.

ETHNICITY

In addition to the double-edged sword of ageism and sexism is the vulnerability of being old and black (Curtis, 1991). While one in five people over the age of 65 years is white, only one in 20 belong to black and ethnic minority groups (Social Trends, 1992).

Skodra (1991) found that in psychological assessments of older black women the content, process and outcome of psychological testing was affected by the ethnicity of women being investigated. First, little reference was made in relation to information gathering about the background culture of the person, how this experience had affected their lives and whether they were able to achieve their expectations and personal goals. Secondly, the beliefs of the health professionals themselves were considered to be at fault since they had a tendency to regard everything as having a psychosocial pathology. Thirdly, there was the important issue of validating the older black women's experiences, concerns, fears and feelings. Culturally biased testing, for example asking for the date of the First World War when this may not have a been part of past life experience or a significant life event, served to work against the older person and relegated them to lower cognitive scores.

Sollit and Hornsey (1990) consider that the status of being 'elderly' must be resumed in the same way that 'black' has been reclaimed as a positive affirmation of the cultural identity, wealth of experience and values and beliefs of black and ethnic minority individuals.

MEDIA IMAGES

The images that society holds of old age are represented and reflected in the various aspects of popular culture and mass media. The presentation of materials relating to older people, including non-verbal aspects, tends to relate to a certain level of emotional appeal. This could be said to be one of the most important ways in which society transmits social norms and expectations. The message, through television, radio, printed matter, advertisements and public entertainment can be a blatant form of ageism.

While a culture of youth is used to advertise and promote health, beauty and leisure activity products, older people are used to promote laxatives, pain formulas and dental adhesives. Advertisements and popular journals present the ultimate image and achievements in younger 'beautiful people' with sexual imagery playing a major part in influencing our lifestyle.

On the whole, older people (with the exception of politicians) are conspicuous by their absence in television or the mass media. Where they appear in fictional works they are generally portrayed as background characters, mostly of middle-class status. Reasonable health and fitness is depicted among the young elderly, although sexuality and dominance are played down. Senility, neglect and abuse is the focus of attention in older elderly people and mostly directed towards women. Covert forms of ageism exist where day to day examples show older people being different and outstanding if they have achieved athletic feats.

Heath (1989) cites covert 'ageism by apartheid', in the form of shops that offer 'reduced rates' – but only on specified days – and birthday cards that strengthen, reinforce and maintain ageist views on getting older, rather than a celebration of life. Heath considers that this subtle form of ageism would not be tolerated by other groups in society who are also the targets of negative stereotyping. There would be a major outcry if statements such as 'people with learning disabilities told to live in one room – to keep warm' and 'Gays and blacks half price – Mondays only'.

PROFESSIONAL IMAGES

Norman (1987) believes that gerontology tends to take a 'victim blaming' approach, looking for problems with the older person themselves rather than looking for a much wider societal cause. She cites the example of hypothermia, which is put down to age rather than the fact that low income and poor housing conditions are more likely to contribute to this condition. It has been these changes that have prompted the perception of older people as a 'social problem'.

Attitudes among professionals

In addition to the economics and rationing of health care in old age, individual attitudes of professionals themselves can lead to further ageist treatment. D'A Slevin (1991) reports the results of a study using an inventory designed to investigate the attitudes of young adults. The study set out to investigate and consider the implications for a caring profession since it is suggested that older people will represent the most common care group for nursing in the future. The study found that the attitudes of student nurses changed for the worse on becoming newly qualified. A number of factors were thought to contribute to this outcome. One factor included the omission of older adults as a specialist area in the Project 2000 educational structure for nurses. 'Doctrinal conversion' was also thought to be one of the contributing factors. Doctrinal conversion considers the internalisation of a body of professional attitudes and behaviour because of a disease orientated approach to care provision that values high technology and devalues less acute care.

The findings supported the fact that professional socialisation, including education, led to nurses having institutionalised and negative attitudes towards older people as a part of professional cultural beliefs.

Working status

Working with older people has always assumed low status in the past, while working with older people with mental health needs has perhaps been the Cinderella of all Cinderella services. A number of health professionals are still shown to believe that older people are the least deserving when resources and services are being distributed (Wetle, 1987). The prestige associated with acute medical care and 'life saving' techniques is not apparent where older people are receiving care. Norman (1987) considers that this has been a factor in attracting less skilled workers in the past, and usually people who are subject to discrimination themselves. Skill mix and the change in ratios of qualified to unqualified staff is a development that has recently been under discussion. The provision of care for older people has been one of the main target areas in which a 'cheaper' option of providing unqualified staff is considered in an attempt to maximise on limited resources. Under-resourcing and the low status and kudos associated with working with older people with mental health needs has therefore contributed to the past problems of providing adequate and appropriate services. While this group of people are the age group most at risk, they are the one group that health and social care services have been least likely to serve (Charney and Lewis, 1989).

Professional language

In addition to low status and under-resourcing, many of our attitudes are shaped and reflected in the language used by professionals. Nurses have been cited as using terms of endearment such as 'gran', 'old love' or first-name terms that serve to embarrass and patronise older people. Day (1988) considers that this is putting the person in a child-like role, submissive, vulnerable, in need of protection and dependent. This also suggests power over a person with the balance towards the professional using such terminology without first seeking permission or asking that person how they would prefer to be addressed. Although there has been a general shift away from the use of 'geriatric' as a noun, terms such as elderly and aged can also give the impression that all older people belong to one homogeneous group. 'Care of the elderly' would not be acceptable if it were applied to 'care of the young' or 'care of the middle-aged' since this conjures up a dependent state rather than promoting independence and self-fulfilment.

HEALTH ECONOMICS

Stammers (1992) considers the expense of providing medical care for older people. In GP prescribing alone, older people are responsible for 41 per cent of prescriptions while some 87 per cent of those aged over 65 years are taking regular medication and one-third will be taking more than three drugs.

Whitaker (1991) describes how the principles of health economics are inherently ageist if used to choose between the provision of care between patients of different ages. He considers that the National Health Service is already biased towards ageist social and demographic trends and that the current reforms in progress will provide much potential for discrimination. Choices and rationing over what services will be offered to patients will become more necessary and more difficult.

Health economics is about making rational choices in order to make the 'best' use of available resources. There are, however, many different kinds of rationality. In order to make rational choices between different ways of spending resources, health economists must compare activities in terms of the costs and the benefits.

Whitaker describes the 'social' model of health economics which advocates that everyone is worthy of treatment and attention. If resources are to be limited they should be limited across the board. Conversely, under an 'economic' model, if resources are to be limited they should be selective so as to maximise the benefit per unit cost. A proportion of the funding therefore is allocated and dictated by the perceived worth of the person receiving them.

When these models are applied using a method such as Quality Adjusted Life Years, two markers are used to estimate the cost and benefit (Harris, 1987). These include the number of years of life gained as a result of treatment or intervention and the quality of those years. It is easy to see that when a scientific value is used to weight a scoring system, younger people are more likely to score highly and therefore be perceived as benefiting the most from any treatment or care.

Day (1988) suggests as an exercise in challenging professional ageism that we conduct assessments or planning exercises without referring to a person's age. The activity of describing the care needs of two people without reference to age can result therefore in two entirely different sets of outcomes.

In outcomes where cost-containment predominates over cost-effectiveness, it is easy to see the potential for hidden discrimination against a politically inert group of people who could be hoodwinked into receiving cheaper substandard services. In addition to this, even charitable funding for services for older people is more likely to be reduced since it does not attract the same public sympathy as, for example, services for children. Age, therefore, is a common factor in deciding the subsequent treatment or way in which a person's care will be planned, offered or managed.

THE NURSING CONTRIBUTION

Nurses need to ensure that their own practice and that of health and social service colleagues is not founded on stereotypical views of ageing. The main areas to be considered include a knowledge of the ageing process and the ability to assess and identify individual needs. Insight, awareness and education into attitudes and guarding against ageist practice are also considered.

Knowledge of the ageing process

Factual evidence on the biological, social and psychological processes in relation to ageing are an important foundation for distinguishing between what is 'normal' and what constitutes myths of the ageing process. Nurses need education and training in order for them to be aware of these various aspects of ageing and to ensure that assumptions about the physical or mental abilities of a person are not attributed simply to an inevitable consequence of the ageing process.

Nurses need to have a knowledge and understanding of the way in which external influences and past life events will have shaped the individual older person's response to their current situation. Making sense of what is happening now to an individual person is dependent upon understanding what has influenced them or happened before. Examples of these influences include cultural and historical perspectives, social order, politics, fashion and custom, and education and employment history.

In addition there are many unique internal biographical factors that affect older people. Examples of these will include the way that a person feels about their past lifetime experiences, how their life has developed and been adjusted and the values and expectations that they have about the present and the future. Finally, a knowledge and understanding of the way in which an individual has prepared for retirement and the types of 'coping mechanisms' that they may have adopted are often the key to understanding their individual position and behaviour.

Assessment and identification of individual needs

Nurses play a vital role in assessing and identifying mental health changes in old age that may prevent the older person from achieving optimum fulfilment of their lives. Nurses can act as a central pivot between different agencies, educating, coordinating, liaising and referring to health and social care services as appropriate. Assessment provides the opportunity to plan future care needs and can be undertaken on an individual basis or with groups of people sharing the same or similar problems.

Assessment therefore needs to be part of a systematic process of collecting information about an older person and the world in which they live. It is not simply about diagnosis as it provides a baseline for further investigation and for planning to meet current and future needs that will maintain or enhance a healthy lifestyle.

The Care Programme Approach (Department of Health, 1990a) and Community Living assessments under the NHS and Community Care Act (Department of Health, 1990b) both provide a framework for allowing the older person to access services. They also provide the opportunity for a nursing contribution to assessment to take place and for nurses to operate as part of a team offering a range of therapies and treatments and practical information. Through advocating on behalf of the older person they can ensure that they have an equitable contribution to make to any decision-making process, providing older people with the opportunity to define their own needs and to anticipate and prevent future problems from being exacerbated or from reaching crisis point.

Insight, awareness and education

Nurses have a responsibility to address both professional and societal attitudes. Through the identification of their own personal needs in tandem with the needs of clients and patients they can set examples to ensure that society starts to uphold different values and beliefs. The power of health professionals still influences the thoughts of many people. The provision of an appropriate, non-ageist role model can do much to negate and change the attitudes of other members of society and and of other professionals.

By developing insight into and awareness of ageism the nurse can avoid prejudgement of the person, the environment or the situation that they are in. This provides a basis for developing sensitivity and understanding the context of past life experiences to which the person relates their current lifestyle. Insight and awareness can also ensure that attention is paid to the use of appropriate and acceptable language that is not patronising or belittling but facilitates a more egalitarian power base between the nurse as a provider and the older person as a consumer. Awareness training therefore needs to include the opportunity for exploring equality of rights, the use of risk and restraint and above all ensuring that disability is not considered to be normal but the loss of an ability that requires thorough investigation.

Staff education, training and professional development needs to consider the attitudes, values and convictions of care providers themselves. The aim should be to make the experience of ageing meaningful to individuals and to the place in which they work. In addition, the overall outcome should assist them to identify what they believe, what they think should happen and how their practice can be changed to reflect effective, acceptable care. Buckwalter et al (1993) consider the use of numerous types of individual and group work exercises that use a questionnaire to identify ageist attitudes and provide targets for addressing them.

It has been shown that older people can be changed by altering the environment in which they live. Older people are not impervious to situational change and may respond to their own dissatisfactions with reality (Carp, 1967). When health professionals are actively involved with older people they develop more realistic and optimistic attitudes to this age group. A non-ageist outlook is therefore fostered where exposure to older people in society takes place. True integration of older people into society, both in employment and as valued members in all walks of life, may promote positive imagery and negate negative preconceptions.

Guarding against ageist practice

Working within multidisciplinary teams provides nurses with the opportunity to check ageist practice. Negotiating aims and objectives for health care with both the older individual and their lay carers can help nurses to understand an individual's personal position and guard against making decisions that do not involve patients or are contrary to patients' wishes. Summarising and confirming that the nurse's understanding matches the individual's can prevent misunderstanding and action that may be based upon stereotypical views of the abilities of the older person. Devolving power, and responsibility and empowering older people helps to ensure that they have control over their health care and that care is carried out with people and not for people.

Self-care may well be an essential strategy of older people in maintaining their health. It is therefore important that they are able to operate from a position of knowledge, have the opportunity to discuss health issues, including personal relationships, and actively participate in health education and health groups as a basic human right. Examples of this include anticipatory work and preretirement counselling and preparation for the effect of retirement can have a major benefit and impact upon older people (Drennan, 1988).

Systematic monitoring of the way in which care is communicated and offered is therefore an essential component to providing appropriate care and empowering the older person. Nursing care needs to be flexible and responsive. It must avoid prejudgement and accept the person regardless of the environment or situation as decisions made on behalf of older people can set up tensions that lead to non-compliance, inappropriate self treatment and poor relationships with health professionals and lay carers (Day, 1988).

Finally, focusing on strengths rather than weaknesses is an important factor in negating self-fulfilling prophecies, guarding against ageist practice and enabling older people to contribute to their own health and welfare. Identifying and promoting individual strengths and abilities minimise the effect of societal attitudes and assist the older person to understand and differentiate between age changes and ill health in old age.

CONCLUSIONS

Ageism, based upon stereotypical views and myths about the process of ageing leads to inequitable treatment and discrimination against older people. The problem with using data that is based simply upon the number of older people to plan health and social care services is that the experience of ageing is then often viewed as being the same for everyone.

Mental health in old age is made up of a complex set of biological, psychological and social interactions. One of the enduring stereotypes about old age is that physical and mental illnesses are attributed to the process of ageing and therefore appropriate assessment, treatment and diagnosis is not sought.

Preparation for old age and expectations for the future have been said to be derived from long-term social changes. These changes occur through an attitude which has in its roots an irrational fear, panic and terror of old age and death. Individuals look to others to compare and validate the sense of themselves. Individual attitudes, values and beliefs about the process of ageing become influenced therefore by what a person believes objectively, what a person feels subjectively and the way in which a person responds to these feelings and values. While growing up is normally taken to be something desirable and almost an end in itself, growing old has traditionally built up very negative connotations.

Current research-based evidence demonstrates that ageing does not bring about an inevitable and profound decline in mental ability. Older people can learn and improve their intellectual functioning given the right amount of time, educational programmes and the right setting.

The myths of ageing therefore are compounded by societal expectations, the value and worth perceived by the older person themselves, and these are perpetuated by professional images and attitudes.

Fears about state expenditure upon the elderly are essentially ideological views which are not always supported by the biological or psychological facts. Discrimination and prejudice shows society displaying an ageist attitude which demonstrates a marked lack of concern about its older members as sexism does to women and racism to black and ethnic minority individuals. In the long term future generations of younger people will lose out as they change from being observers to fully participating members of an older society. The main goal for nurses therefore must be to replace notions of dependency and to foster a framework that places emphasis on interdependence between generations.

REFERENCES

Abercrombie N, Hill S and Turner B (1988) *Dictionary of Sociology.* Harmondsworth: Penguin.

Age Concern (1974) *The Attitudes of the Elderly and Retired.* Mitcham, Surrey: Age Concern.

Age Concern (1993) *A Crisis of Silence: HIV, AIDS and Older People. A Resource Pack for Age Concern.* London: AGCL.

Andrews J (1989) Anti-ageists unite. *Nursing Times and Nursing Mirror* **85**: 22.

Buckwalter K, Smith M and Martin M (1993) Attitude problem. *Nursing Times* **89**(5): 55–57.

Butler RN (1974) Successful ageing. *Mental Health* **58**(3): 11.

Carp F (1967) The impact of environment on old people. *Gerontologist* **7**: 106–108, 135.

Charney M and Lewis P (1989) Choosing who shall not be treated in the NHS. *Social Science and Medicine* **28**: 1331–1338.

Chown S (1972) (ed) *Human Ageing: Selected Readings.* Harmondsworth: Penguin Books.

Cowgill D and Holmes L (1972) Aging and modernisation. In: Miller A (ed) *In The Eye Of The Beholder: Contemporary Issues in Stereotyping*, 3rd edn. New York: Praeger.

Cumming E and Henry W (1984) Growing old. In: Hayes N (ed) *A First Course in Psychology.* Edinburgh: Nelson.

Curtis Z (1991) Redressing the balance. *Critical Public Health*: 29–30.

D'A Slevin O (1991) Ageist attitudes among young adults: Implications for a caring profession. *Journal of Advanced Nursing* **16**: 1197–1205.

Day L (1988) How ageism impoverishes elderly care, and how to combat it. *Geriatric Medicine* **18**(2): 14–16.

Department of Health (1990a) *The Care Programme Approach for People with Mental Illness Referred to the Specialist Psychiatric Services*, HC[90]23/LASSL[90]11. London: DOH.

Department of Health (1990b) *The NHS and Community Care Act.* London: HMSO.

Dowd J (1984) Social exchange theory. In: Hayes N (ed) *A First Course in Psychology.* Edinburgh: Nelson.

Drennan V (1988) *Health Visitors and Groups.* Oxford: Heinemann Nursing.

Evers H (1981) Care or custody? In: Hutter B and Williams G (eds) *Controlling Women.* London: Croom Helm.

Finch J (1989) *Family Obligations and Social Change.* Cambridge: Polity Press.

Fischer D (1978) *Growing Old in America.* New York: Oxford University Press.

Ford G (1985) Illness behaviour in old age. In: Dean K, Hickey T and Holstein BE (eds) *Self Care and Health In Old Age*, pp. 130–163. London: Croom Helm.

French S (1990) Ageism. *Physiotherapy* **96**(3): 178–181.

Gearing B and Slater R (1988) Attitudes, stereotypes and prejudice about aging. In: Gearing B, Johnson M and Heller T (eds) *Mental Health Problems in Old Age*. A Reader. Chichester: John Wiley and Sons in association with The Open University.

Gross R (1987) *Psychology: The Science Of Mind And Behaviour* London: Edward Arnold.

Harris J (1987) QALYfying the value of life. *Journal of Medical Ethics* **13**: 117–123.

Haug M (1986) Doctor–patient relationships and their impact on elderly care. In: Dean K, Hickey T and Holstein B (1988) *Self Care and Health in Old Age.* England: Croom Helm.

Havinghurst R (1984) Successful ageing. In: Hayes N (ed) *A First Course in Psychology.* Edinburgh: Nelson.

Heath H (1989) Old: almost a four letter word? *Nursing Times* **85**(31): 36–37.

Lasch C (1981) The culture of Narcissus. In: O'Donnell M (ed) *A New Introduction to Sociology.* Edinburgh: Nelson.

Macdonald B (1984) *Look Me in the Eye Old Woman.* London: The Women's Press.

Midwinter E (1986) A Time for Age, FACT PACK. London: BBC.

Morris M and Williamson J (1982) Stereotypes and social class: a focus on poverty. In: Miller A (ed) *In The Eye Of The Beholder. Contemporary Issues in Stereotyping.* New York: Praeger.

Norman A (1987) *Aspects of Ageism: A Discussion Paper.* London: Centre for Policy on Ageing.

O'Donnell M (1981) *A New Introduction to Sociology.* Edinburgh: Nelson.

Palmore E (1985) *Retirement: Causes and Consequences*. New York: Springer Verlag.

Phillipson C (1982) *Capitalism and the Construction of Old Age*. London: Methuen.

Sadler C (1993) Positively older. *Nursing Times* **89**(26): 22–23.

Saul S (1974) *Aging: An Album Of People Growing Old*. New York: Wiley.

Skodra E (1991) Ageism and psychological testing with elderly immigrant women. *Counselling Psychology Quarterly* **4**(1): 59–63.

Social Trends (1992) *General Statistical Services*, No22. London: HMSO.

Sollit L and Hornsey J (1990) Tackling ageism. *Journal of District Nursing* **9**(1): 22–24.

Stammers T (1992) What is at the root of ageism? *Care of the Elderly* **4**(7): 288–289.

Stevenson O (1989) *Age and Vulnerability.* London: Arnold.

Stokes G (1987) Self care skills and reducing institutionalised behaviour in a long-stay psychiatric population. *Journal of Advanced Nursing* **12**: 35–48.

Thomas L (1988) A double-edged sword. *Geriatric Nursing and Home Care* **8**(7): 21.

University of the Third Age (1984) *The Image of the elderly on television*, Research Report, No 1. Cambridge: University of the Third Age.

Wetle T (1987) Age as a risk factor for inadequate treatment *Journal of the American Medical Association* **4**(258): 516.

Whitaker P (1991) The inherent ageism of health economics. *Geriatric Medicine* **11**: 57–58.

CHAPTER 9

Involving Users in Developing Depot Phenothiazine Services

Tom Sandford

INTRODUCTION

There is an increasing body of evidence, from sources as diverse as user surveys and inquiries into failures of care, that demonstrates that the current trend towards community care for people with long-standing psychotic disorders can only be sustained if it is founded on services that are appropriate and desirable to the user group. This population, freed from the impositions of institutional life, will assert increasing discretion over their involvement with the mental health service.

One element of this community based service provision is the clinic providing phenothiazine treatment in the form of depot intramuscular injection. Observation of current practice in these services would suggest that they perpetuate institutional dependency, rather than empower their users, but little work has been done on soliciting users' perceptions of the service. This chapter explores the literature surrounding this area of nursing practice. It also reports on a study which retrieved users' perceptions of clinic provision in one health authority and piloted a method of exploring the relationship between satisfaction and compliance with this treatment modality.

BACKGROUND

In recent years, Community Psychiatric Nurses (CPNs) have acquired a creatively developed reputation for state of the art nursing practice and integrity in their field. This is a belief that is promoted and fostered both within and outside the nursing profession. It is harnessed within the profession by commentators such as Butterworth, who proposes that:

> community psychiatric nursing has been a significant force in the strug-
> gle to give mental health issues a meaningful place in the nursing
> profession in the UK. Few professions have moved with such commend-
> able speed to change their ideology, clinical practice... (Butterworth,
> 1990, p. 9)

Butterworth cannot be dismissed as a partisan actor. His claims are supported by accolades from outsiders. For example, Heginbotham, as director of national MIND, pronounced:

> community psychiatric nursing is one of the success stories of mental
> health services over the last thirty years...through it, nursing will be
> revalued as a profession. (Heginbotham, 1986, pp. 9, 10)

This entourage of expectation which conjures up a scenario of robust, well sub-stantiated and evolutionary practice largely reconciles with the reality of the literature developed by CPNs. Comprehensive reviews by Griffith and Mangen (1980), Davis (1986) and Simpson (1989) indicate that while community psychia-tric nursing could not yet pretend to be a research-based profession, there is nevertheless a flourishing plethora of past and on-going enquiries, both descrip-tive and evaluative, into most aspects of CPN work. One of the few blots on this rosy landscape are the depot clinics, outpatient-style clinics where people go to receive intramuscular depot injections of neuroleptic medication. Baldessarini et al (1988) note how this formulation of neuroleptics (otherwise known as phe-nothiazines or major tranquillisers) has dominated the prescribing and treatment habits of doctors working with people with long-term psychotic ill-nesses. This approach is supposed to maximise compliance and ensure a more consistent plasma concentration of the drug. Ayd (1978) catalogues how, as the regime escalated in popularity, the demands of giving the injections led to it becoming a treatment whose administration was passed from doctors to nurses. A few users receive their injections from a GP or practice nurse and some users, particularly the elderly or disabled, receive the injection at home from a CPN. However, in order to contain costs (home visits by F/G graded CPNs are expensive) and maximise the availability of the service, the majority of users are encouraged to attend outpatient-style depot clinics where they receive their injection on a regular basis.

Even a cursory visit to depot clinics reveals that they are often places of disad-vantage. The practice within the clinics is characterised by attending to individuals so swiftly and impersonally that there is barely time to monitor effectively for iatrogenic consequences of treatment. In this respect they reflect with disturbing similarity the elements of institutions that Barton (1959) and Goffman (1961) had catalogued 30 years earlier, and which the role of the CPN was established to redress (Carr et al, 1980).

In direct contrast to seeking creative solutions to practice problems in other areas, CPNs have appeared reluctant to acknowledge the difficulties within the clinics. Users have started to fill this gap. In 1989, for example, the Islington Mental Health Forum published a collection of individual users' experiences of local mental health services under the title *Fit for Consumption?*. It contained a resounding indictment of many aspects of service provision, including the depot clinics. Comments such as:

> treatment should not simply equal medication, but in practice this is what people are offered (Islington Mental Health Forum, 1989, p. 12)

and

> how can a patient discuss his medication when there is little personal contact (Islington Mental Health Forum, 1989, p. 14)

are just two examples from a welter of accusations levelled by the document. This type of publication is still relatively unusual in the literature and its publication and that of other concerns emerging from the user movement provides an important opportunity to focus attention on some of the intrinsic problems of depot clinic services. The reformed NHS, developed under the auspices of the NHS and Community Care Act (Department of Health, 1990), is explicitly instructed to use the techniques of market research to elicit the views and experiences of users.

THE NATURE OF SCHIZOPHRENIA AND THE ROLE OF PHENOTHIAZINES

A predominantly biological organic model of schizophrenia prevailed during the first half of this century. The 1950s and 1960s witnessed a proliferation of research into schizophrenia. The ascendant theory of schizophrenia was the 'developmental' view (Bateson and Jackson, 1956) which proposed that schizophrenia occurred because parents had brought their children up in ways that were aberrant or pathological.

Alternative analyses derived from Laing (1959, 1961), Brown (1959), Szasz (1961) and Scheff (1966) evolved from a movement that was questioning the assumptions on which psychiatry, and the research on which it based its assertions, was constructed. Laing demonstrated that the behaviours and communications of those people diagnosed as schizophrenic could be reframed. His perspective understood their actions as a logical response to social and psychological pressures exerted on the individual, a unique strategy for reconciling the conflicts of an untenable situation.

This work became the catalyst for a great many avant-garde and meticulously detailed projects. A sequence of work, including replication studies by Brown (1959), Brown and Birley (1968) and Brown et al. (1962, 1966, 1972) painstakingly pieced together the influence of relationships on the prognosis and course of schizophrenia and contributed markedly to the contemporary understanding of the condition. Ongoing and standardised research by Vaughn and Leff (1976a, b, 1985) culminated with the development of the 'expressed emotion' concept and a related battery of psychosocial interventions. These are multidimensional and range from the sophisticated to the simple. At the sophisticated end of the spectrum they include family orientated interventions designed to minimise criticism and refocus dialogue about negative symptomatology into a transactional problem-solving mode (Goldstein and Koperkin, 1981). Simple strategies include attention to clear, unambiguous dialogue in everyday situations (Sundeen et al, 1985). These strategies have been demonstrated in well controlled and replicated studies to prevent relapse in of a population with schizophrenia (Leff et al, 1982, 1985).

Almost as astonishing as the success of the findings themselves is the endemic neglect of the material, until very recently, by virtually all of the mental health disciplines. Brooker reviews an accumulation of evidence which concludes that:

> although it was originally envisaged that techniques [of psychosocial intervention] would be widely disseminated to other disciplines, psychosocial interventions have remained largely limited to the research studies themselves. (Brooker, 1990a, p. 275)

A wealth of studies indicate that the treatment strategy most frequently encountered by people with long-term psychotic problems is that of neuroleptic medication (Westermeyer and Harrow, 1990). There are different views of why this is so. Robust historical analyses by Boyle (1990) suggest that the phenothiazines have limited utility beyond chemical strait-jacketing. She proposes that they were a natural successor to popular medical patronage simply because they evolved from, and did not philosophically challenge, a long lineage of disenfranchising control-orientated treatment perspectives.

The more conventional view, and that supported by medical and pharmacological research, is that the phenothiazines have the ability to alleviate the delusions, hallucinations and resultant disturbed and bizarre behaviour of people experiencing a major psychotic illness such as schizophrenia (Silverstone and Turner, 1987). These strengths should not obscure the substantial concerns regarding their use. Although these feature in the medical literature, they are surprisingly poorly reported given the incidence of prescribing. Elegant studies by Johnstone (1990) and Barnes (1990), for example, illustrate the clinical conflicts stemming from their use. Summarised briefly, their irreversible side effects (in the form of tardive dyskinesia) create an ethical dilemma for prescribers who must weigh these serious disadvantages against their relatively successful, though crude, antipsychotic properties. The potential risks of tardive dyskinesia are well documented. Jeste and Wyatt (1981), internationally acclaimed authorities on the subject, reviewed 11 studies covering 3000 users of neuroleptics and found the prevalence of tardive dyskinesia to be between 25.7 per cent and 35.9 per cent. Their own impeccably developed work demonstrated (Jeste and Wyatt, 1982) that the condition is irreversible in two-thirds of all cases and that (Jeste and Wyatt, 1985) there is no effective treatment for the condition. These results concur with the literature considered by Casey and Keepers (1988) and McCreadie et al (1992) in major reviews of neuroleptic side effects.

Historical analysis by Lidz et al (1984) suggests that psychiatrists do not have a very creditable track record in this sphere of decision-making. Given the risks of treatment, one would anticipate that the issue of informed consent to neuroleptic treatment would be well represented in the literature. However, specific interrogation revealed little in the way of analysis. Carr (1984) makes no reference to it in a review of the legal and ethical considerations facing CPNs.

While Turnquist (1983) does draw attention to informed consent in neuroleptic therapy as a nursing issue, there is no subsequent literature describing how CPNs recognise and apply these responsibilities. Dyer and Bloch (1987) draw a similar conclusion in relation to psychiatrists' practice. Cast in the light of studies (Holloway, 1988) suggesting that the medication regimes of the long-term mentally ill, especially those on depot neuroleptics, are inadequately and infrequently reviewed, the situation is one of concern that demands further scrutiny.

The literature also reveals that medicine and the pharmocological industry have been tardy and have given low priority to sophisticating the neuroleptics; even the key advocates and exponents of their use such as Jolley et al (1989) acknowledge that the field is neglected. Furthermore, the disciples of neuroleptic therapy are not able to demonstrate outcomes that strike anywhere close to those achieved by psychosocial interventions. Jolley et al (1989) concede that protection against relapse in approximately 40 per cent of the population taking neuroleptics represents the mean data in the field. These figures can only be enhanced if the drugs are used in combination with psychosocial interventions.

It is in this area of combination therapy, phenothiazines – psychosocial interventions – educative strategies, that some of the most recent and most impressive work has taken place. Hogerty et al (1986) report on a large study carried out over 4 years, in which more than 100 patients were allocated to four different treatment modalities. Follow-up outcomes for the group treated with a combination approach demonstrated that no one relapsed. While this study needs to be replicated, and while no one else has achieved a zero relapse factor, there is nevertheless a degree of consistency in carefully gathered results from other studies (Tarrier et al, 1988; Leff et al, 1989) which suggests that successful relapse management for the vast majority of people with major psychotic illness could be an achievable goal. There is also now significant evidence to suggest that nurses are recognising and testing the importance of this work (Brooker, 1990b, c; Brooker et al, 1993).

CPN ACTIVITY WITH PEOPLE WITH LONG-TERM PSYCHOTIC ILLNESS

Most commentaries describing the genesis of CPN services attribute this innovation to recognition of the need to provide community support to those people with a diagosis of schizophrenia who were being discharged from psychiatric hospital on phenothiazine medication (Carr et al, 1980; Simmons and Brooker, 1986). Early CPN research reflects this orientation; Hunter (1978) is of this genre and his work focuses on a CPN role in the administration of depot neuroleptics and the monitoring of psychotic symptomatology. While none of the information is scientifically impeccable, it would appear that home visiting by a CPN to administer depot neuroleptics offers substantially more in the way of prevention of relapse than the same treatment administered in a depot clinic. Better access to relatives and greater sensitivity to early signs of deterioration by the CPNs undertaking home visits are the reasons cited to explain the difference.

Because CPN activity was excluded from the major studies of psychiatric nursing undertaken by Towell (1975) and Cormack (1976), it was left to Sladden (1979) to develop the first eclectic and substantive role analysis of CPNs. Within the CPN sample, 61 per cent of their users were diagnosed as having schizophrenia. Sladden found the cohort of CPNs lacking in the skills needed to adequately respond to this user group. She noted that in 49 per cent of all sample contacts, the CPN retreated into the task-centred role of giving a depot injection. She also uncovered discrimination in the form of time spent with depot clinic users, the contact time for this group being one-seventh that of users seen on home visits.

During the early 1980s the trail goes cold in respect to CPNs researching their work with users with long-term psychotic difficulties. This absence of related studies coincides closely with a period of significant change in CPN services. Brooker (1987) describes cogently the factors which determined a mushrooming of CPN services during the first part of the decade. The Community Psychiatric Nurses' Association (CPNA) surveys of 1980 and 1985 and the work of White (1993) confirm this but, more importantly, they reveal that the nature of the services had fundamentally changed. A move from hospital to community bases brought about a change in referral sources; as GPs rather than psychiatrists became the principal referral agents, CPNs drifted away from work with people with major psychotic disorders.

The trend is clearly documented in studies by Goldberg (1985) and Wooff et al (1986, 1988a). The latter notes that not only did the caseload population of users diagnosed as schizophrenic reduce to 23 per cent in 1988 (from 78 per cent in 1975), but that interventions with this group were characteristically very short and related to administering depot medication. Pollock (1989), in a very systematic study of CPN work, discovers a similar trend. Brooker (1988) and Wolsey (1990) explore in more detail the integrity of CPN intervention with users diagnosed as having schizophrenia. Wolsey's study included ascertaining CPN awareness of the contemporary literature on the condition. It revealed that:

> CPNs as a body are not familiar with the work. (Wolsey, 1990, p. 241)

Furthermore, his review of actual practice indicated that:

> because of their lack of skills, they [CPNs] tended to manage encounters with patients by trial and error. (Wolsey, 1990, p. 245)

There is a degree of consistency across this work and an absence of even a single study that demonstrates a counter position. This suggests that the scenario described by Sladden in 1979, of CPNs being ill-prepared for a role with people experiencing psychotic illness, has changed little in recent years. The Clinical Standards Advisory Group Schizophrenia Report (1995) confirms this position.

THE DEPOT CLINIC

Until very recently there has been a dearth of published studies specifically constructed around depot clinics. As in the case of the work by Sladden, the material must be retrieved from studies of CPN activity that included scrutiny of depot clinics as a dimension of a wider inquiry.

Of these, the work of Wooff et al (1988a, b) is perhaps the most exacting and meticulous in respect to scope and method, and also emerges as the most critical of actual practice. Using carefully contrived direct observation and well researched content analysis on all contacts, the research team built up a gloomy picture. CPNs minimised contacts, controlled dialogue so as to reduce the possibility of users reporting negative symptomatology and left users with considerable unmet need. The problem was compounded by the CPNs being unsystematic in their collection of information. Although not constructed as part of the study into CPN effectiveness (and therefore not tested within the study), the researchers used the Present State Examination (PSE) interview schedule (Wing et al, 1974) for the purpose of comparing differences between the CPN and social work caseload profiles. In so doing, and by coincidentally comparing the PSE results with CPN observations, they identified major discrepancies; the CPNs appeared to be failing to recognise the full range and severity of their user's symptoms, some of which were quite debilitating. Rotational (rather than caseload) responsibility for the depot clinics was observed to be a factor further prejudicing consistency and contact with the users.

Skidmore (1986) draws conclusions of greater concern. While we are not briefed adequately on either the mechanisms for, or the frequency of, his observations he nevertheless reports that when users on depot neuroleptics questioned or refused their medication, they were not encouraged to discuss their reasons and were coerced by veiled threats. Turner (1984) found poor recognition of depot administration as an important treatment modality.

Recent work has only just started to redress this situation. Turner (1993), in a very significant study, described the standard and content of observed nurse and user contacts involving the administration of depot drugs. He suggests that the way in which CPNs utilised the contact inherent in depot drug administration is determined by caseload size and location of clinic. His findings suggest that there is not a common approach to exploiting the opportunities presented by contact with users to administer depot injections, and that practice standards vary dramatically from clinic to clinic.

From a medical perspective the scenario is equally sparse. Periodically literature has emerged (Marriott, 1978; Johnson, 1981, 1990; Hogerty, 1984, some of which (Marriott's work in particular) is in the form of rigorously developed follow-up studies. However, they all adopt the common theme of focusing on substantiating depot clinics through reference to medical convenience items, such as easier monitoring of the patient, control over dosage given and removal of the potential problem of overdose with oral medication. The contrast between a rather rosy view of the clinics portrayed in the medical literature compared to the rather bleak and deprived observations made by nursing commentators is curious. The scenario becomes even more perplexing when one considers the dimension of user non-compliance. Masur (1981) and Ley (1988) review a collection of studies which unfortunately all use different methods of data collection, but that nevertheless indicate a spectrum of between 15 per cent (Johnson and Freeman 1973) and 66 per cent non-compliance (Marder et al, 1983) with depot neuroleptics.

THE USE OF SERVICE USERS IN INFORMING SERVICE DELIVERY

Although studies describing user views are abundant in the generic literature, they have been relatively isolated in the work produced by psychiatric nurses. In relation to community psychiatric nursing, only those studies by Mangen and Griffith (1982), Munton (1990), Ferguson (1993), Field (1993) and Gournay and Brooking (1993) set out with the primary intention of attempting to measure user satisfaction, although other work (Hunter, 1978; Marks, 1985a, b, Pollock, 1989, 1990) included this as peripheral to other enquiries.

Mangen and Griffith (1982), reporting from the same study as Paykel and Griffith (1983), used the multidimensional methods of the self-report questionnaire devised by Catalan et al (1980), as well as interview, to calculate total satisfaction scores for comparisons between CPN and psychiatrist follow-up. Although the study is an important attempt to evaluate CPN outcome from a user perspective, it focuses on a purely neurotic user group, and a type of intervention that is relatively untypical for CPNs.

Munton (1990), acknowledges that firm conclusions cannot be drawn from what is a relatively small pilot study skewed by bias in sampling. Nevertheless, the work again demonstrates that users do appear to value, and use, an opportunity to discuss their opinions about CPN contact.

Ferguson (1993) scrutinised patients' views on discharge preparation and uncovered the need for greater attention to be paid to what users of mental health services and their carers want to know. In addition, there was a need for a more structured approach to the transmission of the necessary knowledge and skills to enable patients and their families to cope with mental health breakdown, hospitalisation and discharge. Given the opportunities for monitoring mental state provided by depot clinics, the findings are important for nurses' practice in this area.

Field (1993) contrasts patients' and CPNs' views of a CPN service. He suggests that CPNs lack an awareness and understanding of their interventions from the patients' point of view, and that they neglect the social circumstances of their patients in preference for a preoccupation with pathology and cure.

The work of Gournay and Brooking (1993) is unusual in that it attempted to link satisfaction to outcome. They reveal clear differences in the satisfaction ratings of users who dropped out of intervention with a CPN (those who dropped out being least satisfied) although they could not demonstrate a relationship between how well users did in treatment and how satisfied they were with the CPN intervention.

Of the studies that report user views as part of another enquiry, Marks (1985a, b) and Pollock (1989) are perhaps the most systematic. While Marks appears to solicit user views very reliably on a dimension of their care, the uniqueness of the treatment modality (specialist and intense behavioural therapy) and the user group both limits the scope for translating the findings out of the research context. Pollock (1989) in an elaborate study designed to examine the effects of community psychiatric nursing, included retrieval of users' views through the use of the personal questionnaire rapid scaling technique (Shapiro, 1961;

Mulhall, 1976), from which it is possible to extract some interesting consumer perspectives. Of particular relevance is the apparent way in which CPNs shaped the users' view and indeed their needs. The users could only comment on what they were informed about and were encouraged to construct their needs around service availability more than any other factor.

Hunter's (1978) work is refreshingly detailed in verbatim recording both of dialogue and context. As such, it presents a valuable example of the quality and scope of user feedback on experiences of treatment. It is important to note that this was achieved with a population of users all diagnosed as having schizophrenia.

This is an issue which occupies a controversial position in the literature and therefore demands scrutiny. Many commentators (McEwen et al, 1983; Tuckett et al, 1985; Johnstone, 1989) point to evidence of both covert and overt dismissal of the views of those diagnosed with psychotic illness. The literature suggests that this happens on two levels, an assumptive perspective and an analytical perspective. The assumptive perspective presumes that a thought-disordering illness renders one incapable of evaluative reasoning and is reflected in the writings of Roth (1976) for example, and in studies such as that by Koltov et al (1978). The second and perhaps more pernicious approach, evident in studies by Hinshelwood (1987) and Donati (1989), attempts to apply psychodynamic interpretation towards understanding the inner world of someone with a major psychotic illness. This is proposed to be so distorted and bizarre that normal dialogue about issues such as satisfaction is impossible, and furthermore that the skewing of normal parameters and dimensions of understanding renders their views unmeasurable using conventional tools. This type of work is increasingly becoming overshadowed by a commanding body of literature. Meticulous studies by nurses such as Raphael (1977a) and Davidhizar (1985, 1987), psychiatrists such as Wills et al (1990), and other researchers such as Rogers et al (1993) demonstrate clearly the validity of the views of people with psychotic illness.

Given the paucity of CPN work in the field, it is helpful to evaluate the contribution of other disciplines in recovering the views of users. Barker and Peck (1987) review a series of rather anecdotal but fascinating examples of users influencing the nature of the services provided for them once they were empowered to do so. Clifford et al (1989) review similar material in their quest to develop systems of assuring the quality of mental health services. Lehman et al (1982) and Berger (1983) offer a more strident and sophisticated approach, honing complex tools towards maximising the utility of consumer satisfaction within long-stay wards in the former study, and psychotherapy in the latter work. Lehman's work is particularly well developed; working with a population of people with psychotic diagnoses, the study adds to the body of findings demonstrating the potential uniqueness of the perspective of service recipients.

In a study that demonstrates great tenacity in overcoming the problem of poor response rate, MacDonald et al (1990) set out to capture the users' perspective as part of an evaluation of a community mental health team.

In a technically ambitious project, Handyside and Heyman (1990) also attempted to solicit users' perceptions using experimental methods which included contrasting the experiences of two matched groups, one of whom received the services of an additional support facility.

A slightly different dynamic that needs to be explored in these studies is their rationale for using a user perspective. Can this influence the construction and outcome of projects? The issue is developed by Winkler (1987), Brooking (1989) and McIver (1991). The integrity of the researchers' interest is highlighted. The adoption of a credible consumer model of service delivery, where the users' aspirations become a critical influence on service development, is contrasted with the pursuit of service review, the supermarket model of consumerism, where the authority of users is firmly circumscribed. Research undertaken by the Centre for Health Economics at York University (Carr-Hill et al, 1989) and reviews by Winn and Quick (1989) demonstrate clearly the tendency of existing work to fall into the latter category, with managers often being unable and poorly committed to applying the survey information. The dangers of token initiatives obscuring the absence of substantive consumer models, and the problems derived from the absence of feedback and change being perceived by users, are identified as potentially unethical and undermining abuses of the researcher's position by Cartwright (1983), Potter (1988) and Campbell (1990). It therefore is necessary to adopt and honour a definition of consumerism that is relevant to mental health care. Munton (1990) draws usefully on the work of Chambers (1987) to develop what is both a pragmatic yet challenging position for this study; she suggests that it should

> encapsulate the idea of developing an awareness and a sensitivity to the needs and expectations of the consumer in the planning and running of services. (Munton, 1990, p. 82)

METHODOLOGICAL CONSIDERATIONS

The literature also yields an array of material relating to the methodology adopted by researchers enquiring into users' opinions and their satisfaction with services, and the problems encountered as these studies were undertaken. Jones et al (1987) identify ownership and cooperation as essential prerequisites to starting a study, without which any changes suggested by the work would be difficult to implement. A lack of standardisation between surveys is noted by many commentators (Luck et al, 1988) as one of the greatest shortfalls of studies completed to date. Lebow (1982), for example, reviews evidence of the use of 69 different measurement scales in projects to assess consumer satisfaction in community mental health centres. The lack of 'state of the art' instruments appears to compound the problem. In a similar vein, Gutek (1978) focuses on the problem of scant and diverse definition of terms such as 'satisfaction', 'very satisfied', etc. which in turn generates problems of comparison and measurement. Lebow (1982) notes that validity is particularly difficult to assure in mental health surveys and cites sampling bias, in the form of poor user response, as the prime cause of this. This can be compounded by reticence on the part of users to reveal frank opinions, especially those of a negative nature; Fitzpatrick and Hopkins (1983) note these as methodological problems in most NHS user surveys. Reflecting on the particular circumstances of people diagnosed with schizophrenia, and others who have an on-going and possibly life-long dependence on services, Hunter (1978) and McEwan et al (1983) note the legitimate concerns these groups will have about expressing views that could in any way prejudice their already vulnerable position.

THE STUDY

The above-mentioned literature informed a study which retrieved users' perceptions of clinic provision in one health authority and piloted a method of exploring the relationship between satisfaction and compliance with this treatment modality.

It was considered of great importance that the study be grounded in an agenda that was determined by service users; the issues considered important by service providers may not be those which are of most concern to service users (McIver, 1991). Goldman and McDonald (1987) and Social and Community Planning Research (1988) describe the technique of the group depth interview to achieve this, a simplified approach to which was adopted with a group of users identified by a local user forum.

An approach based on a structured interview, determined by a questionnaire schedule, was selected. This minimised the problems associated with poor response rates and maintained rapport with users (Oppenheim, 1966). Given that neuroleptic therapy is risk-laden, users need to understand key elements of the treatment and the questionnaire was therefore designed to explore and illustrate this.

The questionnaire was also constructed to reveal material relating to compliance and reasons for non-attendance which complemented the documentary evidence available to the researcher in the form of prescription charts and attached nursing records. The survey addressed users' views on issues where there was the potential to introduce changes or service developments based on user feedback. Complementing these were questions contrived to develop either a demographic profile of service users or to develop a profile on specific items of pertinence to depot clinic users. The inclusion of questions from which a measure of satisfaction could be calculated raised myriad methodological problems. These ranged from definition to measurement. Fitzpatrick (1984) suggests an approach involving conferring significance on evaluations of specific episodes or events, which was adopted. The scoring technique developed by Ley et al (1976a, b) and Ley (1988) fulfilled the requirement of providing a satisfaction measure for comparative purposes. Validity was maximised by the techniques recommended by Belson (1986) and Fitzpatrick (1991a, b). This included pretesting to exclude poorly understood questions and interviewer deviation and elimination of researcher bias in wording and order effects. The potential threat to validity posed by the possible unwillingness on the part of the respondent to make certain admissions was countered by emphasising in both the interview proforma and the consent form that individuals' information would not be revealed to staff.

A final test for validity lay in there being documentary evidence, in the form of prescription charts and nurses' notes, that could be used as a 'criterion of truth' in terms of comparison with some of the results yielded by the questionnaire.

Reliability was also difficult to assess. Techniques such as the 'test-retest' reliability of the questionnaire, or 'split-half' reliability could have been calculated. However, in the context of the work being largely an exploratory study, it was considered acceptable to proceed with this limitation, the ramifications of which are noted in the discussion and conclusions.

The sample

A complete sampling frame was available in the form of the depot clinic prescription charts. This revealed that there was a total of 217 users using the service. As it was not possible to interview the total population it was decided, on the basis of the time available, to identify a sample of 60.

Scrutiny of the sampling frame, and reference to the literature, suggested that it would be necessary to subdivide the population into homogeneous subsets. The first division was by clinic attended. A total of five different clinics operated. The clinics were observed to be different in many respects (e.g. degree of privacy, the nature of the building they were located in, etc.) and therefore it was seen as essential that the total sample be stratified by 'clinic attended' in order to obtain a greater degree of representativeness. The prescription chart data facilitated this.

The second stratification of the sample related to freqency of injection, the

Table 9.1   Respondents' reported contact with other support services.

GP	17	(29%)
Social worker	14	(24%)
Psychiatrist	18	(31%)
Day centre	12	(21%)
Day hospital	2	(3%)
Ward staff	0	
Voluntary agency	5	(9%)
Hostel staff	7	(12%)
District nurse	0	
CPN	4	(7%)
Probation service	0	
Health visitor	1	(1.5%)
Other	0	
None	20	(34%)
Total (*n*)	58	(100%)

literature having indicated that factors ranging from compliance to understanding could be affected by whether an individual has to make weekly or monthly visits to the clinic. Again the prescription charts provided the means to calculate that 82 (38 per cent) of clinic users attended every week or fortnight, 89 (41 per cent) attended once every 3 or 4 weeks and that 46 (21 per cent) attended every 5 weeks or more. The sample selected from each clinic was therefore stratified as closely as possible according to these percentages.

Random selection techniques were then used to draw the necessary numbers of names from each subgroup. A total of 11 of the sample refused to be interviewed, which necessitated a return to the subgroups of the sampling frame to select a replacement from the same category of clinic/frequency of attendance.

A total of 58 people were finally interviewed. It became impractical to follow-up the last two, who repeatedly failed to attend. A review of user discharges over the last year revealed that only five depot users were discharged or self-discharged. It is unlikely therefore that discharges significantly skew this population and present attenders (the sampling frame used) can generally be seen as representative.

The health authority in which the study was based gave approval for the work.

The interview schedule was piloted on three volunteering users at a depot clinic. While no structural changes were determined by the pilot, several detail changes to the wording of both the proforma and the questionnaire schedule were implemented with the intention of making questions easier to understand or easier to ask.

Selected findings

The cohort of 58 users consisted of 59 per cent men; 67 per cent were single, 17 per cent cohabiting, 4 per cent widowed and 12 per cent divorced. Fifty-nine per cent were white, while 17 per cent were Afro-Caribbean, 9 per cent were Irish and 9 per cent Greek. Only 12 per cent were in full employment and 19 per cent in part time employment. Nineteen per cent lived alone, 21 per cent with friends, 18 per cent with spouse, 24 per cent with parents and 12 per cent in a group home. Half had no admissions to a psychiatric hospital in the past year, 43 per cent had one admission and 9 per cent two or more. Twenty-four per cent were aged up to 30 years, 33 per cent between 31 and 40 years, 19 per cent between 41 and 50 years, 15 per cent between 51 and 60 years and 9 per cent were over 61 years. Table 9.1 records respondents' reported contact with other services.

- Forty per cent of respondents stated that they attended for injection 1/2 weeks, 41 per cent every 3/4 weeks; and 19 per cent at longer durations; 93 per cent were correct in their reporting (from documentary evidence of prescription charts).
- Eighty-one per cent were correct in naming their injection.
- Sixty-six per cent of respondents thought that one nurse regularly administered their injection and 62 per cent were able to name the nurse while 90 per cent reported knowing the name of the prescribing doctor (although two of these reported the wrong name); 69 per cent reported that they knew how to see the doctor, but 12 per cent reported an incorrect procedure.
- While only 53 per cent of respondents reported that the reason for injection had been adequately explained, in the open-ended second half of this question, 78 per cent reported a correct diagnostic or symptomalogical reason for having the injection.
- Eighty-one per cent of respondents reported that side effects were possible and 62 per cent of users could identify up to two possible side effects; 83 per cent of respondents reported that they sometimes failed to attend the clinic and the main reasons given were not needing the injection (36 per cent) and forgetting (24 per cent); 79 per cent could report correctly the number of injections they had missed over the past year.
- In relation to respondents reporting the amount of medicine received 7 per cent felt that they did not receive enough, 36 per cent enough, 45 per cent too much, and 12 per cent didn't know.
- In relation to respondents reporting on provision of side effect information, 26 per cent received more than adequate, 34 per cent adequate and 40 per cent not enough information.

- Twenty-nine per cent would have preferred a home visit from a CPN and 19 per cent would have preferred to receive their injection from a GP or health centre.
- Thirty-six per cent of respondents reported finding it easy to access a doctor, although only 26 per cent could see a doctor immediately or before their next injection if they wanted to.
- Sixty-two per cent of respondents reported that the nurse asked about side effects, while 29 per cent of respondents reported that the nurse asked about the people the person lived with; 62 per cent of respondents reported that the nurse asked about other problems in their lives; only 10 per cent of the respondents reported the privacy provided in the clinic as unsatisfactory.
- Forty-three per cent of respondents thought an information group regarding medication should be provided; 38 per cent of respondents thought an information group regarding illness should be provided; 26 per cent of respondents thought that consultation with the pharmacist should be provided.
- Thirty-one per cent of respondents thought that the clinic should be open in the evening, and 33 per cent of respondents thought it should open on a Saturday; 16 per cent of respondents would value more time with the nurse, and 33 per cent of respondents reported the value of social activities in the clinic.
- Thirty-four per cent of respondents thought a better range of refreshments should be provided and 19 respondents suggested other changes to the clinic. Changes included relaxing the prohibition on smoking ($n=14$), greater continuity of nurse input into the clinic ($n=5$) and moving the clinic to the outpatient department ($n=2$).
- From the results of calculating the Spearman's correlation coefficient r on the variables of mean satisfaction and non-compliance for a population of 58 users of depot clinics, it appears that there is a significant negative association between the two ($r=-0.5254$, $n=58$, $p=0.01$), indicating that as mean satisfaction with the clinic decreases, non-compliance increases.
- From the results of calculating the Spearman's correlation coefficient r on the variables of adequacy of explanation provided for having depot injection and non-compliance for a population of 58 users of depot clinics, it appears that there is a significant positive association between the two ($r=0.5609$, $n=58$, $p=0.01$), indicating that as inadequacy of explanation increases, non-compliance increases.
- From the results of calculating the Spearman's correlation coefficient r on the variables of non-compliance and psychiatric admissions for a population of 58 users of depot clinics, it appears that there is a significant positive association between the two ($r=0.5961$, $n=58$, $p=0.01$), indicating that as non-compliance increases, psychiatric admissions increase.

DISCUSSION

The study was established to obtain users' perceptions of the clinic provision of a given health authority and to explore whether there is a relationship between compliance and satisfaction with the clinic.

An overview of the data demonstrates clearly that users of depot clinics are able and willing to share their thoughts about the clinics. This extends to making both critical and positive observations. In the context of the reviewed literature, which revealed relative reluctance on the part of service providers to explore a user perspective, the evidence of the study provides affirmation that this type of endeavour is worthwhile and justifies enhanced interest and sophistication.

Specific observations substantiate this. As noted earlier, for certain items documentary evidence was available to test the validity of the respondent's response. Respondents were congruent with documentary evidence in 79 per cent of responses relating to non-compliance, 93 per cent of responses relating to frequency of attendance and 81 per cent of responses relating to name of medication. It is also worth noting that 78 per cent of the respondents provided an insightful response as to why they were having depot injections.

In this context, nurses should take seriously the areas of user concern that emerge from the results, as well as the portfolio of preferences which derive from the data.

In relation to concerns, the features of 47 per cent of users feeling that the reason for injection has been poorly explained to them, 45 per cent of users feeling they receive too much medication, 36 per cent of respondents citing not needing the injection as a reason for missing injections, 40 per cent of users reporting that they have received too little information on side effects, together with 62 per cent of users only being able to report two or less potential side effects of drugs, can all be interpreted as confirmation of the literature that suggested that there is a paucity in terms of the quantity and quality of interventions at depot clinics. In the face of these findings one is also left to speculate about the extent to which users have given properly informed consent (as against uninformed consent, see Downie and Calman (1987) and Carson and Montgomery (1989)) to what the literature demonstrates to be a relatively risk-laden treatment schedule. The root of this problem may go back beyond the users' attendance at depot clinics, in that most users are first prescribed depot medication during an inpatient admission. However, if nurses are acting as advocates for users in respect of informed consent, their assessments should include ascertaining what users have been told.

Peripheral observations correspond with the concerns. The evidence of only 57 per cent of respondents being able to state correctly how to access the doctor prescribing their injections and that only 26 per cent of respondents report being able to see the doctor before their next injection if they have concerns to raise, gives rise to doubting the adequacy of medical review. Reports by 71 per cent of respondents that the nurses do not ask them about the people the respondent lives with can be taken as indicating that nurses ignore the wealth of literature pertaining to expressed emotion and psychosocial intervention strategies. These were noted in the literature as effective in preventing relapse in people with long-standing psychotic disorders, but also as complementary to neuroleptic regimes.

These anxieties are compounded when they are seen in the context of the limited access this population has to other health and social care agencies. An astonishing, but believable, 34 per cent report no contact with any agency outside the clinic, which makes them totally dependent on the depot clinic for mental health care maintenance. That only 29 per cent have on-going contact with their GP, and only 31 per cent have on-going contact with a psychiatrist is worrying. It substantiates current concern that community care for groups of the population with significant psychiatric disorders is inadequate and that purchasers should be demanding better systems of case management to assure a minimal level of service provision to this group. From a nursing perspective, it is interesting that only 7 per cent of this population (who probably are representative of some of the most disabled mental health service users in the district) see a CPN outside the depot clinic. One could speculate that covert strategies to marginalise this user group solely into the depot clinic service have operated with great precision and success.

From a more positive perspective the data confirm some of the gains, for both users and service providers, which could be derived from addressing these issues. While 50 per cent of the sample population needed psychiatric admission during the 12 months prior to interview, further data confirmed that non-compliance is associated with an increase in admissions. With confirmation of a relationship between non-compliance and adequacy of explanation provided for having injections it is apparent that staff can take steps to control and minimise non-compliance, and hopefully prevent costly readmissions. These data also support the conclusions of projects such as the Salford study (Whitehead, 1987) which maintained that it is only the movement of fiscal and staff resources from inpatient areas to community services that will facilitate the development of preventative strategies in the community.

The data raise concerns about the passage of people from ethnic minorities through the psychiatric system. Littlewood and Lipsedge (1982) and Helman (1990) note that this group are vulnerable to diagnostic discrimination. These results indicate that ethnic groups (especially those from the Caribbean), are over-represented in the clinic sample in comparison with local population norms.

The findings also reveal a portfolio of preferences expressed by users of the clinic. In addition to the desire to have less medication and better information on side effects, a total of 62 per cent expressed a preference for an option other than the clinic as a venue for their injection. It perhaps reflects present inadequacies in the clinics that such substantial numbers felt that additional facilities such as information groups regarding medication, information groups regarding illness should be included as part of the clinic facilities. About one-third of the sample thought that organisational changes such as opening in the evening and on Saturday, appointment systems and better refreshments should be provided, as should social activities.

These results could be conceived as grim and accusatory by field workers. While they do demand acknowledgement and action, they need to be framed in analysis from other perspectives. First, some positive findings are apparent. In the context of the literature reviewed earlier it is pleasing to note that 66 per cent of respondents regularly have their injection administered by the same nurse and that almost the same number knew their name. A full 90 per cent (perhaps reflecting the importance attached to medical staff by users) knew the prescribing doctor's name and a similar percentage felt that the privacy afforded by the clinics was either fairly or completely satisfactory. Several items were reported as completely convenient by substantial numbers of the sample, and 47 per cent thought nurses and 52 per cent thought doctors always had enough time to discuss their concerns. One needs to regard the success of the work in achieving the aim of exploring whether there is a relationship between compliance and satisfaction with greater scepticism. The evidence that one's satisfaction with the service influences directly whether or not one complies with the service must be seen in the context of methodological limitations of the study. One can, however, safely regard the results as interesting, and potentially as evidence that further supports the proposition that the services can be more proactive in developing users' satisfaction ultimately as a preventative measure against relapse.

CRITIQUE OF THE STUDY METHODS

The representativeness of the sample is prejudiced by not knowing the views of the 11 people who refused interview. It is tempting to interpret their non-response as evidence of service disatisfaction, but this is merely speculation.

It is interesting that while some respondents were clearly able to level criticism at areas of the service, their comments on some of the only questions directly referenced to staff performance, such as time made available by doctor and nurse, were generally favourable. This could be evidence of a methodological problem in soliciting users' frank views, especially when seen in the context of literature that revealed that users are frequently offered very little time by both doctor and nurse. A further area of concern focuses on validity and reliability. Some steps towards ensuring validity were discussed but both concepts remain untested and these features limit the scope to make specific generalisations.

IMPLICATIONS FOR NURSING

It is safe, however, to suggest the following practice changes in relation to the depot clinics. The provision of better information should ensure that users understand the mechanisms by which they can arrange to see the doctor, the reasons why they receive injections and the potential side effects of medication. This should form part of a strategy for ensuring that users give their fully informed consent to treatment and needs to be addressed by medical, as well as nursing staff.

The training needs of staff working in the service should be reviewed in order to expand the repertoire of skills on which CPNs can draw in their work with users in the clinic. This evaluation of skill mix should run in tandem with a review of the nursing human resources available. The present system of employing G graded CPNs to administer a treatment regime that currently consists of little more than injection-giving represents poor value for money. A mixed package of D or E graded nurses organising clinics and working as key workers, while G graded CPNs offered supervision and certain sophisticated psychosocial interventions to targeted user groups, may be more appropriate and achievable.

CPNs also need to experiment with different roles and approaches. It may be that intensive case management could lead to early detection of symptoms and enhance compliance. In this scenario, intensive case management may become the vehicle for titrating doses of medication and perhaps the eventual replacement of depot medication by oral preparations, over which users feel they have more control. Initiatives in the United States support this and commentators such as Turner-Crowson (1993) review the implications for Britain of United States experience.

It may also be worth considering if a role for unqualified support workers or a social facilities coordinator exists. Rather than simply pass an activity from one group or discipline to another, as happened when medicine delegated responsibility for depot clinics to nursing, we should consider who is best placed to fulfil the requirements and needs of this population. With the projected resource and demographic problems that lie ahead for nursing, the profession needs to consider carefully how best to use a relatively expensive and scarce resource.

Changes that facilitate greater user choice need to be addressed. Giving part of each clinic over to an appointments-based system, extending the opening of some of the afternoon clinics into the early evening, offering a better range of refreshments and diversifying the social dimension for those interested and including groups on specific issues, could all have the potential to empower users with more control and raise their satisfaction with the clinic. While the provision of smoking areas would be in direct conflict with most health authorities' policies on the subject, staff nevertheless need to be aware of this as an issue for users. They could be assisted with strategies to survive an hour without a cigarette, or to give up. Many of these issues could be considered collaboratively with users, perhaps through the involvement of user forums.

Medical staff need to take a lead on evaluating how best to enhance access to themselves by users, how a system of regular review of medication should be established, and how informed consent should be dealt with and documented. They should also scrutinise their practice with ethnic groups to ensure that they are not inappropriately using this treatment modality to respond to this population.

THE WAY FORWARD

Directions for future study emerge from these recommendations. The most important of these relates to developing and substantiating this work. If (as is suggested by the findings) CPNs can influence user relapse through maximising compliance, they hold the key to massive savings in both inpatient costs to the service and emotional costs to users. Half of the sample had one or more admissions over the past 12 months. This reinforces the view that attention should be paid to evaluating further the extent to which CPNs can develop a cost-effective role in relapse prevention.

The presentation and uptake of information by this user group demands attention. The suggested changes in information provision could be futile if the problem lies more in the area of communication of information rather than provision of information. The development of a standardised and tested instrument for measuring the satisfaction of mental health service users is an important research challenge which, as the momentum behind effective engagement of service users in service evaluation becomes more tenacious, needs prompt attention.

Other methods of exploring a user perspective also merit consideration. A more qualitative study, for example, could perhaps better inform us as to what really motivates users to come to the clinics. How important is the relationship with the nurse? Do the nurses themselves enact and impose some of the expressed emotion dynamics explored in the literature review? What effect could implementation of psychosocial interventions have on outcomes? It would be interesting to compare the experiences of users who use the clinics with those who receive their injections at home from a CPN or at a health centre from their GP or practice nurse. These merit consideration as important missing pieces in our broader understanding of the services provided.

In the face of evidence of relatively poor practice standards in the clinics, the development of specified standards derived from examples of practice excellence and the literature could form a useful initiative (Kitson, 1987). It would be useful to know if there are characteristics associated with working with this population that alienate or antagonise CPNs. Why is the wealth of work on psychosocial interventions so neglected when these skills so patently complement the existing psychiatric nursing repertoire of treatment strategies?

These and other speculations demand rigorous enquiry by mental health nurses. Without an understanding of these dynamics, services could invest substantially in changes yet find that nursing attitudes and priorities remain static. The welfare of users with long-term psychotic illness demands that they be spared this outcome.

REFERENCES

Ayd FJ (1978) *Depot Fluphenazine: Twelve Years' Experience*. Baltimore: AMC.

Baldessarini RJ, Cohen BM and Teicher MH (1988) Significance of neuroleptic dose and plasma level in the pharmacological treatment of psychosis. *Archives of General Psychiatry* **45**: 79–91.

Barker I and Peck E (1987) *Power in Strange Places: User Empowerment in Mental Health Services*. London: Good Practices in Mental Health.

BarnesTR (1990) Tardive Dyskinesia: Can it be Prevented? In: Hawton K and Cowen P (eds) *Dilemmas and Difficulties in the Management of Psychiatric Patients*. Oxford: Oxford University Press.

Barton R (1959) *Institutional Neurosis*. Bristol: John Wright.

Bateson G and Jackson D (1956) Towards a theory of schizophrenia. *Behavioural Science* **1**(3): 251–264.

Belson WA (1986) *Validity in Survey Research*. London: Gower Publications.

Berger M (1983) Towards Maximising the Utility of Consumer Satisfaction as an Outcome. In: Lambert MJ (ed) *Assessment of Psychotherapy Outcome*. New York: Wiley.

Boyle M (1990) *Schizophrenia – a Scientific Delusion?* London: Routledge.

Brooker C (1987) An investigation into the factors influencing variation in the growth of community psychiatric nursing services. *Journal of Advanced Nursing* **12**(3): 367–375.

Brooker C (1988) High expressed emotion: a new theoretical perspective for CPNs working with schizophrenics and their families. *Community Psychiatry* **1**(1): 11–13.

Brooker C (1990a) Expressed emotion and psycho-social intervention: A review. *International Journal of Nursing Studies*. **27**(3): 267–276.

Brooker C (1990b) The application of the concept of expressed emotion to the role of the community psychiatric nurse: A research study. *International Journal of Nursing Studies* **27**(3): 277–285.

Brooker C, Tarrier N, Barrowclough C, Butterworth A and Goldberg D (1993) Skills for CPNs Working with Seriously Mentally Ill People: The Outcome of a Trial of Psycho-social Intervention. In: Brooker C and White E (eds) *Community Psychiatric Nursing: a Research Perspective*, vol 2. London: Chapman and Hall.

Brooking J (1989) A Survey of Current Practices and Opinions Concerning Patient and Family Participation in Hospital Care. in: Wilson-Barnett J and Robinson S (eds) *Directions in Nursing Research: Ten Years of Progress at London University.* London: Scutari Press.

Brown GW (1959) Experiences of discharged chronic schizophrenic mental hospital patients in various types of living group. *Millbank Memorial Fund Quarterly*: **37**(2): 105–131.

Brown GW and Birley JL (1968) Crises and life changes and the onset of schizophrenia. *Journal of Health and Social Behaviour* **9**: 203–211.

Brown GW, Monck EW, Carstairs GM and Wing JK (1962) Influence of family life on the course of schizophrenic illness. *British Journal of Preventative and Social Medicine* 16: 55–68.

Brown GW, Bone M, Dalison B and Wing JK (1966) *Schizophrenia and Social Care: a Comparative Follow-up of 339 Schizophrenic Patients*. London: Oxford University Press.

Brown GW, Birley JL and Wing JK (1972) Influence of family life on the course of schizophrenic disorders: a replication. *British Journal of Psychiatry* **121**: 241–258.

Butterworth T (1990) Foreword. In: Brooker C (ed) *Community Psychiatric Nursing – a Research Perspective*. London: Chapman and Hall.

Campbell P (1990) Mental Health Self Advocacy. In: Winn L (ed) *Power to the People*. London: King's Fund.

Carr P (1984) Legal and ethical perspectives in the nursing care of the mentally ill. *Community Psychiatric Nursing Journal* **4**(5): 14–18.

Carr P, Butterworth CA and Hodges B (1980) *Community Psychiatric Nursing*. Edinburgh: Churchill Livingstone.

Carr-Hill R, McIver S and Dixon P (1989) *The NHS and its Customers*. University of York: Centre for Health Economics.

Carson D and Montgomery J (1989) *Nursing and the Law*. Basingstoke: Macmillan.

Cartwright A (1983) *Health Surveys in Practice and in Potential*. London: King's Fund.

Casey DE and Keepers GA (1988) Neuroleptic Side Effects: A Review. In: Casey DE and Christensen AV (eds) *Psychopharmacology: Current Trends*. Berlin: Springer-Verlag.

Catalan J, Marsach P, Hawton KE, Whitwell D, Fagg J and Bancroft J (1980) Comparison of doctors and nurses in the assessment of deliberate self poisoning patients. *Psychological Medicine* **10**: 483–491.

Chambers N (1987) Developing a consumer strategy in the NHS (or getting things right). *Hospital and Health Services Review* **83**: 12–14.

Clifford P, Leiper R, Lavender A and Pilling S (1989) *Assuring Quality in Mental Health Services*. London: RDP/Free Association Books.

Clinical Standards Advisory Group (1995) Report of a CSAG Committee on Schizophrenia. London: HMSO.

Community Psychiatric Nurses Association (1980) *National Survey of Community Psychiatric Nursing Services*. Leeds: CPNA Publications.

Community Psychiatric Nurses Association (1985) *The 1985 CPNA National Survey Update*. Leeds: CPNA Publications.

Cormack D (1976) *Psychiatric Nursing Observed*. London: Royal College of Nursing.

Davidhizar RE (1985) Can users with schizophrenia describe feelings and beliefs about taking medication? *Journal of Advanced Nursing* **10**(5): 469–473.

Davidhizar RE (1987) Beliefs, feelings and insight of patients with schizophrenia about taking medication. *Journal of Advanced Nursing* **12**(2): 177–182.

Davis B (1986) A Review of Recent Research in Psychiatric Nursing. In: Brooking J (ed) *Psychiatric Nursing Research: Developments in Nursing Research*, vol 3. Chichester: Wiley.

Department of Health (1990) *The NHS and Community Care Act*. London: HMSO.

Donati F (1989) A psychodynamic observer in a chronic psychiatric ward. *British Journal of Psychotherapy* **5**(3): 317–329.

Downie RS and Calman KC (1987) *Healthy respect – ethics in health care*. London: Faber and Faber.

Dyer AR and Bloch S (1987) Informed consent and the psychiatric patient. *Journal of Medical Ethics* **13**(1): 12–16.

Ferguson K (1993) A Study to Investigate the Views of Patients and their Carers on the Work Undertaken by Nurses to Prepare the Patient for Discharge from Hospital. In: Brooker C and White E (eds) *Community Psychiatric Nursing: A Research Perspective*, vol. 2. London: Chapman and Hall.

Field R (1993) Patients' and CPNs' Views of a CPN Service. In: Brooker C and White E (eds) *Community Psychiatric Nursing: A Research Perspective*, vol. 2. London: Chapman and Hall.

Fitzpatrick R (1984) Satisfaction with Health Care. In: Fitzpatrick R, Hinton J, Newman S, Scambler G and Thompson J (eds) *The Experience of Illness*. London: Tavistock.

Fitzpatrick R (1991a) Surveys of patient satisfaction: 1 – Important general considerations. *British Medical Journal* **302**: 887–889.

Fitzpatrick R (1991b) Surveys of patient satisfaction: 2 – Designing a questionnaire and conducting a survey. *British Medical Journal* **302**: 1129–1131.

Fitzpatrick R and Hopkins A (1983) Problems in the conceptual framework of patient satisfaction research. *Sociology of Health and Illness* **5**: 297–311.

Goffman E (1961) *Asylums: Essays on the Social Situation of Mental Patients and Other Inmates*. Harmondsworth: Penguin.

Goldberg D (1985) Implementation of mental health policies in the north-west of England. In: Wilkinson G and Freeman H (eds) *The Provision of Mental Health Services in Britain: the Way Ahead*. London: Routledge and Kegan Paul.

Goldman AE and McDonald SS (1987) *The Group Depth Interview: Principles and Practice*. New Jersey: Prentice Hall.

Goldstein MJ and Koperkin HS (1981) Short and Long-Term Effects of Combining Drug and Family Therapy. In: Goldstein MJ (ed) *New Developments in Interventions with Families of Schizophrenics*. San Francisco: Jossey-Bass.

Gournay K and Brooking J (1993) Failure and Dissatisfaction. In: Brooker C and White E (eds) *Community Psychiatric Nursing: a Research Perspective*, vol 2. London: Chapman and Hall.

Griffith JH and Mangen SP (1980) Community psychiatric nursing – a literature review. *International Journal of Nursing Studies* **17**(2): 197–210.

Gutek BA (1978) Strategies for studying user satisfaction. *Journal of Social Issues* **34**(4): 44–56.

Handyside E and Heyman R (1990) Community mental health care: Users' perceptions of services and an evaluation of a voluntary agency support scheme. *International Journal of Social Psychiatry* **34**(4): 280–290.

Heginbotham C (1986) Foreword. In: Simmons S and Brooker C (eds) *Community Psychiatric Nursing: A Social Perspective*. London: Heinemann.

Helman CG (1990) *Culture, Health and Illness*, 2nd edn. London: Wright.

Hinshelwood RD (1987) The psychotherapist's role in a large psychiatric institution. *Psychoanalytic Psychotherapy* **2**(3): 207–215.

Hogerty GE (1984) Depot neuroleptics: The prevalence of psycho-social factors. *Journal of Clinical Psychiatry* **45**: 36–42.

Hogerty GE, Anderson C, Reiss D and Kornblith S (1986) Family psychoeducation, social skills training, and maintenance chemotherapy in the aftercare treatment of schizophrenia. *Archives of General Psychiatry* **43**: 633–642.

Holloway F (1988) Prescribing for the longterm mentally ill – A study of treatment practices. *British Journal of Psychiatry* **152**: 511–515.

Hunter P (1978) *Schizophrenia and Community Psychiatric Nursing*. Surbiton: National Schizophrenia Fellowship.

Islington Mental Health Forum (1989) *Fit for Consumption*. London: Islington Mental Health Forum.

Jeste DV and Wyatt RJ (1981) Changing epidemiology of tardive dyskinesia. *American Journal of Psychiatry* **138**: 297–309.

Jeste DV and Wyatt RJ (1982) Therapeutic strategies against tardive dyskinesia. *Archives of General Psychiatry* **39**: 803–816.

Jeste DV and Wyatt RJ (1985) Prevention and management of tardive dyskinesia. *Journal of Clinical Psychiatry* **46**: 14–18.

Johnson D (1981) Oral Versus Depot Medication in Schizophrenia. In: Goffries CG (ed) *Long Term Neuroleptic Treatment: Benefits and Risks*. Copenhagen: Munksgaard.

Johnson D (1990) Organising a depot injection clinic. *Practical Reviews in Psychiatry* **2**: 1–3.

Johnson D and Freeman H (1973) Drug defaulting by patients on long acting phenothiazines. *Psychological Medicine* **3**: 115–119.

Johnstone EC (1990) Chronic Schizophrenia: Can One Do Anything About Persistent Symptoms? In: Hawton K and Cowen P (eds) *Dilemmas and Difficulties in the Management of Psychiatric Patients*. Oxford: Oxford University Press.

Johnstone L (1989) *Users and Abusers of Psychiatry*. London: Routledge.

Jolley AG, Hirsch SR, McRink A and Manchanda R (1989) Trial of brief intermittent neuroleptic prophylaxis for selected schizophrenic outpatients: clinical outcome at one year follow up. *British Medical Journal* **298**: 985–990.

Jones L, Leneman L and Maclean U (1987) *Consumer Feedback for the NHS: a Literature Review*. London: King's Fund.

Kitson AL (1987) Raising standards of clinical practice – The fundamental issue of effective nursing practice. *Journal of Advanced Nursing* **12**(3): 321–329.

Koltov M, Ahmed M and Meyer M (1978) A study of outpatient satisfaction with mental health centre services. *Hospital and Community Psychiatry* **29**: 179–182.

Laing RD (1959) *The Divided Self*. London: Tavistock.

Laing RD (1961) *The Self and Others*. London: Tavistock.

Lebow J (1982) Consumer satisfaction with mental health treatment. *Psychological Bulletin* **91**(2): 244–259.

Leff J, Kuipers L and Berkowitz R (1982) A controlled trial of social intervention in the families of schizophrenic patients. *British Journal of Psychiatry* **141**: 121–134.

Leff J, Kuipers L, Berkowitz R and Sturgeon D (1985) A controlled trial of social interventions in the families of schizophrenic patients: A two-year follow up. *British Journal of Psychiatry* **146**: 595–600.

Leff J, Berkowitz R, Shavit N and Strachan A (1989) A trial of family therapy vs a relatives group for schizophrenia. *British Journal of Psychiatry* **154**: 58–66.

Lehman A, Ward N and Linn L (1982) Chronic mental patients: The quality of life issue. *American Journal of Psychiatry* **39**: 1271–1276.

Ley P (1988) *Communicating with Patients: Improving Communication, Satisfaction and Compliance.* London: Chapman and Hall.

Ley P, Bradshaw PW, Kincey JA and Atherton ST (1976a) Increasing patients' satisfaction with communication. *British Journal of Social and Clinical Psychology.* **15**: 403–413.

Ley P, Whitworth MA and Skilbeck LE (1976b) Improving doctor–patient communication in general practice. *Journal of the Royal College of General Practitioners.* **26**: 720–724.

Lidz CW, Meisel A, Zerubavel E, Carter M, Sestak RM and Roth LH (1984) *Informed Consent: a Study of Decision Making in Psychiatry.* New York: Guilford Press.

Littlewood R and Lipsedge M, (1982) *Aliens and Alienists: Ethnic Minorities and Psychiatry.* Harmondsworth: Penguin.

Locker D and Dunt D (1978) Theoretical and methodological issues in sociological studies of consumer satisfaction with health care. *Social Science and Medicine.* **12**(4): 283–292.

Luck M, Lawrence B, Pocock P and Reilly P (1988) *Consumer and Market Research in Health Care.* London: Chapman and Hall.

MacDonald LD, Ochera J, Leibowitz JA and McLean EK (1990) Community mental health services from the user's perspective. *International Journal of Social Psychiatry* **36**(3): 183–193.

Mangen SP and Griffith JH (1982) Patient satisfaction with community psychiatric nursing: A prospective controlled study. *Journal of Advanced Nursing.* **7**(3): 477–482.

Marder S., Mebane A and Chien C (1983) A comparison of patients who refuse and consent to neuroleptic treatment. *American Journal of Psychiatry.* **140**: 470–473.

Marks I (1985a) *Psychiatric Nurse Therapists in Primary Care.* London: Royal College of Nursing.

Marks I (1985b) Controlled trial of psychiatric nurse therapists in primary care. *British Medical Journal* **290**: 1181–1184.

Marriott P (1978) A Five-year Follow-up at a Depot Phenothiazine Clinic: Patterns and Problems. In: Ayd FJ (ed) *Depot Fluphenazines: Twelve Years' Experience.* Baltimore: AMC.

Masur FT (1981) Adherence to Health Care Regimens. In: Prokop CK and Bradley LA (eds) *Medical Psychology: Contributions to Behavioural Medicine.* New York: Academic Press.

McCreadie R, Robertson LJ and Wiles DH (1992) The Nithsdale schizophrenia surveys IX. *British Journal of Psychiatry* **160**: 793–798.

McEwen J, Martini CJ and Wilkins N (1983) *Participation in Health.* London: Croom Helm.

McIver S (1991) *An Introduction to Obtaining the Views of Users of Health Services.* London: King's Fund.

Mulhall DJ (1976) Systematic self-assessment by PQRST. *Psychological Medicine* **6**: 591–597.

Munton R (1990) Client Satisfaction with Community Psychiatric Nursing. In: Brooker C (ed) *Community Psychiatric Nursing: a Research Perspective.* London: Chapman and Hall.

Oppenheim AP (1966) *Questionnaire Design and Attitude Measurement*. London: Heinemann.

Paykel ES and Griffith JH (1983) *Community Psychiatric Nursing for Neurotic Patients*. London: Royal College of Nursing.

Pollock LC (1989) *Community Psychiatric Nursing: Myth and Reality.* London: Scutari Press.

Pollock LC (1990) The Goals and Objectives of Community Psychiatric Nursing. In: Brooker, C (ed) *Community Psychiatric Nursing: a Research Perspective*. London: Chapman and Hall.

Potter J (1988) Consumerism and the public sector: How well does the coat fit? *Public Administration* **66:** 149–164.

Raphael W (1977) *Psychiatric Hospitals Viewed by their Patients*. London: King's Fund.

Rogers A, Pilgrim D and Lacey R (1993) *Experiencing Psychiatry: Users' Views of Services*. London: Macmillan/MIND Publications.

Roth M (1976) Schizophrenia and the theories of Thomas Szasz. *British Journal of Psychiatry* **129:** 317–326.

Scheff TJ (1966) *Being Mentally Ill – a Sociological Theory.* Chicago: Aldine.

Shapiro MB (1961) A method of measuring psychological changes specific to the individual psychiatric patient. *British Journal of Medical Psychology.* **34:** 151–155.

Silverstone T and Turner P (1987) *Drug Treatment in Psychiatry,* 4th edn. London: Routledge and Kegan Paul.

Simmons S and Brooker C (1986) *Community Psychiatric Nursing: a Social Perspective*. London: Heinemann.

Simpson K (1989) Community psychiatric nursing – a research based profession? *Journal of Advanced Nursing* **14**(2): 274–280.

Skidmore D (1986) The effectiveness of community psychiatric nursing teams and base location. In: Brooking J (ed) *Psychiatric Nursing Research: Developments in Nursing Research*, vol 3. Chichester: Wiley.

Sladden S (1979) *Psychiatric Nursing in the Community: a Study of a Working Situation*. Edinburgh: Churchill Livingstone.

Social and Community Planning Research (1988) *Keeping in Touch with the Talking: the Community Care Needs of People with a Mental Illness*. London: SCPR.

Sundeen SJ, Stuart GW, Rankin ED and Cohen SA (1985) *Nurse–User Interaction*. St Louis: CV Mosby.

Szasz T (1961) *The Myth of Mental Illness*. New York: Harper.

Tarrier N, Vaughn C, Barrowclough C and Bamrah J (1988) The community management of schizophrenia. *British Journal of Psychiatry* **153**: 532–542.

Towell D (1975) *Understanding Psychiatric Nursing*. London: Royal College of Nursing.

Tuckett D, Boulton M, Olsen C and Williams A (1985) *Meetings Between Experts: an Approach to Sharing Ideas in Medical Consultation*. London: Tavistock.

Turner G (1984) A census of out-patients attending for depot medication at a Glasgow psychiatric hospital. *Health Bulletin* **42**(3): 141–145.

Turner G (1993) Client/CPN contact during the administration of depot medication: implications for practice. *In*: Brooker C and White E (eds) *Community Psychiatric Nursing: a Research Perspective* vol 2. London: Chapman and Hall.

Turner-Crowson J (1993) *Reshaping Mental Health Services – Implications for Britain of US Experience*. London: King's Fund.

Turnquist A (1983) The issue of informed consent and the use of neuroleptic medication. *International Journal of Nursing Studies* **20**(3): 181–185.

Vaughn C and Leff J (1976a) The influence of family and social factors on the course of psychiatric illness: A comparison of schizophrenic and depressed neurotic patients. *British Journal of Psychiatry* **129**: 125–137.

Vaughn C and Leff J (1976b) The measurement of expressed emotion in the families of psychiatric patients. *British Journal of Social and Clinical Psychology* **15**: 157–165.

Vaughn C and Leff J (1985) *Expressed Emotion in Families*. New York: Guilford Press.

Westermeyer JF and Harrow M. (1990) Prognosis and the natural course of schizophrenia. *Current Opinion in Psychiatry.* **3**(1): 3–7.

White E (1993) Community Psychiatric Nursing 1980–1990: A Review of Organisation, Education and Practice. *In* Brooker C and White E. (eds) *Community Psychiatric Nursing: a Research Perspective* vol 2. London: Chapman and Hall.

Whitehead CS (1987) *Co-ordinated Aftercare for Schizophrenia: Report of a Pilot Project*. Salford: Salford Health Authority.

Wills W, Dayson D and Gooch C. (1990) Patient Attitudes Before and After Discharge. In: Team for the Assessment of Psychiatric Services *Better out than in?* London: North East Thames Regional Health Authority.

Wing JK, Cooper JE and Sartorius N (1974) *The Measurement and Classification of Psychiatric Symptoms*. London: Cambridge University Press.

Winkler F (1987) Consumerism in health care: Beyond the supermarket model. *Policy and Politics.* **15**(1): 1–8.

Winn L and Quick A (1989) *User Friendly Services*. London: King's Fund.

Wolsey P (1990) The Training Needs of CPNs in Relation to Work with Schizophrenic Users. *In*: Brooker C (ed) *Community Psychiatric Nursing – a Research Perspective*. London: Chapman and Hall.

Wooff K, Goldberg DP and Fryers T (1986) Patients in receipt of community psychiatric nursing care in Salford 1976–1982. *Psychological Medicine* **16**: 407–414.

Wooff K, Goldberg DP and Fryers T (1988a) The practice of community psychiatric nursing and mental health social work in Salford. Some implications for community care. *British Journal of Psychiatry* **152**: 783–792.

Wooff K and Goldberg DP (1988b) Further observations on the practice of community care in Salford: Differences between CPNs and mental health social workers. *British Journal of Psychiatry.* **153**: 30–37.

CHAPTER 10

Changes and Challenges – the Future of Mental Health Nursing

KEVIN GOURNAY

This book was written soon after the publication of the final report of the Mental Health Nursing Review and many of the themes reflect the *Working in Partnership* document.

Tremendous changes are occurring in the mental health field and some of the specific challenges to be faced in the next few years are addressed by the various authors. Written from a user perspective, Peter Campbell's chapter certainly raises many issues for mental health nurses and indicates the way forward. *Working in Partnership* was so named because of the desire by both the review team and many of those who gave evidence that mental health nurses should form an alliance with users to develop services which are accessible and at the same time relevant. Antony Sheehan describes the progress of mental health nursing practice within the context of nursing development units and echoes a theme which now underpins the best of mental health nursing practice, i.e. that nursing practice should be firmly based on research evidence and systematic enquiry. Antony Sheehan also demonstrates that mental health nurses can develop a great deal of autonomy, while at the same time being valuable and equal members of the multidisciplinary team. I hope my own chapter develops this theme of autonomy further, but at the same time I would like to emphasise the need to be much more flexible in our approach and willing to accept that many core functions of mental health nursing can also be seen as the core functions of other mental health professionals. However, this does not concede to the view that there is no reason for mental health nursing to carry on as an entity – this argument is one to which I shall return below.

Jean Faugier has provided us with some valuable insights into the process of clinical supervision. She has made an excellent argument for supervision becoming an essential part of all practice but nevertheless an area which must be developed further.

Paul Tarbuck has described one of the saddest stories in mental health care in the last decade. However, Paul has demonstrated that the situation at Ashworth is now a much more optimistic one with dedicated staff working successfully to retrieve what looked to be irretrievable. As a consequence, it seems clear that the standards of care given to this most vulnerable and needy population have improved considerably. It almost goes without saying, however, that this is but a start and mental health nursing in general will probably take years to repair the damage done to its image by the dreadful events at Ashworth Hospital.

Dave Sallah's material is derived from his substantial experience of working with people in secure environments and although this chapter will of course be of general interest to all mental health nurses, the messages are clearly aimed at those working with this particularly needy group who, with the advent of greater awareness of mental health problems in populations of people who offend, will become a greater challenge to all those working in mental health services.

Stuart Darby's chapter on older people is most welcome as he focuses on a population that have not received their due attention – mainly because of the need of mental health services to refocus their energies on people with schizophrenia and other serious and enduring mental illness. However, mental health nurses must in the future give older people a much greater service particularly, as Stuart points out, because of the increasing numbers of older people in the population. As a corollary of that, there will be many older people who present with an array of problems. This population is often victim to stereotyping and it is my view that mental health nurses still have a long way to go to provide optimum services for this group.

For too long, mental health nurses working in the community have seen the task of giving and supervising medication as being of only peripheral importance and, for that reason, many of them have delegated medication-related tasks to others. As Tom Sandford has indicated, involvement in the area of maintenance medication is much more than giving an injection or monitoring for side effects. It is my argument that to fulfil this role requires the careful development of a collaborative relationship with the client and a number of other skills in assessment evaluation and intervention. To complicate matters further, the pharmacological approaches to serious and enduring mental health problems are widening in their scope all the time, thus testing the skills and knowledge of the mental health nurse. I also believe that at some point it is inevitable that mental health nurses will become even more important in this area as prescribers of medication, adjusting the timing and dosage on their own judgement.

Overall, therefore, this book provides us with much to reflect upon and every chapter gives us pointers to the future and ideas which should help us develop our practice towards optimum levels.

However, all that being said, mental health nursing is facing additional problems. In May 1994 Professor June Clark, then President of the Royal College of Nursing, addressed the RCN Congress. In this speech she put forward the argument that branch programmes should be discontinued and that all nursing training should commence with a generic qualification. Although she did not say this at this specific time, it was also implied (from other speeches made in other places) that this generic qualification should be in the form of a university-based degree. Professor Clark's view that the qualification for all should be a generic nursing degree is one that has support in other areas and, as such, it poses a direct threat to mental health nursing as we know it today. Apart from the fact that her arguments seem completely contrary to all of the evidence gathered by the Mental Health Nursing Branch of Project 2000, and a strong mental health nursing entity in general, there are considerable problems associated with the route that Professor Clark supports.

First, being relegated to a postgraduate programme would drastically reduce the potential pool of recruits. Many students, having completed a 3/4 year under-graduate degree would not wish to pursue further study, presumably at postgraduate diploma or masters level. Thus, another year of training in mental health nursing would be 'beyond the pale' for most. If one had the stamina to follow such a postgraduate course, what would be its content? Presumably such courses would be no longer than 1 academic year i.e. 35 weeks) and, as such a course would be at postgraduate level, there would surely be a great deal of theory to assimilate. This would, at a stroke, reduce practical experience and it is difficult to see how the core mental health nursing skills could develop. Indeed, from this base it is difficult to see how clinical nurse specialists as we know them today in behavioural psychotherapy or problem-orientated case management could emerge. If one contemplates such a scenario as would follow in the wake of the implementation of Professor Clark's ideas, mental health services would be starved of nurses. The majority of nurses would hold a generic nursing qualification only and there would be an elite of mental health nurses with postgraduate qualifications who might provide specific services. The large mental health nursing workforce that we know today, who provide care in all its varieties to the elderly and to people with serious and enduring mental health problems both in the community and in hospital, would disappear and people with mental health problems would receive an inferior level of care.

Mental health nurses working in all areas need to be aware of the possible threat to the existence of the profession and should not be complacent just because *Working in Partnership* has recommended that mental health nursing be retained in its current form. Over the next few years there will be a need for mental health nurses to preserve a form of nursing unique in the world and one which potentially provides the best of possible services to those most in need.

Index

Index

Index

models of 38–9
in old age 143–4
organic 143
see also schizophrenia
mentors, characteristics of 56
mentorship
educational aspects 56–7
role in supervision 65
MIND 6
Stress on Women campaign ix-x, 119
MINDLINK 6
mirror role in supervision 65
mixed-sex wards 112–14, 115–16
Modernisation theory, of ageing 145–6
money management, for clients 46–7
monitoring
in case management 47–8
role in supervision 65
of signs and symptoms 45

NDUs, *see* nursing development units
networking organisations 6
neuroleptics
and informed consent 169, 181
protection against relapse 169
side effects 168–9
see also depot clinics; phenothiazines
Nottingham, advocacy and patients'
councils in 8, 11
nurse–doctor relationship 117
nurse–patient relationship
caring *v.* technical skills 14
compulsion and 13
creative non-intervention 14
differing values in 14
future changes in 15
and independent advocacy 10–11
lack of interaction 12–13
need for greater dialogue in 15
nursing practice and 13
power balance in 12, 13
users' views 12–13, 14, 15
nurses
as abusers 114
ageing process, knowledge of 157–8
ageism, insight and awareness of 158
assessment of older person's
needs 158–9

attitudes to older patients 153, 155, 156
challenges for 1
components of leadership 27
dissemination of information 9
gender of 117
guarding against ageist practice 160
helpful and responsive x
nurse–doctor relationship 117
and patients' councils 11–12
pivotal role 3
working with advocates 10–11
working with older people 155–6
see also Community Psychiatric Nurses
(CPNs); education and training;
nurse–patient relationship
nursing, key principles 2
see also Charter for Professional Nursing
Practice
nursing beds, in nursing development
units 28
nursing development units (NDUs)
agendas for 22–3, 28
alternative models of service xii
clinical supervision in 23
common themes 19
criteria for 19–20
definition 18
elements of service provision 22
empowerment in 25
examples of 23–5
focusing of services 26, 27
future 27–9
history of 17–18
importance of, in mental health
settings 20, 25
King's Fund involvement 19–20
managers' role 23
nursing beds in 28
patient-centred care 28
philosophy 18
risk taking in 20
St George's Hospital, Stafford 20–2,
22–3, 26–7
sessional working 21–2
skills not used 21
Nursing in Special Hospitals, statements of
intent 76

202

Index

patients' councils 11–12
representativeness of 7
user movement
enabling self-evaluation 14–15
growth and organisation of 5–8
impact on user involvement 7–8

'ward in the community', Madison
Wisconsin 33
wards, mixed-sex 112–14, 115–16
Wollongong, New South Wales
monitoring in 47–8
University of 44
women
admissions by diagnostic
group 103, 104
and anorexia nervosa 107–8
castration complex 109
child-care facilities 117, 119
– choice of gender of staff 116, 117
in custody 103–4
enforcement of male values on 105–6,
108, 110
– future service provision for 119–20
greater proportion of mental illness
diagnosed 103–4, 117
and hysteria 106–7
internalising pressures? 110
lesbianism 110–11
and male staff 114–15
in mixed-sex wards 112–14, 115–16
as nurses 117
– nurses' awareness of needs 119
and old age 152–3
as 'Other' to men 104–5, 109
physical abuse of 111
psychiatry for behaviour control 105–6
psychoanalytic theory 109–10
rape 114
rights issues 119
sexual abuse 111–12
society's expectations of behaviour 103
stereotypical role 104, 105
Stress on Women, MIND campaign ix–x,
119
therapeutic approach to caring for 118
treated as naughty children 107, 108

Women's Social and Political Union
(Suffragettes) 110